Praise for A Hard Place to Leave

"These probing, achingly beautiful essays form an indelible portrait of a life. Who is this woman with her many, at times contradictory, facets? She is an adventurer, journalist, wife, mother, daughter, her world set spinning by the brilliance of her mind, the tenacity of her love for her family, and the intensity of her longing to be anywhere but here. Through the very act of interrogating her own restlessness, Marcia DeSanctis provides us with a tantalizing window into a rich and singular world."
—Dani Shapiro, New York Times bestselling author of Inheritance

"Marcia DeSanctis's A Hard Place to Leave is perfumed with lush, luminous language as she sweeps us all across the globe. From Moscow to Cape Town, quiet New England to Sweden, these tender portraits grow on us like a spring garden."
—Aimee Nezhukumatathil, author of World of Wonders: In Praise of Fireflies, Whale Sharks, and Other Astonishments

"Never has a travel memoir put the ordinary and the extraordinary in such tight and revelatory conversation. A Hard Place to Leave brims over with intelligence and human truth. More than just a recounting of a life boldly and peripatetically lived, it's a reckoning with the passage of time, with one's own undying urges. I knew myself better by the end of this book, thanks to the fierce honesty and perpetual questing of Marcia DeSanctis."
—Colleen Kinder, editor of Letter to a Stranger

"There is such honesty and feeling on every page of Marcia DeSanctis's book—her avowal to push past the conventional boundaries of women's lives, her rediscovery of travel and solitude, her celebration of family, friendship, and homecoming—that I felt delightedly transported and deeply inspired."

—Jasmin Darznik, *New York Times* bestselling author of *The Bohemians*

"To read this masterfully composed memoir is to better understand our beautiful, broken world, our complex tethers to home and family, and our own imperfect selves. DeSanctis is brilliantly attuned to the nuances of these subjects, and she navigates the hairpin turns between the three with breathtaking curiosity, elegance, wisdom, and generosity. The essays in *A Hard Place to Leave* are equal parts dark and luminous, ferocious and tender, universal and intimate—and the writing is some of the finest I've ever read in my whole damn life."

—Lavinia Spalding, author of *Writing Away* and editor of *The Best Women's Travel Writing*

"Mountain climbing. Love affairs. Diplomats who may be spies, or love affairs, or both. Marcia DeSanctis's travel essays are thoughtful, stylish, and loaded with charm. It's the kind of book that goes great with a glass of wine and a strong dose of wanderlust."

—Rosecrans Baldwin, author of *Everything Now: Lessons From the City-State of Los Angeles*

A Hard Place to Leave

A Hard Place to Leave

Stories from a Restless Life

MARCIA DESANCTIS

TRAVELERS' TALES
AN IMPRINT OF SOLAS HOUSE, INC.
PALO ALTO

Travelers' Tales and Solas House are trademarks of Solas House, Inc.,
Palo Alto, California
travelerstales.com | solashouse.com

Art Direction and Cover Design: Kimberly Nelson
Interior Design and Page Layout: Howie Severson
Cover Photograph: © Miti (@mitifotos)
Author Photograph: © Elena Seibert Photography

Library of Congress Cataloging-in-Publication Data is available
upon request.

978-1-60952-206-3 (paperback)
978-1-60952-207-0 (ebook)
978-1-60952-208-7 (hard cover)

First Edition
Printed in the United States
10 9 8 7 6 5 4 3 2 1

This book is in memory of my mother,
Ruth Ann DeSanctis

One ghost in search of several others, I trotted dreamily
about, proving to myself that things were in order:
the corners must be sharp and clear, the lines incisive
for my future contemplation.

—M.F.K. Fisher

Some part of me is always left hanging on the places
I travel through—new countries, clear or cloudy skies,
oceans in the pearly gray rain—it's left clinging so
passionately that I feel as if I'm leaving behind me a
thousand little ghosts that look like me, rolling in the
waves, rocking on the leaves, scattered in the clouds…

—Colette

Table of Contents

Introduction

*A*bandon. This is the word we carry when we arrive some-where else. To give ourselves over without restraint. It is a singular thrill, to pitch out of the satisfying but predictable order of domestic life into this state of disarray. We become vaga-bonds, searchers, giddy tourists. Whatever the case, we are, above all, strangers. So in that sense, we assume a second meaning: to desert, as in our own selves. We know who we are in our homes. We have no idea who we'll be in Kigali, Racine, or Angkor Wat.

The voyage usually starts with the same script. How strange and wonderful it is to stash only the essentials into a bag and shut the door behind us. We lift off. We land somewhere across the world, usually alone, usually in the middle of the night. Hunched by fatigue and the weight of our luggage, we find our room, switch on the lights. Sometimes it's decent.

What, exactly, has been left behind? And what might lead us back home? Every arrival is a crash course in possibility, but it does not always open a path to immaculate wide-eyed clarity. Waiting for a bus under a battering sun or breathing the bug spray on a hotel pillow, we crave the safety of our old couch, the comfort and camaraderie of friends and family. But comfort never endures. Restlessness prickles under the skin. Whatever the story becomes, one cannot write about travel without writing about home. Each leads to the other and back again.

Traveling alone and writing about it is my work, a career I began at fifty. It was a discovery at midlife, one that exposed both the escape and the quest I craved as I confronted my life's second half. One that quelled the hormonal tumult that was as unrelenting as weather. And finally, one that reached back to the most elemental part of me, the younger woman I once was, the child I had been.

In third grade, as soon as my mother allowed me to walk to the center of Winchester, Massachusetts, along a half-mile of flat, suburban streets, I always wanted to go alone.

"Why don't you ask a friend to walk with you?" my mother would ask. But I didn't want a friend. Not then, and not now. I preferred to drift unaccompanied, unencumbered, and I grew intimate with my own independence. Even then, I think I understood the restorative power, the joyous exuberance, of these stretches of time spent solo. I loved the company of my friends, but in town— at the record store, the ice cream shop, crossing through the village green—I absorbed it best alone. For a time, anyway.

Sometimes I try to imagine that preternaturally tall girl with a pixie cut, wearing bright red corduroys as she wanders past the worn brick buildings in an old New England town. If the passage of time has offered me any wisdom, it's the knowledge that our essence changes so little over a lifetime.

In my twenties and thirties, I traveled—for my work as a television journalist, for weddings, and, when I lived in Europe, for the heck of it. And then I stopped. I gave up my career as a producer and media executive and moved with my husband and two children, who were five and eight at the time, to a rural town in Connecticut. During the next several years, I barely set foot on a plane. Vacations were a prohibitively high-ticket luxury for a newly jobless, floundering woman and her sculptor husband.

It was as if this phase of life erected a tough membrane I could not cross out of and back into, the way I once had with ease. I browsed travel magazines, gazed at arty spreads about Sardinia and the Maldives—the province of illusion, but always in the realm of possibility that the prospect of a journey held. During this time, home was where I belonged, where I needed to be.

Five years of dislocation in the wilderness later, I was in my mid-forties, the land of reckoning and diminishing reason. Middle age was less an ebb and flow than a relentless tide. "Your children are all that matter," is the bromide foisted on every woman as soon as she gives birth, a vague notion about the primacy of mothering above all else that is deeply embedded into our collective consciousness. There were times I was convinced that these sayings are part of a belief system created to allay the mind-blowing confusion that women experience when they have babies, when our identities are co-opted by a squirming bundle of humanity. My children *were* everything that mattered. But what was I?

The easiest and most satisfying way I grappled with the crisis—the tsunamic love for my children that coexisted with my abundant sense of failure—was to try to be productive. In the daylight hours, I pecked out a novel from the driver's seat during the kids' piano lessons (it never sold). Then I taught French for a bit. Finally, adrift on a sea of shifting hormones, I enrolled in a master's program in international relations. From the opening words of the first macroeconomics lecture, I was galvanized in a way I had not been in decades. The neurons were snapping again.

It turned out that I was primed for something else. While at graduate school, I met another man, an unmarried fellow student, who swept me away. My seventeen-year marriage to Mark was strong, built and sustained on love and respect. He was an ideal husband and for me, the ideal man: optimistic and wise, gentle, handsome, and brilliantly funny. But midlife was a twisted reality disruptor, and with estrogen and sense leaching from my system,

I became wrapped up in the idea of another possible life. But the other man did not want a married woman, or me. In the wake of this episode, I crashed. For a while, I floated into and out of the weathered badlands of depression while my family waited for me to touch back down. With my husband's mercy and goodness, I did.

We were battered but whole, resolute in our love and commitment to keeping our marriage alive and making it better. But if statistics were on my side, there were many remaining years to be lived, and not simply whiled away. I had to figure out how to renew the sensation of hope graduate school had offered me, in realms beyond that of the heart.

After graduation, I could not find a job in policy or development. I knocked on doors in Washington, D. C., and if they bothered to open, it was only to slam shut in an instant. Under the delusion that I could just jump into a job as chief of staff to the Secretary General of the United Nations or as national security advisor to newly elected President Obama, I had a shattered psyche and a school loan that I needed to pay back. Panic-stricken, dispirited, unemployed and on the cusp of fifty, I sought a plan, and something else.

What I found was a voice.

Oftentimes, I recalled the words my husband used to comfort me during the darkest, most terrifying time of my breakdown: "Everything you need is right here, with us." He was half right.

Ideas began to pile up for essays and stories. I wrote them and one after another I sent them out to editors. There were many rejections—then fewer, which felt like the beginning of something. Buried in my depths was a reserve of ambition, and I drew from it.

I traveled backwards, mining my memories for past encounters from long-ago voyages, people and places I had not been able or willing to shake, retracing old maps. I discovered that, from my vantage point, years (even decades) later, small memories seemed more substantial and sometimes, transformational in retrospect. As I culled through scribbles from a trove of diaries, I pondered people to whom I had not given much thought, but who still populated my dreams.

So I began to travel again. I found myself in airports on my way somewhere, seeking an awakening and a story, gathering pearls for a necklace. The mission was two-fold: to devise an exit strategy from whatever was intractable in my life and then to discover the way back into it. On I went, scouring the Earth for windows with infinite views. Once in a while, the lens would turn right back onto me, leading me to understanding, meaning and ultimately home again.

I leveraged everything I could to invest in my new career. I cashed in my measly 401K. I shipped boots to a consignment store in Minnesota. I sold a watch, maxed out a credit card, and asked my sisters for help. I booked one ticket and then another. I left, I came back, and left again, more and more often on assignment, always in pursuit of a story.

Ten years on, I have traveled much and far. Yet, as I cross through Jordan on foot, or follow a herd of elephants in Botswana, or drive from Wyoming toward Montana toward the setting sun, I think of Mark and my children and I wonder: Would we ever come back here together? Is there enough time? How many trips are left? Will I ever see this again? Now and always, travel imparts a liquid language whose sole property is the flow of questions.

Where will I find a pearl?

Like most adults, I've been through the ringer. I've faced elation, disappointment, joy, loss and almost everything in between. I have many regrets that some days, don't burden me. I've been with one man, an artist, for thirty years now, and seen what can happen when one is deep inside a long marriage whose strength is tested. I have raised two children, now grown, who partake in this patient yet unstoppable universe. I have journeyed to five continents and found solace and purpose in solitude. Above all, a life of travel has made me an optimist.

Since my first major print story was published in *Vogue* magazine in my fiftieth year, I have written about 140 more. Although surprisingly few of them were travel essays, it is in these where I find the kernels of truth about love, memory, devotion, aging, even the creative life. In this book, the stories from the road explore the reasons we travel, the ways the past lingers, the allure of escape, and how a life created outside of home can reinforce the love and commitment within it. The essays from home are meditations on (and antidotes to) the sensation that time now passes more swiftly than before. I am fortunate to have both a home to return to and work that allows me to travel. And when I do, I fully and gratefully grasp my exorbitant privilege. A person who can measure life in journeys taken is lucky indeed. But there are enticing mysteries everywhere, even within the four walls of my house. The world is full of them.

It's possible that such an existence, of comings and goings, of departure lounges and arrival gates, might become increasingly rare, and certainly fraught. The reality is inescapable and truly alarming. Burgeoning refugee crises caused by poverty and climate change are causing mass relocation, exposing the inequality between those who travel by plane because they wish to do so and those who travel on foot because their survival depends on it. The COVID-19 pandemic has exacerbated humanity's existential worries, and solidified a shared sense of paralysis. In addition, it has shined a light on what we've known for a long time: that travel can be risky and problematic, a vector for deadly contagions, and that it often exploits local populations and harms the global ecosystem. From carbon emissions to sunscreen residue on the planet's coral reefs, our need to "get away" could be seen as selfish, unnecessary, and harmful.

And yet, humankind is designed to wander, to venture beyond one's own valley into another, to cross oceans and mountain ranges. Whether we seek adventure, connection, beauty, solitude, togetherness, or nothing less than the meaning of life, travel is ultimately about curiosity. Like love, curiosity is an engine that can change fate and move the tides. When we cast ourselves off from customary moorings and expose ourselves to other landscapes and people, we become empathetic, hopeful, worthy citizens. As I said, travel has made me an optimist.

I write this from an airport lounge in Amsterdam, en route to an assignment in Rwanda. The coffee is fresh, and I'm drinking a lot of it—it's a theme that repeats itself in these pages. I am sixty years old, and overnight flights are not as simple or as comfortable as they once were, back when hauling a carry-on and falling asleep in cramped seats was less painful on my knees and neck. Hand sanitizer dispensers are all over the airport and everyone's face is obscured by a mask. But I am on the verge of finding out what my story will be, and it is the most exciting state of mind I can imagine. I have the jitters but mostly I'm exuberant. Perhaps, I will encounter someone whom, thirty years from now, I won't have forgotten.

For now, I will keep going, resolved to travel quietly and lightly, to listen, to observe, to be open to the grace of the universe, to awe and sublimity.

But I will always take the familiar path home.

Schiphol Airport, October 2021

Chapter 1

Masha

*T*he first time I met Maria Konstantinovna, she was wearing a black leather skirt. It was Italian, brand new, and it was mine.

Masha, as I would come to know her, was a *dejournaya* in Moscow. Women like her sat on every floor in every hotel in the Soviet Union. They performed a range of duties—they served tea from a samovar that simmered behind their station. They ordered your phone call to America and came to wake you if it ever went through. They even washed lingerie and tee-shirts, leaving the latter folded like fine envelopes, whiter than they ever deserved to be. They also handed out your room key with varying degrees of suspicion, charm, or ennui, and if you wanted to leave it for safekeeping, collected it when you left the floor. But allegedly, the real purpose of these hall monitors was to observe your comings and goings on behalf of the security apparatus of the Kremlin.

It was my second trip to Cold War Moscow.

One year earlier, I had arrived in the city with a new degree in Russian Studies and stayed in an old hotel in the center of town. On nights when my brain was whirling from too much Georgian wine, I crossed the street and walked past the cupolas and scarlet-brick walls of Red Square. Now I was back as a tour guide of sorts, a *liaison* for a travel company that organized continuing education junkets for groups of doctors or lawyers from the United States. I was a translator, a babysitter, holder of boarding passes, procurer of bottled water, and whipping post if needed when tempers grew hot, which—with wealthy doctors unused to the specific hardships encountered when traveling around the Soviet Empire—they often did. It was part of my job description to be cheerful, but when my busload of jetlagged physicians and I arrived at our hulking mass of a hotel, I despaired.

Our official Intourist guide told us the building had been constructed in 1979 to house athletes and guests for the Olympics the following year. That much was obvious; it was a model Soviet vanity project, from the monstrous scale to the banners out front which erupted with optimism: "Onward!" they proclaimed. Across the street was a giant park devoted to the fruits of socialism, as well as a massive obelisk celebrating the Soviet space program. Inside, it was as sprawling and noisy as a city, and the close air was freighted with cigarette smoke and the grease from several restaurants.

Prior to my trip, a fellow tour guide in New York had informed me that there were fiber-optic cables installed in every room, and that the entire twenty-fifth floor was devoted to surveillance. He claimed to have stumbled upon a wall of reel-to-reel tape recorders there. President Reagan had given the Evil Empire speech only a month earlier, and the country was being run by an ex-KGB chief, Yuri Andropov. Paranoia was everywhere—in bars and on park benches, where locals lurked to change our dollars on the black market. They assumed, as well, that we were listening to *them*.

As my job paid little and I would depend on tips, I was eager to prove myself. But the first morning I woke up with a foggy head and aching limbs. So with apologies for being sick on day one of my new job, I loaded my fourteen gastroenterologists and their spouses onto the bus with their Russian guide and then repaired upstairs, hungry for my bed. I peeled my clothes off and crawled in naked. The sheets were coarse cotton and delightfully crunchy, and the duvet still held a welcoming hint of my own body warmth.

I woke up to the sight of two men going through my suitcase at the foot of the bed. One man's arm was buried in a zipper compartment; the other man was turned toward the window, holding my raincoat up to the light.

"What are you doing?" I asked. Russian literature was full of fever dreams, and I believed I was having one. The clarity was dazzling—two guys in blue shirts, the older one with a pale smoker's complexion and hair all neat like a little boy's on school picture day. The younger one had gray eyes that betrayed a flicker of menace, as if *I* were the one intruding.

Startled, the older man dropped the raincoat into the suitcase.

I was shivering and drew the comforter tightly around my bare body, sleeping bag-style.

"Excuse me," he declared. "We thought you were out."

They scrambled out the door and soon I fell backwards into sleep.

The next day, while my group toured Lenin's tomb, I sat on the bus sweating, too ill to move. I had not spoken of my visitors from the previous day. Many of my charges already supposed they were being watched; some were amused and some were downright scared. They whispered to each other, on the bus or during meals, about the presumed KGB operatives hanging about and a few of them enjoyed the Cold War folklore. But they were all doctors and their American guide was sick, so they insisted on taking me back to the hotel.

I dragged myself through the lobby, into the elevator, down the hallway that was laden with the rotten-fruit odor of disinfectant. My feet carried me, more quickly now, to my room, to that delicious, warm bed. The *dejournaya* was not at her station. I had wordlessly passed her that morning, not stopping to leave my key.

She had glanced up from her book and smiled, which was unusual for a key lady. I had noticed her wide-set green eyes.

And there she was, inside my room, wearing my skirt. She was curvier than I, and the waistband stretched tightly around her middle. The leather pulled across her hips sexily, as if the utterly random act of wearing a stranger's clothes gave her an air of danger and power. Barefoot, she held the pair of black high heels that I had packed along with the skirt. I'd known I would never wear them on my tour of Moscow and Central Asia, but they were new and expensive, and I had not wanted to leave them in the closet of my grim, shared New York apartment. Her own satin blouse was unbuttoned; the remains of trim frayed around the cups of her bra, which, at least a size too small, pinched her ribcage and crushed her breasts.

"*Bozhe moi*," she said under her breath. Oh my God.

"It's okay, really." What else could I say to this poor, mortified creature? "I just need to sleep."

"Just a moment," she said. One at a time, with two hands, she bent to place my shoes on the floor, toes pointed straight ahead like loaves on a baking sheet.

"Just a moment," she repeated, unzipping with shaky fingers. For a second, I averted my eyes, so as not to see her Soviet-issue underwear, hoping at least she wore some. She nodded deferentially, her face creased with shame. In what seemed like one move, she stepped into her wool skirt and slipped on her shoes. She shuffled her breasts around, rearranging them to make room in her bra, and fastened her blouse.

I waved her out the door, saying, "Don't worry, don't worry. Please!"

I scanned the room, flipped through my suitcase. Only my make-up case looked disturbed, with pencils, brushes and compacts strewn about the dresser. Strangely, despite my exhaustion and the fever that seared my brain, I knew I wasn't angry. Rather,

I pitied her embarrassment at being caught. Whoever this woman was, she was now exposed and compromised, and I wanted her to know that I, at least, didn't care.

Still fully clothed in jeans and a sweater, I went to bed.

After my nap, I came down the hall. She was sitting at her station and rose to greet me. She seemed taller and more beautiful having regained her composure and must have been twenty-five or twenty-six, a few years older than I.

"Do you want tea?" she asked.

"Yes, please," I answered. "What's your name?"

"Maria Konstantinovna," she replied, using her patronymic rather than her last name. "Masha."

"I'm Marcia too," I said. In Russian, they sounded the same. "Is there anything to eat?"

She walked me back to my room, where I stripped down and slid back into bed. Soon, Masha returned with rolls, cheese, and black tea. I drifted in and out of sleep. At times, I could hear the door swish open and closed or feel her swab my face with a damp cloth. Once I sat up to sip some tea and felt her hands bolster my shoulders, brace me as I lowered myself back to the mattress, and finally tuck the covers under my chin.

"I'm not working tomorrow," she said. I looked at her, puzzled. "I think you will be well enough to leave for Tashkent."

"Thanks to you, I think I will be," I said.

I had not mentioned my itinerary to her, but she knew. The next day would be my last in Moscow, as the doctors and I would be flying to Uzbekistan the following morning. The shades were drawn. There was still daylight behind them, but I had no idea what time it was. Loud voices erupted in the corridor, and Masha stood to return to her station.

"I'll be back in a few weeks. May I bring you something from America?" I asked.

She pressed the starched napkin that rested under the tea glass, and held her finger there while her eyes caught mine. A corner of a folded square of paper stuck out, barely visible, from beneath the napkin. After Masha had left, I plucked out the note and tucked it into my wallet.

Within a month, I returned to Moscow with another group of doctors, this time seventeen thoracic surgeons. At the airport, a customs official had confiscated my copies of *Vogue* and *Newsweek*, but I still had the illustrated collection of Pushkin fairy tales Masha had requested. She wanted the book, she said in her note, to read to her young son. At a Russian bookstore in New York, I had easily procured what was impossible to find in the shortage-ravaged Soviet Union. Of course, I brought a few extra things—a leather handbag stuffed with lip gloss, eye shadow, rolls of Lifesavers.

The scene had never left my mind—her open shirt, the tattered lingerie, and her eyes that shifted around mine until that moment of comprehension and convergence: had our fates been reversed, I would have discovered the Italian skirt from the depths of *her* luggage. And I would have shimmied it on as she had done to see myself reflected, just once, in something beautiful.

Right after checking in, I hopped the elevator to my old floor and found the on-duty *dejournaya*.

"Is Maria Konstantinovna working today?" I asked.

"She left," the woman answered.

"For the day, or for good?" I asked.

"I don't know," she said, and turned to rearrange the keys, inviting no further questions.

Over the next six months, I was back at the hotel several times with the book in my bag, but I never saw Masha again. In the winter of 1986, I returned to Moscow, this time with an American television network. Change was afoot, Mikhail Gorbachev was in power, and *glasnost* was the order of the day. I was a lowly minion on the nightly newscast I worked for but in those days, I still had a car and driver. Sitting in the back seat of a Volga sedan, I watched the snow fall gently, unstoppably. My old hotel seemed closer to town than I remembered.

She wasn't there.

Rounding the circular drive to leave, I recalled a brief embrace Masha and I had shared at the end of the one day we knew each other. I had recognized her perfume—Amazone—because it had come from my own bottle.

Over the years, I returned many times to Moscow. I went with Peter Jennings, Barbara Walters, and *60 Minutes*. Each time, I packed that book of fairy tales. Each time I journeyed out beyond the Monument to the Conquerors of Space, past the All-Russia Exhibition Center, to the ever-forbidding hotel. Always a fool's errand, to be sure. And each time I got off the elevator, I swallowed harder as I confronted the empty space she once occupied.

After an eighteen-year absence, I recently went back to Russia. As I packed, I slipped the slim, orange book into my suitcase. I was, frankly, surprised when I found it on the bookshelf—after six moves, a couple of renovations, and decades of neglect. The stories were in Russian, so I never read them to my own kids. Yet there it was, shelved patiently, a talisman of guilt, gratitude, and unfinished business.

Even though Moscow had changed beyond recognition, I hadn't. Nor had the feeling of dread and sensory overload I experienced when I got to the hotel where Masha had worked the day shift twenty-seven years ago. The lobby was still garish, but now it was loud with Italian cafés and gift shops selling nesting dolls and amber jewelry. A large man with a "Security" emblem on his suit lapel would not allow me to pass beyond his checkpoint to the elevators, so I went to the front desk.

"Would it be possible to go to the fifth floor?" I asked the receptionist. "I'm researching a book."

"You are writing something on the hotel?" she asked.

"Not really...." I hesitated. "Well, yes."

"What is the nature of your project?" she asked.

"Actually," I said, "years ago, I met someone here."

Her face softened. "I understand," she said, and turned. "Just a minute."

Within seconds, an official-looking woman approached me at the desk.

"Please leave your passport," she said, "and we'll go upstairs."

I handed it to the receptionist and was ushered past the guard.

"Do you still have *dejournayas?*" I asked.

"Yes, of course. It is not the same as it was. Mostly, they just take care of the floor."

"Can we please stop on five?" I ventured. She pressed the elevator button.

"Twenty-five is the only floor non-guests may see," she stated.

The doors opened.

There was no sign of tape recorders, only a fancy carpet runner and an eerie stillness that bore the echo of empty rooms. There was no *dejournaya*, either, and certainly no Masha. As we strolled back down the corridor, I murmured niceties about the lovely, modern décor.

Back in the elevator, I took out the Pushkin volume and turned to the Tale of the Tsar Sultan, the great writer's most famous children's story about the prince who saves the life of a swan, who in turn becomes a beautiful princess. The illustrations were simple but unremarkable, and I skimmed through the pages, stopping at a drawing of a bird flying across a starry violet sky. I closed the book and put it in my bag. It seemed that Masha had at last given it to me.

For all I knew, she emigrated, and I had passed her on a New York City sidewalk. Maybe she got sick or simply quit her job and was somewhere in Moscow now, her son grown. Perhaps she did vanish one night in that hazy time right before her country's dissolution. I would never find out. Masha was in my life so briefly it shouldn't have mattered. But to this day, I have not known comfort like the sound of her footsteps padding in and out of my hotel room as I sweltered with fever. I was twenty-two, in a strange land, nursed by the hands of a woman who, but for her clothes, might have been me.

Chapter 2

The Precipice

I spied it on the counter by the stove as I headed downstairs one morning not long after our move: huge, green, phallic. Had an alien dropped a sex toy in my kitchen last night?

"Did you get the cucumber?" shouted Bob, the contractor, from upstairs. "Straight from the garden." He must have heard me bashing around the kitchen, exaggerated for the slight annoyance of his hammer drills waking me yet again.

"Thanks," I said nervously. I was too embarrassed to touch the curving, suggestive vegetable, especially when Bob walked down into the kitchen with his thermos of coffee.

"The garden is popping," he said. "I think it's all the rain from May."

I was aware of the ungainliness of my favorite old nightgown, which was shorter than was proper, but Bob seemed oblivious. If Mr. Cordiality was not going to bring me coffee, I wished he had given me the time to make some, and to cover up, before he engaged me in cheerful conversation at 7 A.M.

"The tomatoes are growing like gangbusters. Our lettuce is looking good too. I'm trying this new thing to keep the deer away, bobcat urine."

"What? Jesus," I said. "Who collects bobcat urine?"

"I just get it at the hardware store."

I needed to go find a robe.

"And I brought you this!" He handed me a basketball-sized iridescent cabbage that looked like a papier maché fake. This is something people do up here—bestow home-grown specimens of vegetables whether the recipients want them or not.

"Wow," I said, turning the purple sphere around, brushing the waxy leaves with my fingertips.

"It makes the best coleslaw," Bob informed me.

Between Bob, his cronies, and my husband Mark's assistants, who landed in my kitchen each day for banter, our mornings had not wanted for male company during the two months since we first moved here. The weight of logistics and housework had been cumbersome, and I found myself sharing a lot with these men, my anxiety as bare as my legs were that morning. I was overwhelmed by the work that needed to be done and the money it was going to cost to make this decaying weekend crash pad a year-round home for me, my husband, and two children.

One of Mark's assistants, Lionel, was sleeping in the cellar for the time being. Technically it was our responsibility to feed him, but sometimes I just dreaded the sound of his footsteps on the basement stairs. He was learning to read the mood. If it wasn't welcoming, he would smile, fire up his truck, and head for safety and an egg sandwich somewhere else. Make yourself at home, I told him with some uncertainty, but some days, please don't.

Bob had a different status. He'd lived in our town all his life and was a bartender-like repository for housewifely neuroses about paint colors. But I think even his vault full of pithy maxims seemed worthless when he came across me. My raw need was almost a tactile presence in the house.

It was hard to describe, but I think Bob knew that I was molting, in the sweet spot of a total transformation, landing here after giving up my career and the identity I had worked so hard to carve out. He tried to look the other way the previous day while I sat on the lip of a twenty-foot-long dumpster, basking in self-pity.

My four-year-old, Ava, was skirting the perimeter of the bin on high alert. Yesterday, she caught me chucking a few of her stuffed animals, ones that I deemed sufficiently unloved so as not to be missed. Their blank expressions stared at nothing as they lay prone in the garbage. Ava was horrified.

Her monitoring activities might have amused me but for the task I was engaged in that morning. Box after box, memory after memory, I was tossing my past onto the construction debris. I had tackled reams of old files—research, contacts, rough drafts of stories I had worked on as a journalist over twenty years, all now scattered among pizza boxes and ripped linoleum. I found a torn-out page of a diary in a box labeled "Prague, October 1989."

I arrived back in Prague last night at dusk from Munich. The cab driver took me to the wrong hotel, but I was too tired to correct him. He offered to change money at 4 times the going rate. I was supposed to go to the Hotel Forum, but ended up at the Flora, where showing up unreserved is grounds for suspicion. I was exhausted, though, and the desk clerk took heart. Once again, dollars spoke their magic language.

The place is pretty sketchy. I tried to do some research but there was a twenty-watt bulb in the ceiling, giving off a thin brown light. This is my ninth bed in fourteen nights. The sheets so starched they almost scratch. There was lots of drunken noise on the street outside, high heels and laughter. Toilet is way down the dark hall so I peed in the sink.

My story feels like a mangled mess of leads. I have to get coins for phone calls. I have to go the Ministry to apply for official interviews. I have to call Jizi, the translator, who obviously won't find me at this hotel. I have to get to Havel. He was in prison for five years. He's a Mandela type. I hope they don't have me followed. It's hard to

tell if anyone bothers with that Stalinist stuff anymore. I'm excited.
Too excited.

This morning, the smell of coffee and grease settled into my room
from the kitchen ventilation system. My throat aches from the old radi-
ator. The bathtub is about three feet deep, longer than me, and I had
an excellent bath. I dried myself with something that looked like a dish-
towel, ironed like cardboard, with flowers embroidered in the corner.

Now, I am in the dining room and it is almost empty. Cutlery is
clanking, and the air reeks of a man's cologne from the only other per-
son in the room who isn't a waiter. He has those tinted Soviet bureau-
crat glasses and is wearing a brown suit.

"Deutsch?" the waiter asks me, pouring coffee.

"No, American," I say. I don't think he has met many of us, from
the looks of it.

Breakfast is cheese, warm bread, and thick berry jam. This coun-
try has the best food. The soups are incredible, every time.

Oh, it's my birthday.

"How about if today, you and I go to the Agway," Bob suggested.
"It's early enough in the season to plant and still have some vegetables by the end of the summer."

Gardens, in Bob's view, beat drugs and God for self-help. As
with religion, faith is put into something you believe but are not
certain will happen. Is there a heaven after a life well lived? Will
a squash really grow from this tiny, wrinkled seed? One need only
believe. A garden could be a place to find yourself if you are lost,
a reference point that highlights the concepts of possibility and
hope and optimism. It forces you to look ahead, rather than backwards. Yes, diaries are wonderful mementoes, but reading them in
tears over a dumpster is deranged.

The truth was that, despite its disarray, our garden, stretching
along the fence by the flagpole, had issued forth peonies, black-
eyed Susans, mint, crimson spears of bee balm, and ratty clumps of

lavender year after year. It mystified me how this stretch of flowers and weeds never had its spirit broken by neglect. There must have been twenty years of mulchy leaves wedged into the two hydrangea bushes. We were never short of blooms in our yard and I never thought they needed me. Before I lived in a quiet spot of rural New England, I thought the whole business was a pastime—like raising spaniels—enjoyed by eccentrics or the elderly. But Bob was here to tell me that the garden is actually the point. It's the soil's way of thanking us for our forbearance over the long winters.

If I had allowed it, I might have recognized another past closing in, besides the one I was relinquishing to the trash, mourning the city I had left and work I had loved. My mother's mother, a dainty Yankee of no-nonsense fortitude, was a local expert on wildflowers. She knew her fiddleheads and phloxes, and she lived to spot a rare white lady's slipper in the shady woods near her New Hampshire home, through which she would walk in a hand-sewn blue dress and nylon stockings. I pictured her with her little gloves and pruner—no drama, sweat, or sunscreen, just patience.

My father's father was an Abruzzo-born campesino, who grew figs, olives, and avocados in his tiny Tucson backyard. I am certain he never bought a vegetable in his 97 years. He was a world away from his birthplace, but he brought with him an affinity for the land and soil and everything they give us. I can see him, tanned and barefoot, squinting as he reaches high to pluck a plum, or in his kitchen slicing a tomato still warm from the Arizona sun.

That first year, with Bob's help, I started with green beans, zucchini, and basil, all planted next to the flowers in the existing beds. I swear I put no effort into it. I just buried the seeds and made sure they had plenty of sun and water. Each year since, I have taken on a few more plantings. Zinnia. Dahlias. Lettuces and an herb garden. Spaghetti squash, which I bake and load up with butter and Parmesan cheese. Finally, I built two raised beds out of two-by-fours, bought an industrial-sized watering can, and was ready to grow tomatoes—Pink Ping Pong, Isis Candy, Painted Ukrainian. I did not know that tomato plants emit a perfume like a Mediterranean breeze, heady and earthy, which fills the air and stays on your fingertips long after you touch the leaves.

After the pandemic arrived, and I was not sure whether or how we would be able to get food, I called a farmer, who arrived at my house with a dump truck full of composted soil, and then parked it right on the grass. Shovel to wheelbarrow, wheelbarrow to shovel, shovel to garden bed, where I tucked in rows of seeds, which I attended to with the same concern I might accord a sleeping baby with the covers kicked off. I felt lucky to be able to watch up close the alchemy of sun and rain and growth, knowing that life was churning in the dirt. Sometimes, after I watered the beds in the morning, I went outside and could nearly see the spinach leaves growing.

It still astounds me when a green sprout shows itself. Arugula takes all of five days to spring up, all peppery and tart. Stop me when I start to brag about the mellowness of my lacinato kale leaves, the tenderness of my Swiss chard, or the remarkable swirls of gold and red in my tree peonies.

Which brings me back to that first summer and the shiny cabbage Bob offered me, sitting like a talisman, calling me to a certain, still distant, new meaning.

I recalled that years ago, when I was trotting around Central Europe and the Soviet Union, I found that, no matter what godforsaken outpost I was sleeping in, even if there was no hot water, no toilet paper, and no towels, there was always a bowl of steaming and rich soup placed on a starched tablecloth in a dim dining hall. Like the restaurant at the Hotel Flora in Prague, where some new acquaintances and I dined to great abandon on my twenty-ninth birthday, days before the collapse of the Communist regime. I wondered where the fresh dill had come from, not to mention the cabbage, the sausage, or the thick sour cream melting into yellow pools of liquid on the top.

That first summer in the woods, many years later, I searched through my cookbooks. Finally, I found a recipe for zelná polévka—Czech soup. I stopped staring at the head of cabbage and got to work on chopping, boiling, watching and finally tasting the tart, thick and slightly sour concoction. My kids turned up their noses and dug in anyway. I felt something shift when I took a spoonful—and when I watched them take one. This will be good, I thought. Maybe, I thought, this will help.

Chapter 3

Cold War Game Theory

*I*n early April 1990, I arrived in Bucharest to write an environmental story for a magazine based in Paris, where I was living at the time. A catastrophe had been unfolding in the eastern part of Romania at the Delta of the Danube River where, after running its 1,700-mile course through Europe, the great river empties into the Black Sea. One of the most important wetlands in the Eastern Hemisphere, much of the Delta and its pristine wildlife habitat had been dammed, drained, plowed over, agro-industrialized, and otherwise gutted during the 24-year dictatorship of Nicolae Ceauşescu.

Only months before, the last remaining Stalinist-style ruler in Europe and his wife had been overthrown and tried by the National Salvation Front—the FSN—a political party made up mostly of former Communist Party officials, who had assumed control of the government. On Christmas Day 1989, Ceauşescu and his wife, Elena, were executed by firing squad at a barracks outside of the city. Members of the Army, who had turned against the hardline regime, had carried out the killing. The next day, footage of the Ceauşescus' slumped and bullet-ridden bodies was broadcast on state television.

Just weeks after the wall came down with the blows of a thousand hammers, I traveled to Berlin and throughout the German Democratic Republic, also known as East Germany. Over the winter, I had been in Moscow, and back and forth to Prague to cover the Velvet Revolution. But I was drawn to Romania's sinister overtones and the byzantine way in which the coup had transpired. Its revolution was the most violent of all the uprisings that roiled the continent that year.

From Paris, I sniffed about for a feature story I could reasonably explore. Given the uncertainties of the political situation in Bucharest and the tangled agendas that would be impossible to unravel so early in the game, I was on the lookout for leads on something with a less grisly narrative. By then, the bloodshed had ended, or at least seemed to pause. More than one thousand people had died since December, from the early days of unrest in the Transylvanian city of Timisoara through the removal of Ceaușescu and the FSN's consolidation of power. The violence had come from all conceivable quarters: troops loyal to Ceaușescu; rogue members of Romania's own armed forces and secret police—the Securitate—acting on behalf of the revolutionaries ousting the dictator; and dissident groups, some of whom had possibly been armed and trained by foreign intelligence services. Members of all three groups were presumably underground, in the wind, or walking the streets of Bucharest.

I came across a story in Le Monde about the ecological situation Ceaușescu had unleashed in the delta, and the immediate plans—no matter who would eventually end up in power after the late-April elections—to remedy it.

The article led me to Bucharest. There, I began meeting with contacts and sources, and each of them mentioned the name of the one person I needed to know: an environmentalist, writer, and scholar named Andrei, whom I soon met up with at a café in town. The connection was fruitful. Within a day, he introduced me to ornithologists, botanists, heads of institutes, hydrologists—dozens of brilliant bespectacled men in worn Soviet suits. Most of their voices had been stifled for forty years and still bore that burden of weariness, despite the wave of positivity about the delta—its plants, animals, and even villagers that were being rescued by revolution. Romania had been free—relatively speaking—for only a few months, and the information network was scattershot, making for a complex narrative of disparate threads. I was confident that, once I began to write, I would patch together a coherent account of ecological restitution.

Andrei arranged for more interviews in Tulcea, the gateway city to the delta. Not only would he drive me the 180 miles there, but he would skipper me himself along the waters of the Danube for my research trip.

Together with his girlfriend, Dara, we rented a small boat with an improvised cabin for sleeping, and the three of us loaded it up with apples, bread, coffee, several liters of tuica—Romanian plum brandy—and wild boar meat to last the week. Out on the river, Andrei caught fish and, once, a pair of geese to roast with potatoes and boil into soup over a campfire on shore. The birds were small enough to resemble ducks. At a chopping board in the galley, he deftly plucked the geese and, with a carving knife, fileted the fish, discarding the bones, scales, and feathers back into the water. Dara was accustomed to her role as sous-chef, and I helped where I could, rinsing glasses, wiping down forks. She was my age exactly, about ten years younger than Andrei, and I liked her immediately. She regarded her boyfriend's loquaciousness and high state of cheer with slight amusement.

Under the prickly spring heat, we weaved past reed beds, sandbanks, and clusters of willow, stopping at ancient fishing villages where there was no electricity. We seemed a universe removed from Romania's tumultuous winter and even from Romania itself. Parts of the delta had been settled centuries ago by schismatics from the Russian Orthodox Church, and their descendants still spoke their ancestral language. Elsewhere, the country simmered with the unfinished business of political upheaval, and later events would prove that the unrest was far from over. But out in the delta, putt-putting in an old river barge, the country's wounds were obscured by yellower-than-butter spring sunshine and our complete immersion in the wilds.

With Andrei as skipper, guide, and general encyclopedia on wildlife, local customs, and, most of all, the horrific environmental crimes of the fallen regime, we drifted through stands of water lilies and stretches of water both brackish and clear. We hiked through fields of yellow iris, and in the Letea, a primordial forest surrounded by desert that is the heart of the Delta, we crossed paths with falcons and wild horses, meadow vipers and little egrets. "This place must be saved!" Andrei enthused, time and again. He wanted me to love it, and I did.

He had such enthusiasm for the riverine landscape and starry twilights, and so visibly relished a simple bite of perfectly-seasoned game, that I wondered how he had managed his preternatural joy under the stifling dictatorship. "I am Romanian," he said with a theatrical shrug and apologetic grin. There were many benefits to being on the road with an idealist, and such a positive, informed man, but above all, Andrei was the most protective of shepherds. Trust is not rational, but it is immediate, and for a journalist traveling alone on a story, it is fundamental. I trusted Andrei enough to disappear with him for a week into the outback of Romania. Yet, I knew nothing about him.

Crisp with sunburn, we returned to Bucharest, and I checked into the fanciest place in town, the Inter-Continental, right in the center of the city. It was a model of that special Warsaw Pact gaudiness: ubiquitous crimson velvet curtains, chandeliers as big as refrigerators. In the lobby, a fat, grayish man inhabited a chair across from the concierge desk. From his observation perch, he offered, with an oily, close-to-British accent, tidbits to anyone that passed. They all seemed to know him. A woman in thick pancake makeup and minidress walked through the lobby and the man tapped her derrière with the bottom of his cane. She flicked it away with an admonishing grin.

Up in my room, I peeled off my filthy clothes. I had not had a proper bath for days. My trusty leather coat and woolen shawl that swaddled me all over Eastern Europe were saturated with campfire residue. After a long shower, I toppled from exhaustion onto the pleasant mattress. After six nights on a houseboat, my body still rocked from the up-down swells of river current. I awoke to a phone call from Andrei, who was waiting at the reception desk. He was there to collect me for dinner—the last of the fresh goose—at his and Dara's apartment.

He was in a jocular mood, and he resumed his affectionate teasing. "Now, you look like a proper American journalist," he said, when I appeared in a clean skirt, sandals, and pricey Parisian lipstick. By now, Andrei had been my companion for almost two weeks, in the service of the Delta, whose story he wanted to be told. As often happens in the uneven power balance between journalist and source, he gave and gave and gave. All I could offer in return was an article. He refused my dollars to pay for food, the boat rental, even gas.

The next morning, I saw large crowds of people filing purposefully past the hotel, clearly on their way somewhere.

"What's going on?" I asked the concierge.

"Manif," he said, using French slang for manifestation, a march. "On Piața Universității, University Square. But a peaceful one," he clarified.

This was fortuitous. The environmental story I was in Romania to write was on a parallel track to the other story, the one that was outpacing me daily: the precarious and fast-changing political realities three months into the country's revolution. I was engrossed in the subject, but I was still reporting a feature rather than a break-ing news story. But I was still a journalist, always on the *qui vive* for news events. A real-time demonstration on a Sunday morning might be useful for my story, but more than that, I could finally witness something of the revolution up close.

The breakfast dining room had filled up with men wearing suits and too much aftershave. "Happy spring," an American man remarked as he passed my table and stopped. "Care to join me?"

"No thanks, it's a work day," I said, stirring milk into my coffee.

"It's Sunday!" He had wide vowels and an unsparing smile—the kind a witless dad wore in a commercial for cereal or minivans. "And not just any Sunday but Eastern Orthodox *Palm* Sunday."

The man failed to read my face for its clear preference for solitude and sat down across from me. "Waiter," he said. "Can you move my plate over here and bring me more coffee?"

He looked at the notebook I had been writing in, and then at me. "You must be a journalist."

"I am," I said.

"For whom?" he asked.

"*Europ*," I said.

"Writing about the ol' revolution-o-rama?"

"The environment."

It was hard to explain the magazine that employed me. Even to me, it sounded shady. The prior year, I had applied for and won a press fellowship from the Fondation Journalistes en Europe, a group that was funded in large part by the European Economic Community—EEC—the precursor to today's European Union. The writing staff rotated every year, with thirty or so journalists from thirty different countries, who were awarded a stipend to live in Paris and contribute to the magazine the foundation published. Back home in the United States, I was a television news producer, so the year was a sabbatical of sorts, and the editors gave us free reign to explore any topic that interested us. The fact that the Berlin Wall fell a few weeks into our tenure was pure dumb luck.

I was too curious not to ask about him.

"I'm with the embassy. U.S., obviously." His cup clattered against the saucer and he saw that I noticed his shaky hands. "The whiskey is too cheap here," he said with a shrug. "Wild place, Bucharest." He pronounced it the local way: Boo-coo-RÉSHT.

"I can imagine."

"Have you had a chance to look at the tens of millions of bullet holes on every building within a 100-yard radius from here?" he asked. "I'll show you around to see all the beautiful sights, and we can have dinner tonight."

"Thanks," I said, "I have plans. In fact, I actually have to leave now for a meeting. I'm already late."

Excited by the prospect of a demonstration so close to the hotel, I made my move to the front door.

In the lobby, the fat man was in the exact same spot as he had been the night before. "Chumming around with the embassy, I see." His words oozed in my direction. "All the Christmastime festivities," he said, referring, I understood, to the revolution in December. "They lit the match, walked away, and let it burn." The last word was breathy and elongated, like a line in a poorly-acted Shakespeare play. *Buuhhnn.*

"Well…" I said, not knowing how to respond. I wanted to know more about this strange human fixture in the lobby. "And you are?"

"Here eleven years," he answered, "just observing." With a clack of stilettos, the woman from the evening before passed by again. "Heavy perfume for Palm Sunday, Cata." The woman seemed unbothered. "She's been here as long as I have," he offered.

He braced his cane on the floor. "Happy holy day, American girl. Hallelujah. The Lord is risen."

I walked toward Piața Universității in the direction of the march, past the ammunition-scarred parliament buildings, and merged with the crowd on Bălcescu Boulevard. The smell of lilacs mixed with the urban draft of diesel and tobacco. Rebirth was in the wind.

On Eastern Orthodox Palm Sunday, churches hand out willow branches instead of palm fronds at the start of Holy Week, and the newly free citizens waved them gently over their heads, keeping time to the patriotic hymn bellowed by the throng. For now, even the non-faithful celebrated the end of religious persecution that the dictatorship's collapse had delivered. The country had been unshackled and would have its first open Easter Sunday in decades.

According to a young man walking near me, the march was in support of the FSN, and the first gathering in the capital since the seven-ton statue of Lenin in Piața Scinteia was demolished a month prior. I had spent enough time in the Soviet bloc to assume the presence of spies and double agents circulating in the daylight or lurking in the shadows—especially with elections only weeks away. There were probably a few of them walking near me that morning.

I felt a rough tap on my shoulder, and my head jolted to see the American diplomat from breakfast. He brandished a rolled-up copy of the *International Herald Tribune*, as if to indicate what he had deployed to ambush me.

"Hello again." His face was a slick of sweat.

The sudden crackling in my neural pathways signaled an encroaching threat. Until this moment, I had not felt the slightest twinge of unease in Romania.

"Did you follow me?" I asked.

"I hope you weren't late for your meeting."

I broke from the crowd, and he began to walk beside me. He was visibly overheating in the searing sun. A brief story began to emerge. He was from Indianapolis, and his wife was settling in a

26

country in West Africa, his next State Department posting. He had come to Bucharest in November, less than six months earlier.

"I had a front row seat to the big show," he said.

The revolution? I wondered, and then, with horror: the execution?

A makeshift memorial consisting of crosses, photos, and bunches of flowers spread across the circle of grass in the center of an intersection. A steady stream of people arrived to scatter red tulips and white carnations on a growing pile.

"Why did you come to Romania to write about pollution?" he asked as we turned onto Calea Victoriei.

"I've already been to Prague," I said. "Also Berlin. Moscow of course. I was looking for something optimistic to write about. There's no blood in river ecology."

"Tell me again about your *magazine?*" He pronounced the word with sarcasm, as if putting air quotes around it, as if it were something I made up. "I've never heard of it."

"Every office in every department in every ministry in the EEC has it," I said. "Whether or not anyone reads it, I have no idea."

We veered into a park, where a blanket of daffodils shifted in the breeze, and pink magnolia blossoms surged across the landscape. A woman traveling alone, even in the most innocuous circumstances, reads deeply into each interaction with men. Self-preservation, like breathing, is instinctive. I was engaged to my boyfriend Mark, but I was twenty-nine, and understood the laws of attraction. But in this case, there was not a whisper of a flirt, not the merest tug of sexual tension.

"Where did you get your *Tribune,* by the way?" I asked. He handed me his copy of the newspaper. It was several days old, but I had not read any news in two weeks.

"Keep it," he said. I stuck it in my purse.

Linden trees formed neat colonnades, and at one end stood a great ornate clock. "This is a Monet painting," I said.

"Cişmigiu Gardens," he said. "Courtesy of the Krauts, from the 1800s."

Toddlers skipped, lovers held hands, grandmothers chatted. It was a classic scene of a Sunday morning in a European city, with the fresh rush of nature and the clatter of voices. People paddled rowboats across a lake and down a canal, where a couple of black swans glided past a cascade of wisteria and under the arch of a bridge.

"Who is your expert here on the Danube Delta?" he asked.

His questions were unnerving me. I was there for two weeks; I'd met everyone. I told the diplomat so, trying to temper the edge in my voice. I was eager to break from him, his prying, and the pinch of discomfort his presence induced. Plus, I needed to pack and prepare for my last night in Bucharest.

We walked back to the Inter-Continental in silence. The fat man was in his armchair, jabbering his usual madness. "You could find anyone here in December," he said, "CIA, KGB, Stasi, Mossad. It was charming." He waved his hand around the lobby and then pointed it toward the diplomat. "I must say that *you* were completely useless. Offense intended."

"None taken, actually," the diplomat said.

I veered toward the elevator.

"Dinner at 8?" the diplomat said. "I know, I know, you have plans."

Upstairs, I napped, packed and jotted some notes in my diary. *The eeriness of this day will always be marked on my brain.*

After my shower, I took the elevator downstairs to the lobby. The door opened to the jarring sight of the diplomat and Andrei, chatting and laughing at some shared amusement. The creepy man was at his station too, in conversation with two sparsely dressed women.

"There she is," Andrei said with a big smile.

"You are both joining me for dinner," said the diplomat. "I already asked Andrei here."

Andrei, my protector. A dark, tanned Dacian Santa Claus, all bonhomie and mirth, with visible good intentions and genuine concern for the well-being of me, his new friend, all alone in Bucharest. But while he might have been delighted by the idea of not one but two Americans dining with him, I dreaded it. Disappointment reverberated through me, followed by disquiet. The diplomat, in his blue blazer and with a glass of Scotch in hand, was unsettling company. He was tipsy, his moist face a blot of red. I viscerally disliked him.

Dinner was just the three of us, as Dara stayed home. He wondered about the guy in the lobby. "A journalist?" the diplomat asked. "British? Usually, we register such suspicious characters."

"He's been here eleven years," I said. "Not sure how you missed him, since he never moves."

"Andrei, you must know," he said.

"He's a fixture, like the chandeliers," Andre said.

We were drunk after several bottles of wine, and the waiter kept delivering new dishes. Smoked ham soup. Fried cheese. Roasted eggplant. Long, thin spicy sausages. Our tiny crystal glasses were filled multiple times with tuica. Finally, a loud, drunken gangster type in a tough black leather jacket came over to us and gripped Andrei's shoulder.

"I love you. I've read all your articles, my friend. You are a friend of the Romanian people." He was blubbering, and Andrei seemed amused. The man made a grand gesture to buy us a bottle of champagne. We declined but the man sent one over anyway. Andrei rose to thank him at his table, and to say hello to the mobster's wife, whom he had once met.

Our waiter, also drunk by now, leaned over and spoke lugubriously and low, an inch from my face. "Be careful." He murmured a warning to me and the diplomat, pointing to the gangster. "He's dangerous. He hid Nicu Ceaușescu." The dictator's youngest son, Nicu, was a flamboyant and cruel playboy and a Communist party chief who had been arrested around the time of his parents' execution. "Your friend should not be seen with him. He is putting you in danger."

The diplomat's whole demeanor changed. He froze, falling silent as his face transformed into a blanched expression of fear. I felt a rippling twang of adrenaline as Andrei and the mobster roared with laughter on their way back to our table.

"Did you like the champagne?" the mobster effused.

"Very much," I said, "thank you. But I'm afraid we need to get some air. Romanian wine is powerful."

Outside, I told Andrei what the waiter had said about the mobster, and he laughed, swatting his hand. "He's a petty crook. A nobody."

The three of us strolled under a brilliant full moon that cast a spotlight on the scarred buildings in central Bucharest. The diplomat walked behind us, tense. It was hard to enjoy the still beauty of the spring night. "He must be very drunk," Andrei whispered to me.

"Why did the waiter say that man was dangerous? And maybe you too?" I whispered.

I had just asked my friend, whom I trusted on a houseboat, who had dropped everything in his life for two weeks to usher me through a complicated story in a complicated nation, whether I could trust him.

His expression became weary. "The whole of Romania lost the ability to trust over the last decades. It is true, I'm afraid."

"What is true?" I asked.

"The entire world—Moscow, America, Hungary, all of Europe, has something to gain with wherever Romania ends up," he said. "And when this book is written and we see who is still standing, whenever that might be, and I hope it is soon, we have to believe that some people helped the winner to win. But most of us, like me, will simply continue doing our work, regardless."

"And the gangster guy at the hotel?"

Andrei sighed. "He was showing off for you. He wanted to show you that Romanians are generous, so he bought you champagne. A simple moment of vanity."

We returned to the hotel, and I embraced him gratefully and apologetically. Journalists put so much faith in trusted sources, and Andrei had become my ally and advocate. I could discern his disappointment.

In my room, I unfurled the newspaper and glanced at the headlines. All the news concerned Eastern Europe. Germany prepares for reunification. A meeting between Secretary of State James Baker and the Soviet Foreign Minister Edward Shevardnadze. Lithuania declares independence from the USSR. Returning it later that night was my excuse for one last conversation with the diplomat. And where I might not ever be inclined to knock on a strange man's hotel-room door, I was lured to this one because I was eager for an explanation, even a drunken one, as to why he mistrusted my only friend in Romania. It was a necessary coda to a disturbing day.

When he came to the door, his aspect frightened me. He was damp with sweat, his face putty gray, tie askew and loosened as if from a tantrum. The grilling began and his words spun fitfully.

"How do you know him?" he asked.

"He runs the group investigating Ceaușescu's destruction of the Danube Delta."

"Do you know who his friends are?" he asked.

"Why the hell do you care?" I asked.

"Where have you gone with him? Who was with you? Whom did you visit?"

"Stop," I said. "I'm writing a story for a tiny European magazine. He caught fish for my dinner."

He thought Andrei was a spy. He thought I was a spy. I thought he was a spy. Andrei was spying on me, on him, we were spying on each other, and the strange oracle in the lobby was spying on us all. We might all have been suspected double agents or plants gathering intelligence. As for his diplomatic credentials, it now seemed to be a transparent cover. It was difficult to know, however, who wanted what from whom, or who compromised whom, who was using whom, or what potential damage was even being done. I was quite certain that here, in the crucible of revolution, I could offer nothing to anyone and that my value was almost nil. In my notebook was a fairly solid story on the plans for rehabilitating the Danube Delta, and if any classified information slipped between the lines, or if any of my contacts marked me as an enemy asset, it was by accident. It was a harrowing mind game.

Waves of popping nerves, and all that brandy, incited in me a swerve of nausea. The diplomat was silent and visibly panicked. I looked at his desk. The Scotch bottle was almost empty, which must have exacerbated his tailspin. His hair was matted with perspiration, and underarm circles darkened all the way through his blazer.

Foolish woman, I thought, so naïve. I continued to defend Andrei, even as my own doubts swirled. I told him everything. He was a banned writer, brilliant, well-connected, who made a few mistakes, such as joining the party decades ago because he had to in order to survive in Stalinist Romania. "But I am sound in life and limb thanks to the care he showed me and my situation in the Danube Delta. Something the embassy should be thankful for. I would do anything for Andrei—he wants a U.S. Army sleeping bag and I'm going to send him one." All of that was true, but I could not speak about what I did not know. Shame flowed through me as my trust in Andrei wavered.

"What flight are you on tomorrow?" he asked.

My stomach flipped. "Are you saying you don't know?" I asked and turned to leave.

When Andrei arrived at the hotel to take me to the airport, his reassuring confidence and usual ribbing were a balm. In daylight, I had no reservations about him or his loyalties. Kind, generous

Andrei wanted to help me because as a writer, he knew what a journalist needed, and he wanted the story of the Danube Delta to be documented, printed, and read in Europe and elsewhere. It scarcely mattered if the truth was otherwise. I had little to offer besides my interest and commitment to his story. Perhaps that actually meant something in the obscurity of the shadows, but I will never know.

"Your diplomat must have a big headache," he said, heaving with laughter.

"Me too," I said.

"You will forget about me when you get back to Paris," he said as he deposited me at the airport. Andrei had shared his country, his food, his time, and his knowledge with unwavering generosity. It had happened all winter, in small towns in East Germany, in Prague living rooms. People giving their all to an American journalist, expecting—and receiving—almost nothing in return.

"I will have to write to Mark to remind *him* to remind *you* about the sleeping bag!"

At the airport, he ringed his great arms around me, as we both said "goodbye."

It had been two weeks since I arrived in Romania, and I was eager to get home to Paris, to my apartment, to Mark, to my office filled with friends. But as I waited at the gate area, I was shocked to see the odd man, the British cipher of the Inter-Continental lobby, wobble in on his cane. I paused to ask myself what, exactly, I feared about him. Gripped by paranoia, I fixed my eyes downward to my knees and pretended not to see him.

I saw him climb onto a Swissair loading bus and was relieved as he disappeared. Soon I boarded another bus for my Lufthansa flight to Paris through Frankfurt. But when I entered the plane, there he was, seated in the row—the seat—directly behind me.

"Going back to England?" I asked. My voice quavered and I felt utterly unglued.

"Frankfurt," he said. "Sometimes God or Muhammad or who-ever, calls me away. Did you get a good story, American journal-ist?" he asked. "Your new friends will miss you. Andrei and the State Department buffoon." He chuckled.

Heart hammering, I sat and closed my eyes. He hummed a nondescript melody. The bottom portion of his cane appeared beside me on my armrest.

Encoded with meaning, obliquely mysterious, or simply absurd, his ravings sounded to me like nonsense laced with threat. He may have been a lunatic, or he may have been a world-class spymaster. But whoever he was—a spook for the Kremlin, an asset for Great Britain, one of our own, just an ordinary eccentric—he was surely wise enough to know that his words and his presence had by now unraveled me, and that pleased him. When we landed, he vanished into the folds of the Frankfurt airport, and there was no sign of him when I went on to Paris.

In mid-April, violence began again in Bucharest, through elec-tions in May and the landslide victory of the FSN. More protests lasted through the summer. Hundreds more perished in the vio-lence. In June, hunger strikers protesting the former Communists now in government sought refuge in the Inter-Continental.

I wrote my story about the Delta, Xeroxed it, and mailed a copy to Andrei, along with a letter promising the sleeping bag when I next went home to the States. I sent one that summer in a parcel, along with a copy of The Joy of Cooking.

He continued to send newsy letters written on smooth blue vellum, ripe with his wry humor. At first, he rehashed the high-lights of our adventure, needling me about my fear of snakes—the slithering kind we had seen when hiking in the Delta. He tempted me with details of dinners he was cooking up for Dara in Bucharest, especially when the wild boar he roasted gave plenty of crispy skin of the sort I had devoured on the boat. He inquired about Mark, my family, my work and life in Paris, and he updated me on the situation in Tulcea. He expressed his deep affection for me, his one American friend, and wrote of plans to come to Paris. Maybe he would come on foot like the great Romanian artist Constantin Brancusi, he joked.

And then his tone became more pleading, seeking assurances that I would remember him and Dara, my dear friends in Bucharest, and the wild place in eastern Romania he adored so fervently. In 1991, he announced in a letter, "SUCCESS!! THE DANUBE DELTA HAS BEEN PRESERVED!!" He included a newspaper clipping. The headline in Romanian was close enough to French for me to understand: *The Danube Delta was named a Biosphere Reserve under UNESCO and a Wetland of International Importance.* It was excellent news, and Andrei gave me credit that I did not deserve.

But he was right. I stopped writing back, and I did forget him. I moved on to other places, and other sources who, with complete faith in me, gave tirelessly in hopes that I might also recount their stories.

Years later, I mentioned his name to a classmate from graduate school, also a Romanian activist, and learned that Andrei had become a celebrated television chef, and had passed away three years earlier.

The story of the December revolution and the fall of the dictator Ceaușescu is still being told and disputed, and declassified CIA documents have revealed only a few gritty details. Like most revolutions, it is unlikely that the one in Romania transpired without the covert intervention of one or several foreign powers. The Soviet Union wanted Ceaușescu gone. The United States, too, wanted to get rid of Washington's only palatable Stalinist, whose stepped-up repression in the face of Eastern European reforms that year would prove untenable for the rapidly changing continent.

When I'd landed in Bucharest in 1990, the regime had been felled and the old order shattered, making way for a new one that was tentative and rife with complexity. The dissidents and clandestines, assets and sympathizers, plotters and planners, mercenaries and carpetbaggers were not necessarily sitting back to watch fate take its course. And a young American journalist on assignment for a magazine that no one had heard of, on a story that few cared about, might have seemed, for some, too innocent to be true. But Andrei simply wanted me to love the Delta as he did, to tell the story, and help it—if possible—recover and rise again in glory.

That's what I believed then and that's what I believe now. Most of the time.

Chapter 4

To the Man at
the Urinal in Prague

ou must have heard the click of my boots on the stone path as I approached, or felt the swoosh of cold air when I accidentally blew into the men's washroom that January morning in 1990, or heard the metal door slam with a crack. But your head stayed gooosenecked forward, shoulders curved like an egg. Your figure was in profile, so I noticed the deflated wrinkle of your trousers, and the slightly rounded belly indicating a healthy intake of Pilsener.

Your eyes were focused on your hands, which bunched at the level of your fly. I blinked, froze. I swear, that's all I saw in that passing second. But, may I note? Nothing about a public urinal is private: guys lined up, face to the wall, flaunting the simplicity of their biology, convivial and ritualistic like starlings on a power line. It's not so easy for us girls.

I began to tiptoe toward the door, leaving you to the business of your body and me to pursue the urgent business of mine. At 9:00 am, my boss, Barbara Walters, would conduct the first on-camera interview with Václav Havel, who had been president of Czechoslovakia for all of three weeks. We were ten minutes away from rolling tape upstairs, and all morning, our crew had been cursing the Soviet-era wiring inside Prague Castle.

I'm sure you recall those heady times. Only two months earlier, the Velvet Revolution had deposed the communist regime without a single window being broken. A beloved playwright, dissident, and national hero was the new head of state, president of the country he had, for decades, toiled tirelessly to set free. The whole world watched with amazement. The previous day, the crew and I had begun the absurd logistical horror show of loading cameras and lighting gear into the new president's office inside the castle. We had only slept a few hours before we headed back in the morning, crossing the Vltava River and climbing up to Hradcany. Seen from below, the castle, its fortifications, and St Vitus Cathedral were sheathed in sleet and wintry light. Its celestial perch in Prague allowed it to shimmer high above the city it defined, floating like a gilded ship through fog.

The staffers in the office on hand to help were, for the first time, free. Some, I had heard, had just gotten out of jail. As we set up our massive control room to accommodate our multi-camera shoot, it was clear they had not anticipated such a grand production. But it was a joyful frenzy. We all understood that we were participating in something momentous. Each of us collaborating that morning—Barbara's crew, our Czech counterparts, and Havel's new team—sensed the weight of what would soon be recorded in this room. In those days, before the Internet, before everything as we now know it, the first, big, exclusive interview on American television was a Rubicon every new leader crossed as a kind of introduction to the world.

After several blown fuses, we scrambled to access the electrical switchers for the lighting set-up. Barbara's questions needed to be revised on the large note cards she liked, and there was no typewriter to be found in the building. The windows rattled. There were no pens. There was nothing to sit on. The communists had left only a couple of desks, which we moved to the edge of the worn brown carpet.

At last, chairs were located for Havel, his translator, and Barbara, who was getting her touch ups. The set was ready, and it was almost showtime. Adrenaline made my nerves zing and fizz, and though I loathed this sensation, I had grown to crave it, too. I worked in broadcast news. I was wired for this. Buoyed by purpose while wringing my hands with anxiety, electrified by excitement and anticipating doom—that just about sizes up the young associate producer who accidentally walked into a men's room at Prague Castle.

And then, just as I began my turn toward the bathroom door, you happened to look up.

Your eyes were a vivid blue. You disarmed me with a look of utter calm, as if we were not in a stinking public bathroom; as if my face were not pink with embarrassment; as if you were not straightening your navy wool sweater over your trousers. As if you had not been jailed as a political prisoner four times, most recently only a few months ago; as if your story were not by far the most astounding to emerge in the last few months since the Berlin Wall was sledgehammered into oblivion; as if you were not about to go face-to-face with the world's leading television journalist.

"Mr. Havel," I stammered. "Mr. President. I'm so sorry."

"Everyone gets lost," you said, with the vaguest curve of a smile, patting the longish curl at the back of your neck as you exited.

Ten minutes later, standing well out of frame but very much in the room, I closed my eyes for a moment as Barbara Walters leaned in toward you and asked her first question: "In your wildest dreams, did you ever think this could happen?"

Chapter 5

Un Matin de Septembre

I remember, along with so many others, how bright the sky was that morning. There was no premonition—no bruised veins in the clouds, no horizontal rain—that hinted to anyone that within a few hours, all the clocks would stop, and we'd begin to measure time again in a different way.

Mark and I had just gotten back to New York from an anniversary trip to Paris, where we had married ten years earlier. With one baby, and then another, our days as new parents passed in a blur. Except for work and a wedding, I had barely been on a plane for a decade, least of all for vacation. Like travelers throughout the centuries who returned from France with trunks full of chocolate, silk undergarments, and gloves, my bags were bursting. The franc was still used back then, and it bought a lot of stuff. I had new brown suede boots, a black wool suit, and a pair of satin slingbacks that were on sale at BHV, with the soles already scuffed from one last, late dinner on the Rue de Lappe.

At Charles de Gaulle, I headed to duty-free to snag three jars of face cream, $250 a pop, which my friend had asked me to mule for her.

The next morning, I chastised her on the phone: "You owe me $750," I said, "which frankly is a huge waste of money."

"It's amazing cream," she said.

"It's a boondoggle," I declared. "It's basically Neutrogena."

I unwrapped my spoils on the couch, a festive sight. Torn sheets of tissue paper—violet, white, mottled brown—rested beside semi-opened boxes, resembling the aftermath of a birthday party. Pulling my bathrobe behind me with one hand and hiking up my pajama pants with the other, I slipped on the heels and modeled them in the mirror.

"They're perfect," I crowed to my friend.

"Turn on the TV," she said.

The news anchors were going live from downtown Manhattan, scrambling to explain two consecutive plane crashes and the billowing trails of smoke. I froze. It was my son's first day of school, just a mile up from the site. My husband had dropped him off early and immediately drove north to a work project two hours away.

We hung up. I regarded my new packages with confusion, as if they were already relics from a simpler time, one that was suddenly and forever gone.

I shed the heels, threw on trousers and flip-flops, and stood by the door, frantically awaiting our babysitter, who walked in with her customary good cheer. She knew something was amiss but hadn't heard any details while racing to work. I kissed my daughter, Ava—who would soon be four—and left her with a pile of new trinkets and coloring books and Babar figurines.

Running down Hudson Street to collect my son, I watched the first tower collapse.

It took a while for me to eject him from his first-grade class; the school encouraged us not to alarm the kids, who were sitting in a circle and singing "Down by the Bay." I argued with the principal. All my reason had abandoned me, and was replaced by panic and conjecture. "How do you know the plane wasn't loaded with a dirty bomb?" I asked, or maybe shrieked. She eked out a gentle smile. My insides were erupting, my arms twitching so desperately from wanting to feel my son's moving, living body in my arms. "What I mean," I said, emulating calm, "is that we could all be dead by the end of the day, and if that's the case I want to be home with both of my children."

I drifted into the classroom in that haze that arrives alongside tragedy, where faces blur and even nearby voices sound as if they're piped through a distant, malfunctioning P.A. system. I relaxed when I saw him, wearing his Derek Jeter jersey, which he usually wore to taunt me, a Bostonian genetically prone to loathe the Yankees and their fans. I thought I'd made him wear a dreaded collared shirt for his first day of school. We'd argued about it, and he held back tears while I combed his hair and told him to put it on. He'd marched off to his room, and I'd piled a ham sandwich, pear, and bag of Fritos into his lunchbox.

As we exited the school and began to walk, our faces kept turning south toward the single burning tower, and I kept wondering whether he snuck the baseball shirt into his lunchbox on his own, or whether my husband had been in on it. A call came through to my cell phone—Mark, hysterical. He couldn't make his way back. The toll station at the Saw Mill River Parkway had already closed.

My son and I clutched each other's hands and kept walking, but finally we stopped. It didn't occur to me to shelter him from what I knew was imminent.

"This is bad, isn't it," he said, eyes fixed on the smoking building.

"Yes, baby. It's very bad."

The second tower snaked its way down to the ground and as it did, I struggled to keep my knees from buckling.

"I'm glad everyone got out," he said, looking bewildered as he scanned the transfixed crowd. The people made fists or clutched their chests, but they did not make a single sound.

I pulled my son close, and for a second, or an hour, we stared at the plume of ash that rose to the sky. Already, you could sniff poison in the wind. I didn't consider what I might be taking from him, or what, as his mother, I might lose as I held my son that beautiful, dreadful morning, frozen within the stunned and silent crowd on Hudson Street.

All I remember of the rest of the morning is the sound of my flip-flops and the warmth of Ray's hand as we walked home to Chelsea—that and the sight of my daughter when we arrived back in the apartment, dressed in her pale-pink nightgown and my new Parisian shoes, wobbling on the impossibly high heels, laughing like there was no tomorrow.

Chapter 6

Halloween

ight doesn't fall in the wild so much as it crashes. In one minute, you can run from pruning rose bushes in the sunlight to slamming the door behind you, shuddering from the chill and predatory howls.

It was our first Halloween in Connecticut, 4:30 P. M. and pitch dark. The air outside was narcotic with smoke and apples. The kids were in costume: Ray, feeling absurd in a leather vest, bandana, cowboy hat and cheesy moustache painted on with Match-Lite; Ava dressed for a Viennese ball in an elaborate royal gown. She wore thick cotton tights and dainty gold slip-ons that had belonged to my grandmother. The news was on in the kitchen, and we caught the tail end of the forecast: "You might want to dress up as a polar bear this year because it's *chi-hi-hill-y*." Ray was toasty in an alpaca wrap, but Ava refused to put a ski parka over such finery.

When I was younger, Halloween was usually something for me to get past on the way to my early November birthday. If anything, I preferred the candy to the costuming. When we moved to Paris, however, I was all in: searching the produce markets for pumpkins to carve and other gourds to display. The former are redder (or entirely green) in France, but the flesh is a deep, rusty orange. Once, on All Saints' Day, the day after Halloween (and a public holiday in France), I scooped out the skins and made *graines de potiron grillées*, toasted pumpkin seeds, and ate them on a bench in the Place des Vosges.

In New York, Halloween was boisterous and crowded, a loud street festival that sometimes felt genuinely dangerous and undeniably weird. This year the holiday seemed to belong in the windswept Connecticut hills, awash by day with fall's startling oranges, and by night with winter's gloom. We walked out the door, two excited children holding their mother with one hand and Mylar bags with the other. I knew they imagined streets teeming with costumed kids marauding about happily, just like in the cartoons.

We attempted the steep trek up the driveway until Ava's shoe came off for the tenth time, and I was left inevitably carrying my five-year-old, baby style, on my hip. She hugged me for warmth under my flowing navy-blue wool overcoat, the one I wore the day Mark and I shopped for an engagement ring in Paris.

After a significant hike up the street, we passed some de rigueur jack-o'-lanterns and rang our first doorbell. There was no answer. Then we noticed a sign on the doorway: "Take just one!" it read, with an arrow pointing to a large empty bowl on the ground. "There's no candy?" Ava asked. Confusion generated a woeful expression on her face. It was not helped by my attempts at logic. Maybe we were just too late, I thought, though it was not even five o'clock.

"Probably some teenagers came and swiped it all. Let's go over to that white house," I said, noting to myself that night vision binoculars would be helpful in pointing it out. "I can't carry you, honey. It is too dark and I can't hold my flashlight."

We moved slowly up the country road, with no other kids in sight. There were no sidewalks, either, and it was dangerously unlit. In our haste, one of Ava's shoes slipped off her little foot again and fell into the surrounding blackness. The gusty winds were doing an excellent job of blowing my limited enthusiasm for Halloween about ninety miles south to New York City.

We trudged up a snaking driveway and pressed the bell. An old woman answered the door. "Finally!" she said sweetly, making her deposit into the children's bags. "Not too much action on this street."

"Isn't this an exciting night?" I asked my kids after we marched away, and to my surprise, they agreed.

Chapter 7

The Substitute

*T*here were times when my stamina gave out. Teaching, I'd discovered—or teaching French anyway—is not an ideal profession for introverts. Or for journalists, even ones gone temporarily to pasture like me, who tend to listen, rather than speak, for a living. I had to find ways to still do my job without feeling as if I were performing five one-woman shows a day in front of a live audience. So I started to resort to movies during my French classes, delighted to present the sangfroid of Jean-Paul Belmondo in *Breathless,* the glamour of Catherine Deneuve in *The Umbrellas of Cherbourg*—subtitles only for the beginning levels. The assignment to follow would be to write a critique and read it aloud. This day, though, my enthusiasm served only to underscore how little I understood both teenagers and my new, temporary profession.

I was excited to introduce my third level students to *Diva,* a film that I saw and loved when I was twenty, and that epitomized for me the coolest, most stylish aspects of French cinema. With a flourish, I pressed "play" as if to assert that this was, indeed, their lucky day and that I was, indeed, a terrific teacher. One by one, almost the entire class fell asleep during the first ten minutes, as if opium smoke seeped through the air ducts. "Madame," a student who was still awake politely asked, "what is this movie about?"

The call came in the morning between cups of coffee as I stood in the kitchen searching the room blankly for a map to follow in my now familiar quest for a meaningful day. Outside the window, the sky was blue and sparkling, and though the September air was chilly, the grinning TV weatherman had promised ninety degrees of summer heat by midday. I knew the time when I could shed my heavy sweater would present itself in an instant. It was the only plan I had for the day, one that would unfold like many in the two years since I had left New York and my work as a news producer and moved with my family to rural Connecticut.

My husband had lobbied for years to relocate from our six-hundred-square-foot apartment to our crash pad in the country, an unfinished wooden house on the side of a leafy and very remote valley. He is a sculptor, a carver of massive stones, so it stood to reason that he would seek permanence and happiness in the place where he could actually do his work. Also, our children were already strapping schoolkids and had fast outgrown our tight space on the fifteenth floor. The decision to pull up stakes and leave the city I loved was more complicated for me. I stood on the precipice of middle age and was terrified of isolation, geographical and otherwise.

That September morning, with the kids at school, the phone rang and shattered my aimless reverie. It was my new friend, the wife of a faculty member at a nearby private school. We had met through my son and her daughter, who were second-grade classmates.

"You speak French, don't you?" she asked.

"Sure," I said, figuring she needed help with a recipe.

"Well enough to teach?" she asked.

"Well enough, I guess," I answered, genuinely unsure of what else to say. I began taking French in seventh grade and studied until I graduated high school. In my twenties, there were a couple of Frenchmen from whom I learned the saltier bits of the language, and one upstanding Soviet citizen who preferred intimacy in Voltaire's native tongue, rather than in Stalin's. Later, when I worked for ABC News, I sallied forth to the Paris bureau whenever I could finagle a stopover there from Moscow or Berlin, an obvious ploy to butter up my colleagues in the hopes of getting hired to work at the gilded bureau on Avenue d'Eylau. When I was twenty-nine, I moved to Paris anyway, and on my own steam, after the European Union—then the European Economic Commission—gave me a press fellowship. Once I dug into Paris, I stayed for four years. Living there, I learned the cadence, the slang, and the quirks, and I broke all the rules I mastered so diligently in high school. So, yes, I spoke French—clean, dirty, vernacular. But I had not thought about grammar in decades.

The school, my friend reported, was on a frenzied hunt for a French teacher to fill in for a woman on urgent medical leave, and she was certain I was up to the task. Mostly, she knew I needed something to take me away from ruminating. I could use a project, something to fill my day and give my life a point and a paycheck.

"I think you can do it," she said.

"Is there really nobody else?" I asked.

"French teachers don't grow on trees in northwest Connecticut," she said.

How hard could it be?

My interview was a formality. The school hired me to teach twenty classes—five levels of French—each week. Their leap of faith made me incredulous. The parents who could afford it paid about $45,000 for their kids to attend this rolling idyll. My appointment felt vaguely fraudulent. The head of the language department delivered two towers of textbooks and teacher's companions, which I stared at for a couple of days.

Finally, I scattered my prep material all over the kitchen table, the glass and steel one Mark welded together another lifetime ago in his Paris studio that abutted Père Lachaise Cemetery. Sunlight from the end of the day made one side of the room glow like an altar. Color blasted through the picture window that flanked the couch; in the distance, a band of yellow sat above striations of pinks. The sky embellished our early evenings and painted in me a sense of finality. Another day of life had passed, and here's to it. So far, midlife was an infinite bummer, and I hoped to change that with my new job.

I was unprepared for the reaction of horror when I flipped through the workbook for French 3. An invisible hand seemed to grip my throat and choke off my air passages when I saw the chapter title, *Nos amis a Quebec!*

I groaned and read a passage out loud. "*Marcelline est une jeune étudiante en ingénierie de systèmes à l'Université de Montréal.*" Mark laughed.

"What am I doing?" I asked.

"This will be great," he said.

"Did I forget to mention that I immediately have to correct essays on Charlemagne for French 4?"

"King of the Franks, son of Pepin the Short...."

There was no date or historical lineage that Mark couldn't rattle off.

"Want a beer?" he asked.

He went to the fridge and took two Coronas, opened them, and sliced a lime. I squeezed and mashed the pulp into the bottle, and I tried to shove the mangled slice down the neck. It stayed at the top, gulping for air.

As the day approached, I decided to jettison all that. Screw the deadening, mundane curriculum. I would teach them real-life

French. I would be the teacher they'd all remember in future awards-show acceptance speeches. I would be the teacher who changed them. Instead of trudging through grammar, we would screen *Les Enfants du Paradis* and *The Passion of Joan of Arc*. I wanted them to know the devastatingly gorgeous sixties pop singer Françoise Hardy, and to understand why "Non, Je Ne Regrette Rien" was not just Edith Piaf's song but an anthem for all of us. And to avoid, at any cost, the anguish of Marianne Faithful's melancholic "The Ballad of Lucy Jordan," when she sang, "At the age of thirty-seven, she realized she'd never drive/Through Paris in a sports car with the warm wind in her hair." I wanted to inspire them to make off for Paris as Audrey Hepburn did in *Sabrina*—as every sensible person should—and know the singular thrill of standing at the Place de la Concorde at midnight gazing upon the Eiffel Tower in its spangled dress.

I would urge them to first close their books, then their eyes, and to speak—really speak—the language, imagining the thrill of mastering another tongue. To feel it: pucker the lips, shrug the shoulders, add dramatic inflection to every other syllable; to act like a French person and fly. I would tell them about an American news bureau chief I had once known in Paris who did not speak a word of French, and how embarrassed I was for him, and by him. My teaching gig would be *du gâteau*.

The following Monday, my anxiety rose like steam off a lake as I walked across the green toward my first day at work. My boots thudded past sugar maples and teenagers with backpacks, faces rife with curiosity and secrets. Were some of them my students? I wondered whether and how I could teach them. I hoped they would like me. My confidence vanished. When I crossed under the two-hundred-year-old arch into the school and realized the enormity of what I was called upon to do, it was too late to run home.

I had a strong sense that I had jumped, all too readily, into roiled waters. The stone hallways gave me a dark premonition, as if to imply the reality that all teachers know: soon I would meld into the corridors, become part of the building, and barely leave the place. This would be my new home, locked as I now was into pure, low-paying devotion. It was ludicrous. I was no teacher. I belonged in the dark corner of a bar somewhere with a notebook and a pen.

I had fifteen minutes to introduce myself to other faculty members before my first class. But my nerves had emerged, chafed and raw, so I spent twelve of those fifteen minutes fighting nausea in the restroom and finally vomiting out of sheer helpless terror. When at last I took my place at the head of the classroom in front of twenty teenagers and realized I had to put on a show, I understood the gastric upset: it was stage fright. Now I had to entertain them, the kids in Honors French 2, my first class of the day.

"*Bonjour classe*," I said. "*Je m'appelle Marcia DeSanctis.*" I turned around to write my name on the blackboard. I had labored over my outfit for an hour in the darkness that morning, and suddenly I felt too flashy and a bit ridiculous; my skirt was way too tight and my boot heels way too high. I was dressed as I had been for years as a television producer, but for a new French teacher in a bucolic boarding school, I was all wrong. I realized with horror that all eyes were now on my forty-three-year-old backside in a very snug skirt. "But I guess you call me Madame DeSanctis, here at school." I was certain that my cracking voice revealed my insecurities and scant qualifications to lead them on any academic pursuit whatsoever. I desperately wanted to add, "And I am not a French teacher, just a French-speaking former journalist who was lucky enough to be handed this job. And I have no fucking idea what I'm doing."

My knees wobbled as we went around the room, as each earnest student gave me his or her shortened biography. When Tanya, a perky blonde, asked if I was collecting the homework, and Donald, a serious, brown-eyed boy, asked whether the chapter exam would still be the following day, my deep shame was illuminated. I had taken every teacher I'd ever had, and every teacher my children had ever had, for granted. This was going to be work, tons of it, and all my fantasies of real-life French went out the window. These were serious students, some of them brilliant, and they needed to learn, get good grades, and get into college.

"Madame, will the extra vocab be on the exam?" asked one girl.

"Madame, will the test cover just chapter five or everything since the beginning of the year?" asked another.

I had not prepared a test. Neither had the regular teacher, the one I was replacing who had been incapacitated. I had barely opened the textbook. I assured them that there would be no break in their program, not to worry a bit. "I am going to postpone the test until Friday," I said.

"We don't meet on Friday," said a student. "Hi, I'm Hannah. How about a week from today?"

After class, a boy named Grayson came to see me in my office. "I need some help on the imperfect," he said.

You and me both, buddy.

"Sure thing," I said. "Let's see. Can I borrow some paper?" I wrote down a verb: *manger*, to eat. "The imperfect is easy. I'll show you." After fifteen minutes with him, a swelling sense of resolve rose to greet me. He was my student now, and I wanted, almost needed, him to do well.

"Is this any clearer?" I asked, a blatant cry for validation.

I had four classes left to teach that day. I needed a drink.

Those first days, I moved as if floating on water, propelled by the relentless and satisfying current of the school day. I taught five lessons, tried to learn the students' names, and already, I was ashamed to say, had formed opinions about them. I could already see who was serious and who hated French class and who hoped their substitute teacher would give them a free ride. I sensed who was sucking up, and who made excuses for missing homework, and I tried my best to nod compassionately and believe them. It surprised me how quickly—sometimes just by an intensity in their gaze—I could spot a student with a ferocious drive to excel and they popped up regularly.

I did not realize that, despite how democratic the process was in theory, a teacher was only a human being, and being fair was sometimes a necessary contrivance. I was supposed to like them all equally, and the best I could do was to pretend that I did. Similarly, I had to possess an equal trust in their abilities and efforts and not penalize them for lack of enthusiasm in a subject they despised. Even if I knew that Billy, for example, found French class to be a torture chamber, I could not hold that against him.

I was partial to two kids, both stars of the school drama program who had a way with accents. Neither of them could complete a homework assignment or hand it in on time, but their mistake-riddled spoken French was gorgeous. It would propel them, I hoped, around the streets and cafés of Paris or Aix-en-Provence and serve them well. They were better suited to dream and work their way across the world as I once had, more than anyone who scored perfectly on grammar but could not speak a decipherable word.

I tried to look the other way when a student fell asleep in class. It happened all the time, and who could blame them? Grammar is a deadly hell. High school students have enormous demands on their time and, to be truthful, for those not born with a gift for languages, it can be a struggle to stay awake, let alone alert. Of course, I was mortally wounded when a student dozed off, but I wailed only on the inside. When they checked their watches or craned their necks to see the wall clock, I was crushed. They were right: I was boring. I took to throwing candy at my first-year students in a shameless effort to buy their love and attention in the long, starved hour before lunch. I kept bowls of Halloween-sized

Snickers and Twix bars on hand, and once even gave a kid money to buy snacks for everyone at the vending machine.

I am certain my students did not know the hours I put into making up tests, correcting homework, planning the next week's lessons. I had no idea myself until after the first few days of standing reluctantly in front of a classroom. My family life went on hold while I negotiated the learning cliff of a first-time teacher. When I was rewriting a student's stilted homework paragraph at midnight, eighteen hours into my workday, I did it with the same passion and facility I remembered from writing my own stories as a journalist.

Like an actor who gets her big break, I got used to, and even motivated by, the performance anxiety, the brief wooziness from adrenaline, and finally the complete clear-headedness that was required of me as I stood in front of the students. I enjoyed walking in as the figure in charge. Usually, my nerves quickly settled into the classroom's groove. I was working harder than I ever had, and though the schedule was grueling, I looked forward to my lessons and the responsibility that came with them. And yes, when I was depleted and could speak or give no more, I fell back on the occasional movie, even if they often weren't big crowd pleasers.

The students, for their part, may or may not have sensed that I was growing fond of them (or protective) and of the teaching rhythm that had become the engine of my life. I anticipated some of their essays with curiosity, and I felt a new intimacy. You can learn a lot about a person by their homework—that he did not make the varsity hockey team, or that she hates the violin her mother forces her to play, or that his greatest wish is for his parents to reconcile, or that she dreads the upcoming holiday vacation with her stepfather, who drinks too much and *n'est pas sympathique*.

By the time the semester had ended, it was December vacation and my job was over. There was no party for me, of course. Everyone was exhausted from correcting final exams that bleary week. There was snow on the path when I crossed the green for the last time toward my car. With the stone building behind me, and the arches at my back, I wept tears of near grief. I cried for the students who had affected me so deeply, but who I feared had already forgotten me in their exuberant exodus for the holidays. I had gotten myself out of the house and rejoined the family of man again, and it was just as I remembered it: overflowing with motivated, committed people, who demonstrated all manner of goodness. All teachers know that the reward is mutual—you give, you get—and now that sweet secret was mine to hold as well. I had laid myself bare before my students and, in so doing, got a lesson in what mattered, and it wasn't me.

But I also missed the breakfast and dinner routine with my own children, whose Christmas lists sat folded up and neglected in my wallet.

I sat a spell in the parking lot. The life before me seemed vacant, the one just behind me was full. I looked up to see a smiling Hannah at my car window.

"We'll miss you, Madame," she said.

"I'm sorry to be leaving, Hannah," I said. "I loved teaching your class."

"Then stay," she said.

"Madame Mazarine will be back in January," I said. "She's a great teacher and much more qualified than I am."

"So, what do you do normally?"

"I am—I was—a journalist."

"That's cool," she said, "but why don't you teach French instead?"

Why, indeed?

About two years later, my phone rang again just before the Christmas holiday. It was the head of modern languages at the school. There was a new crisis in the French department: a beloved teacher had fallen ill, and it was just the start of the winter semester. Would I consider coming back?

"Depends how long," I said.

"It could be indefinitely," she said.

For a moment I said nothing, as the possibilities tossed around my brain. I still had not come up with any ideas for the second half of my life, and was still puttering around the kitchen. This never was the plan, but I missed the students, the adrenaline, the human race. Hell, I missed speaking French.

"What do you think?" she said.

And I tried to find the words to say that it might not be so bad to go back for a while.

"Sure," I said. "Love to."

Chapter 8

Love's Labour's Won

Sixteen years into my marriage, I fell for another man.

For months, I was in crisis, splintering from a heart that shattered in slow motion. I barely functioned as a mother and citizen or, most important, wife. So I turned to the only person I knew who loved me enough to give a damn and was man enough to forgive me: my husband.

Though I considered—even pursued—an extramarital affair, I'd like to think I wasn't a cultural cliché. But in fact, I am probably the emblematic midlife mother of two who wakes up one day and wonders if all of life's mysteries are behind her. I was in my forties, enduring a daily, robotic cycle of carpooling and cupcakes. I had lived for five years in the professional and literal wilderness, having left New York City and my career as a television producer for rural life with my artist husband. During that time, I wrote a novel about marriage and the sacrifices we make when we decide to commit to one other person in this one life. I began to feel itchy, impatient, a sense that something new might be imminent.

When my son turned thirteen, the pinprick of light at the end of the parenting tunnel suddenly turned into a hole the size of a quarter. I started wearing lipstick in the morning. I retired the unkempt ponytail. I was less aware of the dwindling supply of estrogen left in my body—the female's tragically nonrenewable resource. I knew I had to begin to plan life on the other side of mothering.

Lacking the courage to sell my novel, I decided to go back to school and got accepted to a master's program in international relations. I left that July to plunge into the first of three extended academic residencies—two at Tufts University and one in Asia. The bulk of the curriculum would be taught online, in coffee-fueled all-nighters, as I wrote papers on Nigerian terror cells and Argentine banking reforms over the course of one sleepless, invigorating year.

It was while pursuing this degree that I met him.

I have thought a lot about why women stray, and I have known plenty who have. Some suffer from a love-sapped marriage. Others can't tolerate their husbands but stay with them because of financial necessity or the children. A few want a little midlife sizzle after years of routine sex with the same person. In my case, the explanation was beautifully simple and weirdly complex: I fell in love. It's not that I had a bad marriage; far from it. I have a larger-than-life, hugely talented husband. He makes me laugh, and we adore each other. But somehow, this other man—a relief worker with loose trousers and premature crow's-feet—got under my skin.

It snuck up on me. R. seemed an odd sort at first, a Midwesterner stationed in a crisis zone overseas. He didn't much like to hear himself talk, but others did. We sat beside each other in lectures, and I began to feel his gestures—the way he poured his Coke, the delayed smile when he swiveled his head to look at me, the amused flicker in his eye when one of our professors said something insufferable. I started to crave his company because, despite all that separated us, we saw the world through a nearly identical lens. I led a busy life, and he lived in war zones, but our sense of loneliness was the overwhelming constant for both of us. In our class of diplomats, military officials, and businesspeople, I recognized his self-perception as an outsider because I felt like one too.

OK, it didn't hurt that he was literally feeding starving children. Altruism was an aphrodisiac. He was also not just spare in his lifestyle but also in his thinking. I am not sure I have ever met anyone quicker to slice to the essence of things. R. had absolute clarity pondering a macroeconomics conundrum or the benefits of flood relief in Myanmar. I was drawn to his strong opinions, which reminded me of many cocksure journalists I had worked with in my past—the past that was getting farther and farther away from me. We sought each other out—the married housewife and the younger aid worker—with a burgeoning attraction I assumed was mutual, and about which I was stunningly unconflicted. I was away at school, disembodied from my life.

At the end of our first two-week session in Boston, we hugged each other goodbye in the lecture hall. By all appearances it was chaste, but I swore it was loaded with meaning. I was in the throes of nascent unconsummated love, wondering how I could breathe, run a house, or keep up with the impossible course deadlines for the four months until I saw him again in Asia. How would I sleep with my husband when I longed for a man—one I'd never touched—in Africa?

My husband believed my emotional absence was due to the crushing amount of schoolwork. He picked up all the slack, despite the grueling demands of his own work. I was a fraction of a wife as I buried myself in my studies and my infatuation.

Like that of Governor Mark Sanford, and probably many other lovesick fools, my relationship with R. gathered steam over email. I slept fitfully, waking early to check the in-box, feeling euphoric when his name was there and despondent when it was not. His writing was sparse, elegant, and full of self-deprecating wit. When he described smoking a cigarette under a desert cloudburst, he was Hemingway to me, or Graham Greene, every mysterious adventurer framed by solitude in a foreign land. I was sure he pined for me, too, looking up at the sky and wondering if the earth's tilt or the sun's rays connected us at that very moment.

I planned to be intimate with him when we were reunited. My inevitable betrayal scared me, but nothing—not morality, reason, love for my husband and children—could stop me. How simple it was to rationalize my approaching transgression as necessary. Suddenly, I believed that life is lived but once, and I owed it to mine to be with him. To ignore this romantic love would be a crime I would rue on my deathbed.

I did not consider that R. might not want to sleep with me.

In Asia, we were inseparable. After school hours, in his or my hotel room, we talked about writers Lawrence Durrell and Richard Ford, the careers we still hadn't been brave enough to try, the ways our childhoods helped decide our fates, all the subjects almost-lovers cover to milk connection out of every second together. We discussed a thousand what-if scenarios: if we had met at some other point in our lives; if I were not married. We drained the hotel minibar daily and greeted the sunrise, exhausted, with room-service coffee. But despite some passionate embraces and a few long kisses, there was no physical affair. He explained why: I was someone's wife. We barely touched each other again.

Nevertheless, I galloped toward a future with him. With no logic to speak of, I tried to will him to rethink it, to love me back, to come with me to some imagined place. I knew it was selfish and reckless, and I guessed that the cost would be high if he actually reciprocated, but this feeling had made me remarkably nonjudgmental about myself. I assumed he would be similarly unable to deny something so obvious, so powerful. I had given him all the permission in the world to have this affair.

Looking back, I'm sure that I did, in some way, need him. I could see only the gaps in my life, and R. filled in all of them. And there was something else crouching in the back of my mind:

If I failed to have this, it would be the end of me as a woman. No doubt something was whispering to me: This is your last chance.

At the end of the master's program, I was chosen by my class to give the commencement address. It was a warm July morning in Boston, and R. was seated right in front of me in his cap and gown, listening. I avoided his eyes, fearing a total breakdown right in the middle of my speech. All the while, my proud husband and children beamed at me

After the lunch reception, after all our friends and relatives had left us to gather our things, R. and I faced each other to say one final goodbye. I fell apart. He was returning to the desert, to his work, to the tanned, French NGO girls. His life was moving along quickly, but mine had stood still in that hotel room in Asia. Yes, I was returning to a beautiful family, but all I could see ahead was the grayness of my old routine—the same five-mile drive to school, the same grocery aisles—and no R. in my life ever again. He was gone for good. I felt his absence every second of every single day.

I imagine that in many unfaithful marriages, at one given moment, the life of deception becomes unbearable. And so it happened with me. There was a long, agonizing silence. Finally, one day, I received an e-mail from R. After many women I'd heard too much about, he'd fallen hard for someone in Africa. I shouldn't have been surprised, but I crashed nevertheless. And then I did the only thing that seemed proper: I confessed to my husband.

I explained that I loved a man an ocean away, whom I barely knew, who had rejected me before we ever got off the ground. I told him that I needed my best friend to lead me out of this morass, to save me fast. I explained that the only way I could regain my sanity was with his help. Amazingly, he was the one who loved me enough to comfort me, who knew me well enough to clear my head. Only he could explain why this fantasy had demolished me, and only he could make the pain stop. I told him I was sorry, that

I couldn't discipline the urges of my flailing heart. I told him that I never stopped loving him all the while, but I'd understand if he kicked me out.

He didn't. Nor did he scream or throw things. Yes, he rolled his eyes; yes, he was irritated and fed up with my moodiness and mooning. But he saw it simply: Our marriage would survive if it was meant to. He loved me enough to see beyond my betrayal and even told me this guy didn't know what he was missing.

He made me see that my erotic obsession was disconnected from our genuine, actual, tactile life. One was in the sky, the other was on the ground, and here on earth, people loved me back and needed me.

And then, with my husband grasping me, sometimes from a distance, I began to grieve. Like an addict, I tried to get through a minute, an hour, a meal. I read Ezra Pound's poem "Camaraderie" a million times, always haunted by the line "Sometimes I feel thy cheek against my face." In two frantic days, I wrote six chapters of a novel about an affair with R. I slept all day or not at all, and when I was awake, I cried and stared at things out the window. My kids wondered what was wrong, and when I couldn't get out of bed, they stayed out of my way while their father poured their cereal.

And one morning, I woke up and didn't check my e-mails or disaster reports from R's war zone. I removed the photo from my wallet, of the two of us deep in conversation. I went downstairs and ate bread and butter. I got dressed.

For my husband, forgiveness was not an act of heroism, or even of complacency, but an instinctive gesture of compassion and the deepest friendship. He owed me that much, he said, and he believed we could make it through anything. Fidelity is not to a person, but to devotion and to memory, and it was not worth giving up easily. He knew that nothing could stop a human heart that was racing out of the gates, even his, and should that happen, he would expect the same dispensation from me.

"I loved him," I said. "I thought I could leave you."

"I know," he answered. "But you can make this easy or make this hard. And it really is much easier to stay."

"Do you feel sorry for me?" I asked. "Just a little? That I got dumped?"

"No," he said. "I feel sorry for you because everything you need is right here, in front of you."

Who can predict each of our capacities for understanding? My husband redefined the parameters of empathy. Maybe he had his own story with some other woman on some other dark night. I can only allow him that, and believe that if so, it has made him love me better. And if he has wandered, it gave him the flexibility to see through his wife's heartbreak, to know how fleeting her detour would ultimately be. Through it all was his certainty that romantic disappointment—even wedged into the middle of a long, solid marriage—could make me more of a partner, and not less of one.

My husband obstinately believed in the simplicity of commitment, not as a default but as an act of will, a decision. We choose to stay in the lives we ourselves have chosen. But he also understood that my ache had been real. It's called life, and no one knows where it's going to take you.

As for R.? I took a deep breath and let him go.

Chapter 9

The Language of Sculpture, and of Words

My husband is a sculptor, and he worships stone.

Travertine, granite, marble, onyx—these are the interlopers in our bed, the other women in my married life, and I cannot compete with their charms. The love my husband professes for me exists in the shadow of the love he has for his work, the pieces he fashions from the great slabs of rock which appear with regularity at the top of our rural driveway. They are his constant, devoted companions, and they feed his passion in a way that no person ever can. I don't begrudge him the objects of his obsession, but I do get twinges over the easy partnership he has with his material, so unlike my own relationship with words. A writer can learn a lot from a stone carver, and I've been watching him a long time.

Our accounts differ as to when we got together, which is another story from the wholly empirical *slept* together. That was three years after we graduated from college, or about seven years after first laying eyes on him in Geology 201. He was a big, muscular man with a kind face that was often obscured behind facial hair, the kind that betrayed an unconscious lack of grooming, like that of a shipwreck survivor. I was enrolled in Rocks for Jocks to fulfill a science requirement and compensate for my left-brain shortcomings. I assumed he was taking the course for the same reasons. He was a rugby player, at the center of the scrum, the place where brawny gentlemen dig their feet into the grass and move other giants with their shoulders. It was more fun than football, which he had played in high school, and the guys were smarter. After hours, he could be seen running around campus with his teammates, singing bar songs. He did not appear to be capable of splitting atoms, as others were doing elsewhere on campus. He was a nice guy and I liked him enough, but I never imagined myself as his wife.

I had no idea that he spent his free time making pottery in the entrails of the fine-arts building. He was soon to be a sculptor, with stone as his medium. It was what he wanted to be since he was nine years old, when he traveled to Italy and saw Michelangelo's *Slaves* at the Accademia in Florence and a marble carving of two men fighting at the Palazzo Vecchio. He was struck by the thought that a story could be stuffed into a chunk of stone.

And rocks were in his DNA. His paternal grandmother was born among the artisans of Massa-Carrara, Tuscany in the breast of great marble mountains, and his other side was brute force Scottish, bred in the Orkney Islands, with their coastlines battered for eternity by the harsh Atlantic. Earth science, along with art history, was starting to lay a direct intellectual pipeline to the passion that has fueled him through every day of his adult life, a majority of which has now been spent with me.

His life revolves around shipments of stone. They come from quarries in northern New York, Minnesota, Georgia, Turkey, Italy or Iran, via trucks or containers, sometimes in the hundreds of tons. The stone usually arrives at our property later than scheduled, in an eighteen-wheel rig driven by a trucker who's been lost for hours since the end of his union-mandated, ten-hour break that morning. The driver (and the stone) is met by my husband with hot coffee and great arm waving, a one-man crew on a supply ship, greeting ocean-borne sailors. Then begins the process of loading them onto forklifts for multiple trips to his outdoor studio below our house. There, they get stroked, admired, stacked, and queued for the final journey into sculpture.

I know the lingo now—roughbacks, cores, endcuts. My husband inspects these raw chunks of the planet much like a butcher scrutinizing his chops and roasts. But I don't pretend to understand the fire ignited in him, possibly at birth, that makes him an artist above all else. On a recent winter day, I stood in the warmth of the kitchen and watched his trips up and down the driveway. He was impervious to the cold, ginger with his payload, which he treated as if it were crystal stemware. I saw his mouth moving and eyebrows lift brightly. I asked him what he was saying. A prayer? No, he said. He was singing. Just a tune in his head, while snow and wind pounded the windshield of the forklift, which bore a twenty-ton, ice-cold slice of blue granite. The drill marks were visible. Stone freshly and visibly hewn from the earth excites him, as if it connects him to the ages, his Paleozoic lifeline. On these days, his normal state of high contentment turns to giddiness or even ecstasy.

When he carves a hefty sculpture (and I differentiate here, because he will devote some stretches of time to smaller, more mobile pieces for indoors or the wall) he positions the stone with the forklift onto the center ring of the clearing where he works. This is the area that is equidistant to all the tools and machines and the big, covered space: the wet saw that is plugged into one wall, the compressor that, when activated, sounds like an idling 767, and, resting on a rusting job box, a vulcan's wet dream of chisels, hammers, rasps, and pickaxes.

He lays into the stone with a jackhammer affixed with a foot-long rock bit. Chunks, some the size of a toaster, tumble to the ground with a thud. Next, with one stroke after another, he confronts his medium with hunger and lust and reverence the way some of us tear into a rare steak. His focus, though, is unbreakable. He is sheathed in a one-piece suit, mustard yellow or Santa Claus red, made of dense gauge, flame-retardant cloth. His knee-high boots were once black, but they are so caked with dust and water they appear, from a distance, to be pale white. A respirator covers the area from the bridge of his nose to his chin, and safety glasses obscure the rest of his face. A pair of chopper-issue headphones with a thick, padded brace covers his ears. He is oblivious, a study in concentration. He does not notice me; if I have an urgent message to convey, I have to throw a pebble at his feet to break the spell.

I would not say that the workshop is welcoming to me. It is a precarious festival of blades, edges, and sharp objects. It is bitter cold most of the year as well, rife with the kind of fine-particle dust that not only will ravage your lungs with silicosis but will also smear and smudge and release itself in puffs. It is akin to cake flour, and the handprint that ends up on the thigh of my jeans will stay there until the laundry washes it out. When polishing granite, my husband feeds water to the road saw, and the stone powder on the ground turns to clay. When I walk down there, I'm never wearing the right shoes.

I seemed to be unusually present the time he sculpted a 3½-ton pillow to perch astride a wealthy person's swimming pool. I had to interrupt him a lot because of a family crisis that demanded more of us than we had, and he always seemed delighted to see me, as if it was a great joy to be pulled back to the parallel world of responsibility and human connection. I witnessed the rock hammer give way to a slimmer drill, then to hand tools like the chisel. He intervened often with the wet saw, a brutal conglomeration of steel that shreds the granite while spewing water with a screeching metal-on-metal din that makes my teeth ache. The pieces got smaller and smaller as they landed on the ground and began to form a carpet of refuse, all the bits of stone that were in the way of forming this object.

Within a week or so, he honed away the roughness with a grinder affixed with a diamond blade that spun at 3000 rpm. A pillow about 40 inches long by 28 inches wide emerged from the stone. I could see the crystals and veins—blue, black, teal, specks of gold that will reflect the sun—emerging in the soft, undulating space that he fashioned, a warm rock on which, soon, someone will be able to drape herself comfortably.

Next, he will fire up the acetylene torch and flame the sculpture to make it smooth like velvet. Or, in some places he will use diamond paper to sand and polish to a high gloss if he's inclined. This end phase can be painstaking. He insists that it is where the ordinary becomes transcendent.

When I can no longer stomach something I've been writing, I tell him, "There's no more I can do."

"You have to hone the edges," he says.

"I'm done," I whine.

"You have to grind and whittle," he says. "It's the most important step."

My husband contends that little separates our creative worlds, mine mental and stationary and his physical. After all, don't I spend the day banging my head against the corner of the desk, trying to make a sentence, just as he bashes his own thoughts into meaning? Maybe so, but the comparison seems to end there. His artistic life consists of the transference of ideas to the tactile world through the medium of mostly igneous rock. Every cut he makes is deliberate, joyous; an action with a purpose: to tame the stone and the edges into something that exists already, one that—maybe decades ago—took shape in his head. His tools provide him with a sense of measure, balance, even logic, because they guide him to the sculpture's inevitability. He's an artist, who offers an object of beauty for people to love or buy, and he needs to justify the space it will take up in the world.

My words live in a swarm of chaos, and I have no idea how I'll lay them down until the deed is done. My need is for concentration while I untangle the knots and wrangle the pieces into a linear thought. When I manage to do this, a couple times a day, if I'm really lucky, I'm buoyed by a sense of reward that makes the tortuous act become a pleasurable one.

Sometimes, the differences between our artistic lives are highlighted by circumstances—usually his, which shift more than mine. At the end of a recent truck delivery day, for example, I've written six hundred words; he's unloaded 120 tons of granite from seven trucks and carted it to his stone yard. We uncork a bottle of wine, and I ask him how he's doing.

"Lotto, baby," he says. "This is the most secure I can feel. I have a couple of hundred tons of stone, and I know pretty much what it's going to look like. Once I have the material, the physical act of making the piece is almost insignificant."

"That can't be true," I say.

"All I need is time," he says. "The pieces are already in my head."

It can be hard for me to share in his joy, and not to envy him and the confidence he has in what he calls the "slow language" of stone, as opposed to the fast one of words, the one I live and breathe, the one where I disappoint myself regularly. That is my world, the purgatory of high expectation and low output. I tend to measure my work in what I *haven't* yet done, in what remains unwritten. For him, productivity is quantifiable, in the dust and shards that fall away.

"If I never had another idea in my life, I still couldn't execute half my ideas," he continues. "I'll always have a twenty-year backlog. That's the beauty and disadvantage of working in a slow language. But the upside is that nothing ever comes out that isn't severely scrutinized and edited."

Even though he insists he's just a "physical writer," I respectfully disagree. There's no "delete" key, no cut and paste, no teeth gnashing over a mistake he can't change, but, instead, must integrate into his plan. My writer's life is not filled with his, or any, lucidity. In this sense, sometimes togetherness can feel like solitude.

Many people are in awe of his work, especially when they witness (or know about) the brutal setting where he creates it. He never makes me feel like the philistine that I am when I struggle to understand his sculptures, especially the most conceptually obscure ones—hollow torsos and ten-foot-high, padded granite cells. Maybe those narratives should be clear to me, but they aren't. But they are beautiful, and I do try to impart enthusiasm as best I can, especially knowing the physical price he pays so willingly.

His work involves constant exposure to elements and danger that seems to emanate from another century—like the third B.C. The drills and wet-saws and compressors could slice off a limb or his head, and he shrugs off the anecdotes of constant near misses. I try not to worry about his forklift capsizing under the groaning weight, or about him getting a hand or himself flattened during an offload. Nicks, lacerations, abrasions, and stitches are everyday occurrences, but he is careful. At least he says so.

I prefer not to question him, or even to watch him work. It frightens me to see him engaged in his backbreaking daily activity. I wonder whether he has no fear out there precisely because he has no doubts. There's not a man in the world that can do what he does—I'm pretty convinced of that—but nor would they want to. I know a lot of writers who fake it, myself included half the time, in my motionless little space. Such posing would be impossible for a stone carver, a real one at least. Confidence gives him sure footing, and conviction makes the days and years fly by. This happens as a matter of course—with or without commissions or gallery shows, and with or without me panicking about his safety or our family's finances.

When we first started dating, I was interested in prepped-out bankers with BMWs and Europeans with no visible means of support, but fully loaded with beach houses and refrigerators stocked with Dom Perignon. He was an unlikely match for me; no longer exactly the wild man he had presented at college, but still summarily dismissive of his fancy pedigree and all manner of creature comforts. He was making his life in Carrara, where he carved identical marble copies of classical statuary for wealthy Texans to put in their Fort Worth rose gardens. He was armed with an honors history degree, rudimentary Italian, and nothing more than a feeling that home would be anywhere there was a hammer and chisel. If he had not been so pure about his mission, his drive might have seemed put on. But it came to him naturally, whether it was the simple exercise of making a woman's figure out of *giallo di Siena* while grappling with its pocks and veins, or the adventure of experimenting with patina, textures, and finish.

I was in love with him, but I also loved the *idea* of him. I believed that an artist so skilled at turning crags into living forms so lovely they seemed half alive would be soft as a cub with me and would make my flesh feel worshiped. His hands were chewed up, but he was gentle, and the allure of how he spent his days imbued him with a mystery that, even back then, I didn't bother to fathom. Our backgrounds were similar, but we were turning out as opposites. I worked at jobs I loved but quickly tired of, and he studied history, collected oversized art books, carved stone, and made art. I went off every day to an office where I carried out that day's duties, while he met the day elated to go to some dingy, unheated studio. I filled up my desk drawers with the first chapters of novels I wanted to write, but I abandoned them for the paycheck I thought I needed. He, meanwhile, was determined to change the way we look at things. I saw in him the courage I lacked, and so I tagged along, marrying him and his unbendable spirit, hoping some of it might transfer to me.

I left behind the men with health insurance and suits and ties, as well as any semblance of security or what I then called "normal life." I didn't acknowledge how ill-suited I was for adventure, nor could I predict *how* unpredictable my life with the stone carver would remain. I wasn't sure of my place on the creative continuum, but even before he started his life as a sculptor, he knew his, and it had little to do with anyone's—especially his—definition of success. But I learned how to be an artist, even if his encouragement was a tad simplistic. "You should be writing!" he'd say pretty much every day, as if it were as easy as changing my shade of lipstick. I was fueled by all the stories living inside my head, but unlike my husband, I couldn't pound them into being with a pile of tools. The courage would have to come from somewhere else. I would have to will them into being, and I waited for the day when I could do just that.

Before we had children, I was second in line, and once they came, I was third. He's a good husband, and he's a better father, but best of all, he is an artist. I still envy his indisputable belief in the order of things, his certainty about what he was put on earth to do. I am used to the tenderness he has for the stones he sculpts so masterfully into pillows and chairs and giant megalithic landscapes and female forms and other shapes we call art. We humor him on the highway when he sees a jutting cliff in the distance, jams on the brakes, and marvels at the striations or the crevasses—the absurd lure of the granite. Wherever we are, he pulls over to visit a quarry, to swim in it, if possible, to feel the rock with all of his body and read its lines. It is, in a way, how I treat books and language, but it seems easier to quantify passion when you can feel it beneath your feet.

Our children see a man who is devoted to his work and keeps hours as rigorous as any corporate lawyer. Whether or not they know it, his excitement fills up the house. He has imparted to them and me the singular beauty of getting up and doing what you love, and never needing to complain about your job. For him, and by example for me, every day (even a dark one) is a great day at the office. In the evening, sometimes long after nightfall, he walks back to the house covered in dust, with satisfaction brightening his aura. He believes that what he is doing matters.

But I will always be left out of his creative life, removed from the intersection of man and material. This means that I will always be removed from him, even if he genuinely believes that our work is more than just parallel. Aren't we both just unraveling stories, wherever they manifest themselves? Yes, maybe, but mostly no. His single-mindedness comes at a cost, even if it has taught me how uncomplicated an artist's creative life can actually be. I admire his certitude, and the psychic effortlessness of his pursuit. He masters the material, whereas words tend to rule me until one of those moments of ecstasy, which fades and tries to make way for the next one.

The question I ask many years later is: Would I have chosen differently? It's because of him that I finally quit my last office job, the kind that made me pine for the life I knew I was missing. And I would rather live with a passionate man than a searching one, even if the object of his obsession will never be me.

Chapter 10

Waiting for the Sun

I hadn't considered the rain.

If I had been thinking, I might have figured out that the beach resort was dirt cheap because it was June, the beginning of the low season, which, here, meant the wet season. What did I know? We are a two-artist family for whom a Caribbean respite consists of take-out Jamaican beef patties from a bodega in Waterbury. At the time, my children attended the kind of schools where many, if not most, of their friends bolted for Telluride or Costa Rica or Nantucket or at least Orlando over spring and summer breaks. Some years, when we had room on our credit cards, we hauled off to Tucson to visit family and fill up on guacamole and those saguaro-studded vistas that wipe the winter from the brain. We were used to getaways being synonymous with winging it at the last minute, if we could find a way. But even my kids claimed to genuinely love down time at home, our freezer stocked with Heath Bar Crunch and their mother always willing to sling up eggs to order.

It had been a tough year, even aside from the bills. I was on the upswing from a leave of my senses that had nearly derailed my marriage. For almost eighteen months, I had been unable to discern any strip of daylight above the sea of midlife regret on which I found myself suddenly adrift. It was the riptide of hormones that took me under until one spring day, I crawled out the other side, squinted at the sunlight, and loaded up a few vases with tulips I had planted in the darkest moments the previous November. I was exhausted but hopeful, bursting with apologies I wasn't sure I could ever articulate. What was I supposed to say to my beautifully unscathed children?

I had let them down. What we needed, what I needed most of all, was to get out of town. I wanted to leave my house, and in so doing, to sweep the melancholy out of my house as if cleaning a post-plague hospital. I wanted the kind of togetherness that only a vacation can allow. I wanted my kids to see me as I was meant to be: smiling, at peace, the multi-lingual journalist at ease anywhere on earth and in her own skin; the rock-solid foundation of the family; the woman who could function alongside other people and not sequester herself from humanity; the person who wasn't a basket case.

What we needed, when school ended for the year, was a white-hot beach. I wanted to scour tide pools for shells with my children or drape myself along a patch of sand and watch their bodies leap over the turquoise waves. And then came the solution, courtesy of my Inbox and American Express: a five-star hotel opening in the Caribbean. Forty percent off rooms, free this, complementary that, on a gemlike little island studded with sparkling beaches and a sprawling nature reserve one jet and one tiny plane hop away from Hartford. Sold! We would leave when the kids got out of school and return tanned and whole, the family tighter than ever.

Securing the cheapest flights for all of us meant that my daughter, Ava, and I had to leave a day early, and we set off with our books and carry-ons, our checked luggage crammed with filmy sun dresses and quarts of sunscreen in every SPF. On the plane, we riffled through the research I had dug up: food trucks and coves to explore, the bakeries and drives and promenades that we would squeeze in between our beach expeditions. Ava pored over an article about the bioluminescent bay on the island, the brightest in the world, filled with billions of small organisms that glow when the water is disturbed. I read about the history of the US Navy's weapons testing on the island, which the Pentagon had ceased in 2003.

"I'll be happy just to hang under a beach umbrella all day and body surf and read," Ava said.

"You're my daughter alright," I said.

As we changed planes in the sultry heat, the sight of pineapple-juice carts, and of vendors dispensing *café con leche*, signaled a singular delight: that Tropical Brain Suspension was imminent. For the next week, we would give ourselves over to relaxing on sandy beaches and plunging into the salt water to mitigate the sun.

When our little Cape Air Cessna flew into chunky, black clouds, I was worried less about the plane being banged around by lightning than I was about the weather on the ground. After we landed, the rain was driving with enough force to pummel my shoulders, optimistically bared upon takeoff in anticipation of our midday arrival. My daughter and I braved the downpour in our flip-flops and ran across the tarmac to the tiny terminal, where we found our way to the welcome lounge for our hotel. It was air-conditioned to suit a much drier day; under our soaked clothes, our skin prickled into goose flesh from the chill.

"Welcome!" the host beamed, holding forth two glasses of juice.

"Was this rain in the forecast?" I asked, referring to the forecast I never bothered to check.

"It is supposed to rain all week. Too bad, because it was beautiful until yesterday!" The man's good cheer was so close to infectious that, for a minute, I thought he was delivering good news. Instead he handed down a death sentence on my beach vacation fantasy.

"Ava, let's call the boys," I said. "We're going home."

"That's not funny," she said.

"You heard him," I said, pointing to the picture windows that shook from the force of the storm outside.

"We like the rain," he volunteered, still grinning.

My bloodless face clearly had alarmed my daughter, who looked as stricken as I felt. She had already witnessed my blues so often over the past year. I needed to find a way to shroud the misfortune, but I was despondent. It was the heat that I'd craved—blinding sunshine that browned my skin and steamed the cold and sadness out of me. That was meant to be the antidote. My high hopes had blurred what should have been obvious (or at least, easily researchable). I felt tricked—by this man, the whole conspiratorial island, and, in fact, the entire Caribbean Sea.

We attempted to peck on a cookie, finished our juice, and slogged through the cyclone to the shuttle van, which brought us to our hotel. The reception staff greeted me with similar bonhomie, as though there weren't a river where the driveway had once been.

"So you don't want to go home?" I asked Ava as we made our way along the flooded walkways to our room. In my mind were the ripe, candy-striped peonies I had left behind in Connecticut, and the waning light of an early summer evening on our back porch.

"I don't care about the weather," she said. "And neither should you." Now that my 13-year-old daughter was parenting me, for her and all of our sakes, it was time to buck up.

Our room was refrigerator cold, and I marched straight to the tub to blast it full of hot water.

"Look," Ava said from the porch, "the beach is right there." I went to join her in my robe. The sky seemed as thick as putty and the air bore close upon our skin. The sand blended into the mist and we listened to the swish of the waves below. "The palm trees look so green," she said.

After my bath, I perused the contents of my suitcase, which was devoid of any stitch of rain gear. It would have been easy to stick a few plastic ponchos in among my bikinis and coverups. I'd bought dozens of them over the years, for camping and overnights and soggy track meets.

"I guess I won't be needing this," I said, brandishing the bag full of sunscreen.

My daughter shrugged. "You still might," she said.

While Ava napped, I paid a visit to the front desk. As much as I could fake it for my family, I needed people trained in hospitality to help keep my spirits up. I approached the receptionists near tears and one woman touched my hand with tenderness. I apologized, but I felt foolish for being so surprised by the turn of the weather.

"Take your family to El Resuelve. It's the best place to eat on the island," she said. "Do the bio bay and drive around the old military barracks. Visit the beaches, even if it's not sunny. There is more to the Caribbean than the sun."

After a few hours, with borrowed umbrellas in hand, we hopped a taxi to town. We strolled along the soaked streets, looking for signs of life. Yellow light from street lamps glowed, casting a misty glaze but illuminating nothing on the sidewalks. I took note of a bar on the main plaza that I intended to check out when my husband and son arrived. A shopkeeper pulled the metal grate over the door of his haberdashery, and the mannequins in pressed guayaberas and straw Trilby hats vanished for the night.

We hadn't reserved a table at any of the island's good restaurants, but we found one on the second floor of a pink stucco building on a side street. Ava and I, the only diners there, installed ourselves by the wide-open window overlooking the desolate town. Rain pounded on the tin roof above two paddle fans made of sheet metal. I had a margarita, cold and sweet, and we shared crispy cod fritters and an order of mofongo, served with geometric flair under a fan of sliced limes, and devoured it in no time.

We met my husband, Mark and my son, Ray, the following day, during a respite from the rain showers. The van sloshed through gullies on the airport road to the car-rental agency. In the office, I pulled my husband to one side and gave him my woebegone best as the sky darkened, about to unleash a fresh downpour.

"Are we just going to pretend it isn't pissing down rain all over our first vacation in years?" I asked.

"Actually," he said, "yes."

"You don't think this is a huge waste of money?"

Mark jingled the keys to our new PT Cruiser, and his smile both confused and relieved me. "Who the hell cares?" he said. "It's just rain."

Just rain? My daughter, my husband, and everyone I had met so far on this island had repeated those words. Perhaps it was my childhood in New England, where beaches turn charcoal dark during summer storms that cast gloomy reminders of shipwrecks and lonely widows. I spent one cold July on the seacoast of Maine, waterlogged during an aberrant wet spell. For weeks, my hair frizzed up under the hood of my rain slicker. I was heartsick for the empty restaurants with tanks full of lobsters and for the hopeful owners who prayed for nothing more than a passel of sunburned tourists.

Now that the boys had arrived, the stakes seemed even more perilously high. I had to keep two teenagers busy and make the family (and myself) whole again. Under the circumstances, there was little to do besides eat; and as much as he loved the manicured grounds and heated pools at our hotel, Ray wanted to venture elsewhere for meals.

We took the car south toward the beaches. On the way, we stopped at El Resuelve, which was shuttered. The rain fell steadily, and we drove to the coast. We parked the Chrysler and ambled along the perimeter of the marina to settle upon a food truck that served *pinchos*—snacks to eat with your hands. The odor of roasting meat and hot cooking oil wafted from the grill as we waited for sizzling chicken kebabs, *pastelitos* filled with spicy beef and green olives, and crispy *papa rellenas*. We strolled along the avenue through another tourist town. It should have been packed with vacationers, but it was almost deserted. But the air was tranquil and, perched on the edge of a seawall with my family, sharing a mound of homemade potato chips, so was I.

Next, we headed for the place I'd craved the most in my dreams, Playa Pata Prieta, also known as Secret Beach. As we cruised the road leading to a clutch of hidden coves, we passed herds of feral horses, some with white seabirds perched on their backs. We scaled a small hill and Pata Prieta revealed itself below, the strip of blush sand and electric-blue water from the photographs now shades of steel gray. Mark, Ava, and Ray wanted to swim, and they had worn their bathing suits in anticipation of a brief dip. The water churned under the black sky as my family whooped headlong into the surf. I walked the horseshoe of the cove, back and forth, wading in periodically to let the water swirl around my ankles and rinse the sand off. I repeated this as if it were a ritual. For a moment, the clouds parted, and I saw the seat of my daughter's bright pink bikini pop above the wave as she dived.

"You've got to come in," she cried. "You can't even feel the rain!"

It made perfect sense, and maybe one day I'd believe her.

We continued to eat our way around the island. In the morning, we had breakfast at a *panaderia* in the city, with *café con leche*, donuts, and fried eggs. I didn't bother with sunscreen because the clouds loomed above us, relentless and threatening.

"Isn't this great?" my husband kept asking, or saying. The kids were excited for the excursion to Puerto Mosquito, the bioluminescent bay, which we planned to make that night after dinner at El Resuelve.

Instead of waiting pointlessly all day for the sun to appear, we took a drive along the military road to see the old naval bunkers. After a while, we began to see eerie-looking doorways buried into the hills, barely visible through moss and vines. My husband was intrigued enough to stop and photograph each one that we passed. We were alone out there in the rain, on this abandoned road, and these structures had a neglected beauty that could inspire both a fairy tale and a horror story.

"Are we near the beach?" Ava asked.

I sighed and gazed around at the mist, indistinguishable from the sky. "I will never dry off after this week," I said.

Ava made sandcastles and Ray ran sprints along Playa Caracas, also known as Red Beach, while I went to sign up for the bio-bay tour and fetch lunch. On the way to the car, I walked past the horses and envied them for their peaceful countenance. I wondered how long it would be until the children started making noises about ditching this wet island.

We sat on towels on the damp sand, eating spicy jerk chicken and massive Cuban sandwiches from a food truck painted with blue sky and white clouds. The sun flashed through as I was pulling on a cold Presidente. I felt it, briefly: a quick toasting from the sky, the closeness of my family, the narrowing gap between resentment and acceptance, the growing distance between this beach and my own home, which I'd needed so badly to escape.

On the way back to the hotel, we saw that El Resuelve was closed again, the patio furniture stacked on the drenched terrace, and the neon lights turned off in a scene of total dejection. Sheets of rain made the driving treacherous, so we stopped at a café with an orange metal roof. It was not on our (or anybody's) list of things to do here, but it was clean, and the chicken smelled glorious. We all ordered *pollo asado al carbón*, and I volunteered to drive to the boat launch for the bio-bay tour, to see whether the rain would thwart us.

In truth, I wanted a few moments alone. Like most mothers, I'm the cornerstone of our family—my mood sets the tone for all of us. The last year and a half had been rough on everyone, especially my husband, who had weathered my midlife crisis almost more than I had. But the rain had put a damper on my contentment, and I was well aware of the destructive power of an unhappy mother, no matter how gamely she tries to hide her misery. My incessant fretting about the weather was tiresome, and I knew it. And as much as I craved this old-school family vacation, aloneness was always my default. The only way I could ever make sense of anything—misfortune, circumstances, adversity, or turmoil—was by myself.

As I headed east, rain lashed the car, becoming so heavy and impenetrable that I could no longer see the road. I kept driving, trusting in the sanctity of landmarks I might recognize. The wheels of the PT Cruiser slid beneath me, even at five miles per hour, and when I plunked into ditches along the perimeter of the road, or veered into swales, I jerked out of them, praying that this low-riding pleasure-mobile would stay intact. It was June 20, the second-longest day of the year, and though it was just 6 P.M., there was only a vague glow of sunlight.

I clutched the wheel tightly, feeling panic coil in my stomach. I pictured my cell phone, which I'd left on the table at the restaurant, believing I'd be gone for fifteen minutes. It had now been more than an hour. I could see no signs for the bay, no hotels, no roadside attractions, no other person, even, to whom I could ask directions. I didn't know whether I was on the north or south part of the island, or anywhere near the bio-bay boat launch, but I knew I had to stop. I parked at the dead end of a tiny patch of road hugged by a cluster of jungle. I took the keys from the ignition and, barefoot, stepped out of the car and sat on the hood, my back against the windshield as if it were a chaise longue.

The rain poured on me, drenching my blouse and skirt, soaking my underclothes, and penetrating deep into the pores of my skin. I listened to the leaves of the kapok and mango trees shake overhead. I waited. I collapsed. All winter, I had sought solitude, believing that, in order for this or that crisis to pass, I needed to distance myself from the people I loved, and now I'd done so again. How wrong I had been.

Within ten minutes, I hopped back into the car. It was almost night, and there were still no people, not even a goat or a chicken, to guide me home. Eventually, I spotted a few semi-familiar signs, one to a hotel and bar, another marking an entrance to the national wildlife refuge that covers much of the island. Onward I crept, grasping onto anything I recognized as a crucial knot in a lifeline. Finally, I pulled up to El Mesón Criollo, where my family stood on the porch, unfazed.

"Hi Mom," Ray said.

"I guess the bioluminescent tour is canceled tonight?" Ava asked.

"I never got there to find out," I said. "Was anybody worried I'd driven off a cliff?"

"No," Mark said calmly. He held a brown bag soaked with grease spots from my roast chicken. "Not hardly."

"Tomorrow is the first day of summer," I said.

The skies opened up again the next morning. When the showers halted, for an hour here or an hour there, we bolted for the beach. I lay back in the muggy heat, closed my eyes, and heard the waves and my children's voices. It was unlike any Maine day I had ever known. I was far away—we all were.

We had one last chance for the bio-bay adventure, and on the way to the boat launch, we stopped at El Resuelve. Closed again. The rain was spotty (at times heavy), and we hoped our tour would proceed as scheduled. Fortunately, it did. Unless there were threatening winds or waves, our guide explained, rain was an important and very ordinary part of the cycle of weather in the tropics. It would take a hurricane to cancel these excursions.

We got in a van and bumped along to Puerto Mosquito, where we covered ourselves in bug repellent. We paddled out in kayaks to see the mangrove swamps, whose decomposing roots allow dinoflagellates, those unicellular protozoa, to proliferate. It is these microorganisms that, in some strange alchemy, glow when the water they inhabit is agitated.

Eventually, the guide gave us the go-ahead to lower ourselves into the water. The effect was immediate. The more I waved my hand, the greater was the micro-organisms' excitement, and the brighter was the glowing swoosh of green. The four of us swam a bit from our kayak, under supervision from our guide. We knew we had to share this phenomenon, this astonishment, this rare bit of sorcery arising in this remarkable pool of tropical waters. As we stirred our arms and our feet, I was aware, probably, that the eruption of light in my wake had a greater purpose than to make me feel alive and unified with the people I loved. You can't look at life's mysteries and think they exist only for you. And yet it is so tempting to do just that.

Ava was correct: I could barely feel the rain when I was in the water. It began to fall softly, then more urgently; warm Caribbean rain, the same temperature as the sea.

"Mom, you've got to see this," she said. "Go under and look up."

After I submerged, I looked skyward, and imagined the June solstice as something I could see, hear, even touch. Somewhere above the vast blanket of clouds the planet and the sun were aligning, just for a moment, heralding the longest day of the year and the beginning of summer. Just under the surface, the water erupted with ghostly flashes of blue and green light. The individual raindrops that constituted the downpour caused an unknowable and dazzling reaction for a girl, her brother, their father, and his wife to see. Together.

Chapter 11

Cape Town

It was January in Camps Bay. We'd arrived the day before from Johannesburg, where I had barely exhaled. After dealing with that city's razor wire fences and ceaseless warnings about car-jackings and too much pointless crime, I was relieved to reach Cape Town. That first morning, after a tough hike up Table Mountain, my three best friends from graduate school and I were primed for a swim with penguins at Boulders Beach. We drove our little rental car about an hour down the coast. Through the window, salt air pressed upon me, and the stone outcroppings jutted from the waves like idols.

It had been a long holiday season back home: God knows how many sparkling pomegranate martinis served, how many chunks of peppermint bark scarfed, how much money and energy blown on too many packages under the tree. Snow fell steadily, and the temperatures had been frigid through the gatherings and the endless trips to the mall. Family and friends created a steady tide of love, and—first stressed, then buoyed by it—I was ready to put December and all the trimmings behind me for another year.

My friends had planned this journey across the world to coincide with high summer in the southern half of the earth. One of them was South African, and she was eager to show us her country, the tip of the continent.

In Hout Bay, about halfway to the penguins, I was surprised to see Christmas decorations lingering on the wooden posts that separated the beach from the restaurant where we had lunch. Windswept strands of garland were spun around the fence posts and touched the sand. Artificial evergreens, dragging from a month in the sun, were draped with yellow foil stars and red and green metallic balls. I drowned the broiled kingklip in peri-peri sauce and washed it down with ice-cold water, which felt like pure deliverance.

There were clear coastal skies, fizzy lightheadedness, and otherwise ideal conditions for our dip with the penguins, not far from where the chilly currents of the Atlantic met the warm ones of the Indian Ocean. I looked forward to seeing these creatures dart and dive around me, and wondered how it would all transpire. Would they swim toward me? Would I be scared? Exhilarated? Both? This was something only these three friends, knowing my underwhelming lust for adventure, could have urged upon me. I remember thinking that I could not recall such a hum of anticipation. It was almost tactile: weariness subsiding, energy replenishing, the heat bearing down on my neck and shoulders.

Our toes gripped the sand as we crossed it, through a colony of penguins parading and flapping in a configuration only they understood. Finally, onto one of the titular domelike crags, off of which the birds and I plunged into a small cove. The water was translucent, like a molten pool of turquoise glass. I lay on my back and floated in place while one penguin, then two, dove in and emerged beside me. The birds' black wings turned into paddles below the surface, and their playful, purposeful movements propelled their bodies. Together, we skimmed the shallows, their flippers flipping and my hands making ballerina motions in the water. Below us, on the seabed, moved the pale-gray shadows of our three bodies. If not for the sudden passage of clouds under the sun, which cast a shadow on my face, I might have drifted off to sleep.

Chapter 12

Strangers on a Train

hen traveling alone, my preference is to keep it that way. I'm not one for chatting people up in hotel bars, reeling out my anecdotes or listening to theirs. Which is why, when a man entered my chamber just as the overnight train left Moscow for St. Petersburg, my heart sank.

I thought I had reserved both beds in my first-class compartment—a private suite, so to speak. The day before, I had paid with cash at my hotel service desk. When I got to Leningradsky Station, the woman at the ticket kiosk, annoyed and clearly ready to call it a day, nevertheless barked a confirmation at me through the glass.

The purpose of this trip, after all, was contemplation. I had spent much of my twenties in Russia, back when it was part of the Soviet Union, and I'd traveled this train route many times. I always loved to head north at nighttime, across the Volga River, toward the Gulf of Finland and the Baltic Sea. But I hadn't been back for years, during which time life simply did what it does: it carried on, through ecstasy and despair, but mostly, through everything that lies between those two extremes. I wanted to reflect on the decades that had passed, and do so alone.

Twenty-eight years earlier, I took my first trip to the Soviet Union with my parents. Ten days in, I kissed my father goodbye at the Hotel Rossiya, and my mother took me to this same station. With the help of the state tourist authority, they had booked me on the night train to Leningrad, where I would spend a couple weeks. Just before I left, my mother said simply, "Keep your eyes open and be sensible. You are in for such an adventure." Putting me in a passenger coach, alone, in the Brezhnev-era USSR was as nerve-wracking for her as dropping me off at piano lessons. She had tried to raise me as a can-do New Englander who feared nothing—not foreign travel, and even less, solitude.

As the train to St. Petersburg departed, I looked out the window and imagined my mother waving from the platform, as she had done all those years ago. She was precisely the same age then as I am now.

I unfolded the sheet left by the train crew, and draped it on the bunk, making hospital corners as if it mattered. I unpacked a nightie and my toothbrush. Then I kicked off my flats, sat on the bed, rearranged my skirt, and studied my feet for a minute. They were smudged with a day's worth of urban grime, and my pedicure—which had been painted Beach Party pink in a packed New York nail spa—was showing signs of wear. The linen felt cool under my sticky legs. It was 10:30 on a June evening, and Moscow had been sweltering.

The gentle vibration of the wheels beneath me caused my head to get heavy while the rest of me grew weightless. As I began to doze off, a man walked in. He looked at me with what was surely a reflection of my own expression, which said roughly, "This isn't happening."

"I don't think this is your room," I said. My Russian was rustier than usual thanks to my having been jolted awake, but my displeasure was unambiguous. I looked over at the other bunk.

The space between them was about a foot. I stood, and together we examined his ticket, then the number on the door, and finally each other.

Damn, I thought. *Damn, damn, damn*. He was a hulking tree of a man, easily 6'6" tall, red face, shaved head, wearing a scarlet warm-up jacket with English words on it that clashed with his ruddy complexion. I imagined that he would grunt or worse in his sleep, and he probably had foul breath too. And now I was stuck with him. Tantalizing fantasies about strangers on trains were the furthest thing from my mind. My night passage, my meditation on where all those years had gone, my sentimental journey: all dead on arrival.

He was as flustered as I was.

"I didn't think they'd put me with a woman," he said.

"Tell me about it," I replied.

We puttered about awkwardly. I stuck my nightie under the pillow. He checked his phone. And then we sat and looked at each other. My knee brushed his briefly, and we both instinctively scooted in the opposite direction. He had a kind face.

"I'm Marcia," I said.

"I'm Igor," he said.

No kidding, I thought.

"Where are you from?" he asked.

"The USA," I said. "What about you?"

"Vladivostok," he answered.

"Siberia," I remarked.

"No." He smiled. "The Russian Far East."

"Got it," I said, and asked, "Do you have a family?" But I misspoke, using the word *familia*, which means "surname," instead of *cemya*, which means "family."

"Umm, yes," he answered, looking slightly panicked.

"I mean, a *family*," I said, correcting myself.

"Yes!" he said. He took out his phone and displayed a shot of his wife and kids, tall and smiling—a girl, twelve, and a boy, fifteen. Just the same as I had.

So I fired up my laptop and showed him my own tall, smiling son and daughter.

The attendant brought us tea in glass mugs, and we drank in silence. Then, our dinner came: chicken, noodles, a chunk of bread wrapped in plastic. He ordered water, not beer. I was relieved and, I admit, surprised.

Our dishes were crammed onto the tiny, shared table. We chatted about our kids, sports, work, his travels and mine. He had taken an eight-hour flight from Vladivostok that morning. Four days earlier, I had taken an eight-hour flight from New York. Igor was exactly as far from home as I was.

"I'll let you change," he said. He stepped out of the compartment and closed the door. The nightie was a tad inappropriate, considering, so I dug out some sweatpants and a tank top. Igor returned in his version of pajamas—basketball shorts and a t-shirt—and shut the door behind him.

"It's better to lock it," he said, turning the bolt. A polite look passed over his face, which soothed the worried one on mine. I thought of my husband, who at that moment was probably picking up our daughter from school in Connecticut.

"Nudge me if I snore," he said, covering himself with his sheet and blanket. Our bunks almost touched.

"Oh, I know the drill."

"Sweet dreams."

I didn't get much shut-eye that night, between the intermittent squeals of drunks somewhere nearby, the wide-awake children, and a man who paced the corridor while talking loudly on the phone or to himself. Because it was June, darkness never fell, and even though our blinds were drawn, the compartment was awash in half-light. I stayed awake with the steady hum of the wheels against the rails, the shadows that moved and shifted, the crisp bedding, the fresh pillow under my head. There were my restless hands adjusting the covers, and memories churning through my mind of a much younger me, riding this very train. There was Igor's breathing—not loud, but present, rhythmic, safe.

In the morning, when the attendant knocked to rouse us, I jumped to unlock the door. She delivered bread and tea, again in the lovely glass mugs, and we both looked down at our trays as we stirred in sugar for longer than was necessary.

"Did you sleep well?" he finally asked.

"Yes," I lied. "Very."

"Let's look at the scenery," he said. "It's beautiful."

"Of course," I agreed, and rose.

"Sit, sit," Igor almost whispered. He stood, grabbed the curtain and shoved it to one side. The rush of white light pierced my eyes, causing a flash of sightlessness.

Condensation glazed the windows. Outside, a million birch trees stood deep and wide along the flanks of the tracks, interspersed among stands of aspen and evergreen. Silvery light strobed through the branches and leaves. We sped past them all, through the Russian forest. Soon the landscape widened, and small houses gave way to industrial outposts on the fringe of St. Petersburg, indicating that we were not far from Moskovsky Station. I slowly gathered up my things, feeling both tenderness for this small room and the thrill of arrival.

At the station, Igor held my elbow as I negotiated the chasm between the train and the platform. A driver from my hotel who had been waiting for me took my bags. I immediately turned to say goodbye to Igor, my arms half-opened to embrace and thank him for his kindness, but he was already gone, disappeared into the crowd.

Chapter 13

One Day, Three Dead Men

*T*he concierge told me it was the hottest June day in Moscow on record. A cloud of downy poplar seeds thickened the air in front of the National Hotel. The Russians call it "summer snow," and in the heat, the white fluff stuck to my neck, shoulders, and legs as I drifted through the streets of the city I once had known well but now barely recognized.

It was a homecoming of sorts. Twenty-eight years had passed since I first traveled to the then-Soviet Union. I arrived there in June of 1982 with a shiny-new degree in Russian Studies. I was a wide-eyed Cold War baby who had spent four years in college reading deeply into the tortured Russian soul. It had been an obsession since tenth grade, when I won a school essay contest. I have no memory of the topic, but I do recall the prize: a collection of novellas by Dostoevsky. The stories validated a certain bleak corner of my heart while welcoming and giving relevance to the sensitive wallow. I began to study Russian on weekends and in the summer. No doubt it was my enthusiasm for the minutiae of its complex grammar, rather than my otherwise okay high school academic record or vice-directorship of the blood drive, that gained me acceptance to Princeton in 1978.

Stalin had been dead for only twenty-five years. The Iron Curtain was the central geopolitical divide at the time, and the United States needed Russian speakers to interfere with the ideology of Brezhnev's Soviet Union and Lenin's enduring anti-capitalist legacy. The admissions committee might have seen a potential heir to Ambassador George Kennan, the father of modern Kremlinology, who, since resigning from the State Department, had continued to formulate policy toward the Soviet Union at the nearby Institute for Advanced Study.

But it was the books I loved—their modern, relatable sheen. There was nothing nineteenth century about Chekhovian self-awareness; Anton Pavlovich might as well have been writing about the people in my life. Women like Ariadne, who "woke up in the morning with one purpose: to make an impression." Or Gromov in *Ward 6*, who says, "There are times when I am seized with a thirst for life—and it's then that I'm afraid of going mad." Chekhov wrote about me, articulating my absurd conundrum of privilege and discontent, but transported to promenades in the south of France, a steamer on the Black Sea, or provincial estates lined with avenues of fir and linden. The word "depression" was not part of the vernacular at the time, but the chronic and heavy sensation of longing I carried with me had a perfect and otherwise untranslatable Russian word: *toska.*

I spent my college years in the Department of Slavic Languages and Literature, a daylight-free warren of rooms occupying the basement of a building in the center of campus. The classes were crowded, but only four of us that year had declared Russian as our major. I took courses in politics and history to examine the centuries-old ties between the rulers—Czars, Bolsheviks, the Politburo, or whoever held the reins at the time—and the writers, who belonged to the people. I devoted myself to the literature, to Chekhov's stifling parlors and Gogol's lunatics wandering the streets of St. Petersburg, but also several contemporary authors and poets, some of whom were in exile, and some of whom, through compromise, cleverness, or both, survived the system as Soviet writers.

After graduation, I turned down the chance to translate inter-office memos for our country's security agencies to work for tips as a tour guide for professional-exchange programs. I crisscrossed the Soviet Union, starting in Moscow, winding through the Caucasus or Central Asia, and finishing up in Leningrad. Two years later, I began a career in network television, and as I climbed the ladder, I traveled frequently to the USSR. Three times, I fell in love on assignment during Moscow winters, always finding some magic of chemistry, or coincidence, in that barren place. In 1992, I spent two months researching weapons facilities. I had recently married and would soon move back to the States, have a son, and then a daughter, and duty and domesticity would curtail my travels almost to extinction.

But my forays to Russia continued, at least for a while, through its literature. I loved to re-visit my college volumes—Lermontov, Gorky, Tsvetaeva, Aksyonov, Ahkmatova, and especially Chekhov—and skim my margin notes, scribbled at a time when there was nothing on earth more important than the book in my hand.

At 49, in the throes of unhealthy midlife nostalgia, I became preoccupied with the notion that the unrelenting passage of years had extinguished most of the passions that had fueled my younger self. I had begun to work, write, and travel again, but at the same time, my old obsessions began to surface. I started to miss, then crave, and then positively require the connection to Russia that had once defined me. A classic mid-life epiphany, to be sure, in which I felt a desire to stitch the known past together with the unknown future, and to soothe myself with the knowledge that I might yet be the same person after nearly three decades. My whole life was ahead of me back when I first went to the Soviet Union, and in a way, with two nearly-grown kids, it was now as well.

So, on Memorial Day, I left my family in the middle of a summer barbecue to catch a plane to Moscow, to replicate that first post-college journey. I wanted to know whether landing on Russian soil would feel like home again.

It hadn't begun well. I'd spent two full days—one of them in a torrential rainstorm—standing outside the Russian consulate in New York applying for a visa, with a restless throng of other document-waving hopefuls. I made the mistake of not hiring an outside procurement service, and I spent hours on the sidewalk chastising myself for that fateful decision. Eventually, the document came through, but I already felt done-in by the great Russian obstacle machine.

Round two greeted me upon landing in Moscow. Passport control was interminable; it gave me severe Brezhnev-era flashbacks. I couldn't find an open bank to get rubles, so I used my credit card to pay for a train ride to Belorussky Station, where I discovered that I'd left my fluent Russian somewhere in 1992. It was pretty much gone, especially the part that might have helped me negotiate with a swarm of drivers, all clad in leather jackets, who lurked curbside ready to shake down the next sucker—in this case, me. There were no official taxis. What had I ever liked about this goddamn place? I fumed as I doled out fifty US bucks to a man who ferried me to the National, right on Manezh Square.

From the outside, it was as magnificent as I'd remembered, but the inside was infinitely grander. Back then, it was run by the state but, because of its fine bones and classical architecture, was slightly more upscale than the bland places Intourist usually put up visitors. Even so, it was stuck with the same standard-issue furnishings, same dim lights, and same sour smell I would get to know intimately at hotels throughout the USSR. Now, it was a paragon of five-star luxury, and my room was decorated with crimson brocades and dainty settees, and it was equipped with a full mini-bar from which I procured a double vodka, straight up. From room service, I ordered a thousand rubles' worth of plump little straw-berries to round out my cocktail hour. Thirty-four US dollars for seven berries.

I walked and walked, looking for a bakery where I might find something tasty and cheap. I found one on Varvarka Street, beside the Znamensky Monastery. For pennies, I snacked on pirozhki, one filled with apples, one with potatoes, and one with cheese. The elderly woman who served me was a relic from Khrushchev's time, wearing a boxy blue baker's coat and chef's cap atop her teased hair. Later, I bought a sack of tiny ripe strawberries at a kiosk, this time for the sum of ten rubles—roughly forty cents. They dis-solved rapidly in my mouth, and tasted of candy and sunshine.

After my first full day in Moscow, I ate osso bucco and gnocchi alla Romagna in a palatial, new Italian restaurant adorned with frescoes and bas-reliefs of Roman gods. The dinner was courtesy of an old friend whom I met in Moscow years ago, and who hap-pened to be passing through. He escorted me past a trio of thugs bursting out of their suit jackets—security for an oligarch's lavish birthday party upstairs. I marveled at the dinner, as I recalled the scarcity of everything—meat, milk, even cucumbers—back in the eighties, even in hotels for westerners, and how I lived on small cakes, black bread, and the rare steaming bowl of Beef Stroganoff.

The city had changed, had become full of glitzy boutiques and women with tan legs and towering heels—the Miami Beach of the Steppes. In the Soviet era, even young women plodded through Moscow's grim streets with their backs hunched over; now it seemed they all stood eight feet tall, their shoulders back and breasts pushed forward.

On the third morning, I went to Red Square to see Lenin in his tomb. It had once been among the safest places on earth, patrolled by army troops and teeming with police. When I was in my twenties and had insomnia, which happened often to me when I was in Moscow, I would stroll alongside the Kremlin's crenellated walls at 3 A.M., admiring the cupolas of St. Basil's that maintained their frenzied brilliance even in darkness. Uniformed men were stationed at broad intervals, and I nodded greetings to them as I tried to walk off the blini, caviar, and vodka from dinner. At nighttime in those days, Red Square was well lit but totally deserted, and I recall that the strength in my limbs felt buttressed by this very emptiness, as if its palpable historical significance was mine alone to feel.

Now, nothing remained of the moody atmospherics from the Soviet era. Parts of the square felt like a seedy theme park, with kiosks selling balloons and overpriced lemonade. It never seemed possible that Vladimir Ilyich Lenin, the tiny gray figure in the depressing permafrost, whom one network correspondent I knew referred to as Dead Fred the Head Red, had overthrown the monarchy and set his nation on its roughly 70-year course. But in 2010, that history seemed ludicrous.

My Russian was slowly coming back, and I experienced glimmers of recognition, flashes of the familiar, as faded postcards of 1980's Moscow came into view—the woman at the bakery, for instance. But I still felt disconnected, rudderless, and emotionally blank, as though I'd arrived in a place that I could only identify because I had seen images of it whoosh by a couple of times on film. It didn't feel like mine anymore. I was a stranger, in spite of the years I spent working here, the love affairs, and the great trove of Russian books that had inspired and sustained me, and to which I returned again and again and again.

That afternoon, a taxi driver named Pavel took me to the Novodevichy Cemetery to visit Anton Chekhov, the only dead man I have a crush on. He knows my mind as if he were inside it, and he grasps the confounding equation of marriage more than any writer living or dead. I murmured small devotions to him, thanking him for his clairvoyance and bits of wisdom uttered through characters like Samoilenko in *The Duel:* "The principal thing in marriage is patience. Not love, but patience." Standing in front of the headstone, I hesitated before plucking two sprigs of jasmine blossoms from an overhanging tree. I tossed one flower on the soil above Chekhov's body and stuck the other between two pages of a notebook in my bag.

The sky darkened and without warning split wide open—thunder, lightning, a curtain of rain that in an instant washed the poplar seeds clean off my shoulders. I took shelter against a low building, beside gravedigger tools. After about a half hour, the sky turned a blinding blue. The storm had passed, leaving puddles of water that I waded through in flip-flops.

As I walked toward the exit, I saw a crowd of people gathering in the main courtyard, along with eight or so television cameras. A man wearing an officer's cap and gloves stood in front of an oversized, red funeral arrangement. He held a framed black-and-white photograph of a man I recognized as the poet Andrei Voznesensky, who had died earlier in the week, and upon whose burial procession I had apparently stumbled.

Voznesensky was one of the great and most controversial poets of the Soviet era. He was introduced to me by my college professors, who had the wisdom to convey that a literary tradition perseveres even—especially—when a writer is at risk, which they so often were throughout the histories of the Russian and Soviet Empires. With the exception of a nasty run-in with Khruschev, Voznesensky managed to preserve his humanity and his voice and not run afoul of the Soviet literary watchdogs. Many, especially dissidents who had to leave the USSR, despised him as a sell-out. In the 1960's, he gave readings in stadiums packed with fellow citizens, who needed poetry like we in the West needed the Rolling Stones.

As the crowd of mourners swelled to the hundreds, a hush began to take hold. I fell in line, and we marched down the cemetery's tree-lined alleys, past silhouettes and gravestones and little manicured patches of grass. It was a long shuffle to the burial site, in and out of shadows. The resting place was clearly delineated, exploding with a thousand bouquets draped with ribbons. The crowd, still silent, watched as the poet was lowered into the ground, taking his place alongside Gogol, Mayakovsky, Bulgakov, and of course, Chekhov.

After the service, I found Pavel, my driver, at the appointed meeting place outside the cemetery gates. As I slipped into the passenger seat of the car, I asked him, "Who were all the mourners?"

"Just Russians," he said. "We love our writers." And then he said, with a low flourish as if he were alone on stage, *"Life like a rocket flies/Mainly in darkness, Now and then on a rainbow."*

Sunlight poured through the passenger window and onto my lap. Moscow sparkled from the thunderstorm, and Pavel drove through pools of rainwater.

"*The Parabolic Ballad*," Pavel said.

I had read it in college.

Back at the hotel, I cracked open another $20 vodka and looked up the verse. Outside, the cupolas of the Kremlin were shining as they have for hundreds of years on June evenings like this one. Finally, it all made sense.

During that first trip to the USSR in 1982, a bus driver in Leningrad recited to me the entirety of *The Bronze Horseman*. Aleksandr Pushkin's poetic masterpiece weaves the story of the epic flood of the Neva River in 1824 with an ode to Czar Peter the Great, who envisioned and built the magnificent city on the Gulf of Finland. Another time, an Intourist guide with whom I traveled to Samarkand, and who knew I couldn't sleep, handed me a bootleg copy of Gogol's stories. "If you are awake, you may as well be reading these," she said. Another time, I spent a few nights with a handsome Muscovite who was probably a KGB agent. Upon my departure for New York, he handed me a book called *Nerve*, a collection of poems by the Soviet poet and singer Vladimir Vysotsky, and inscribed it: *To Marcia, my American dream.* "It's not much of a present," he told me with a knowing shrug. "I am Russian, so it's the only present."

That day in Moscow, Pavel honored the death of Voznesensky the only way he knew.

"Do you think he was a great poet?" I had asked him.

Pavel stopped the car and turned around for emphasis, as if this were something I would never understand without seeing him say it. "He was *our* poet," he said with a vigorous slash of his raised finger. "And *that* is what's important."

Chapter 14

Green Pastures

*K*igali was opaque with night when I landed there. As always, I already envisioned myself on the way out of the country, in two weeks' time. Airports have this effect on me. They are my hello and goodbye, the places I cross with an exhausted shuffle when I arrive and impatiently want to ditch when I leave. They are miserable, inhuman places, churning people in and out like an automatic dishwasher; places where you line up for expensive coffee just to kill time.

But on this arrival, my normal excitement—the one I always experience when I venture into the unknown—took on an unusual cast. I wanted to have already seen and felt what was still ahead of me. I knew that Rwanda would be different, like some extraordinary blind date with someone who had a chilling backstory, and the prospect was frightening. Most everything I knew about Rwanda concerned the genocide, and the books I had read about it recently had filled my head with the most horrific details of those two months of terror in the spring of 1994. My challenge was to allow something else to sink in.

Because of its famous mountain gorillas, and the country's efforts to resuscitate its national parks, Rwanda was on the way to becoming one of the most sought-after (and expensive) places to vacation in Africa. But this was a distinct sort of trip for me, a low-budget hybrid of work and pleasure. With both kids now away at school, just as my urgency to flee the reverberating emptiness of my house began to teeter toward despair, I was asked to do some pro bono consulting for a small NGO.

I was delighted. My magazine assignments had taken a turn toward the beauty-and-wellness department. While I was thrilled to be a working writer, I was relieved to finally integrate some of what I had learned from my master's program, having studied national security and humanitarian diplomacy in the disparate corners of Africa. Aimee, a young woman from the NGO, had composed my itinerary. I would spend most of the time driving to remote villages or trekking up hillsides to visit cassava plantations and apiary construction sites. I would occasionally break to see the gorillas, detour to a game preserve, or stretch myself out on the shores of Lake Kivu. But as the days spread out before me, I suspected it would be the spaces in between—the long drives, the solitary hours and wakeful nights—that would really inform my stay.

The taxi drove me from the airport to the Kiyovu neighborhood and the guesthouse Aimee had arranged. My room smelled slightly of age and disuse, but it was well-appointed, and the bathtub was big enough for me to soak in, with the water plenty hot. I was hung over from a travel bender. Complimentary champagne, and lots of it, was the only way I could hack 24 hours with a pinched nerve up and down my shoulders. My teeth felt like they had sprouted fur, and my head grew heavy as the alcohol drained from my system. I walked to the edge of the property. Lights were strewn before me in the distance, so I knew I was on one of Kigali's many hills. I returned to my too-quiet room and fell back on the bed. There was an occasional ping-ping on the tin roof, and a sniffle from the lone guard outside. Sensing something more akin to mortal sickness than terror, I imagined the thousands of people who were killed in the neighborhood where I would be sleeping, and I pictured their souls swirling around in the windy night.

The next morning, two women collected me for breakfast. We walked a good distance into Kigali's downtown, directly to a café. With hunger knotting my stomach into a tight burl, I washed down a slice of banana cake with two large coffees. President Kagame's face smiled from behind the cash register, something I would see again and again. It was a sparkling morning, with prosperous city dwellers breezing past, going about their business. Still, there were embers everywhere. It was uncomfortable to have death still so stubbornly on my mind, as if it would blind me against Rwanda's beauty and hope and promise. But everyone seemed to bear a mark of the recent terror, each man a perpetrator, each woman a survivor, each teenager a victim, everyone a witness. "Who did you lose?"—I wanted to ask everyone I met. How does a country repair the irreparable? How do people survive the knowledge that, where they live, ghosts outnumber the living?

Aimee took me to the Kimironko open-air market, where tables groaned with yam and kale and passion fruit, and vendors haggled away. We scooped up a handful of garlic and looked for pumpkin, carrots, and mangos. The air hung with the smell of soil, sweat, and ripe fruit. A toddler teething on a raw potato clung to her mother. A manicurist painted tangerine polish on another woman. American hip hop blared from the flower section, where I was beckoned by the vendor. I grabbed a handful of calla lilies, pressed my nose in the blossoms, and suddenly swooned with dizziness and then nausea.

"Are you okay?" Aimee asked. I planted my hip on the corner of a table. Still lightheaded, I inexplicably clutched the flowers. "You look awful," she said. "Wait here."

She returned with a bunch of finger-sized bananas, peeled one, and held forth the open skin with the fruit inside. "Try this."

The banana tasted tart, like the inside of a key lime pie. Thankfully, my wooziness, wherever it came from—jet lag, fatigue, too much coffee and too little food—passed.

"*Muzu*, over here!" A man waved me over to a table piled high with tree tomatoes (a fruit that I soon learned tastes like a mix of papaya and kiwi) and avocados. "*Muzu*" is short for *muzungu*, a Bantu word that literally means "aimless wanderer" but is vernacular throughout East Africa for "white person." He looked to be in his mid-forties, which put him around twenty-seven during the genocide. I looked harder at him, at his facial features, and found myself trying to profile him: Hutu, a perpetrator? Or Tutsi, a victim? If the latter, it likely meant that he had been a member of the great diaspora that settled in Burundi, Uganda, Tanzania, Kenya, and the Democratic Republic of the Congo after fleeing from earlier persecution. In the summer of 1994, after an estimated 800,000—nearly all—of the Tutsi in Rwanda had been butchered, those in the surrounding countries began to return from exile.

"I don't need any avocado today," I said. He laughed, and I followed suit.

The next two days were a tornado of activity—a bus ride to Butare in the rain to visit two development projects, both seemingly more desperate and optimistic in the downpour. Men in straw hats and women in bright floral prints sang their gratitude to the NGO and detailed the progress of their community-improvement projects. Mothers nursed babies, the sick hooked onto their neighbors' arms to walk, and children in faded school uniforms, with mischievous grins, kicked a ball with bare feet. At each stop, I had a curious sensation—so subtle I was almost unaware I was feeling it—from the inescapable subtext of every moment spent on Rwandan soil.

More visits, and gallons of stout coffee, then South African chardonnay at Hôtel des Mille Collines, and a party at Aimee's house with creamy sweet potatoes the flavor of pound cake, and curry boiling on the stove.

The next day we drove north, where billboards advertising mobile phone companies lined the highways, construction sites bloomed in the distance, and the countryside sped by in a green blur of trees, farms, and flowering orchards. My neck swiveled back and forth, trying to absorb it all. Banana palms stretched like figures across the horizon, and rainwater caused the tea plantations that curved along the landscape to glow with incandescent brightness. Riverbanks were lined with bean plants and coffee trees, and the soil was a violent shade of red. Scarlet mud spilled down the slopes and onto the street, and flecks of clay splashed onto the car's windshield.

On the way to Akagera Game Preserve, a heavy downpour made the route impenetrable. We had to slow down, inching between currents of rainwater that ran along both sides of our vehicle. The delay was fortuitous. Just ten yards in front of us, a tree fell across the road, barely missing our car. The driver hit the brakes, and suddenly men with machetes emerged out of nowhere, one after another, to hack the tree into bits. I exited the car to witness this quick and efficient road-clearing project. Aimee and I exchanged a glance. The machete—panga in Kinyarwanda—is to Rwanda as a freight car is to Germany—an image so loaded and closely identified with genocide it can never be benign. The sight affected me, and I was unable to speak for a while.

A troop of baboons waited for us at the lodge, as if they had been dispatched by some casting director to offer comic relief. One of them stole my bottle of orange soda, and I filmed him trying to open it like a skid-row drunk. In the park, giraffes nuzzled each other's necks, marabou minced around, and a leopard vanished into the bush. Fishermen trod lightly around hippos and crocodiles. The animals patrolled the waters with unblinking eyes that skimmed the surface with vigilance and a touch of menace as they swam. I filled my lungs with the damp air of the rainy season, and as I walked upon the sturdy ground, my emotions toggled between awe at these living wonders and a foreboding of uncertain provenance that still nagged at me.

Back in Kigali, I ordered dinner at another guesthouse, this time in Kimihururu, a neighborhood where key events early in the genocide were unleashed. I steamed in the shower and dried myself with the only towel, a small red one, and hung it over the lip of the tub to dry. I went to the miniscule lobby, ordered a cold Primus beer, and tried to engage the night clerk as I nibbled on a plate of vegetables and rice. I was the only customer for the night.

"What was this guesthouse before...?" I asked.

"It was always a house."

"Did the same people always live here?"

He shrugged.

"Where are you from?" I asked.

"I'm Rwandan. But I'm from the Congo. When I was little, I went to live with cousins there."

Tutsi.

"Are your parents..." I stuttered, "I mean, your family...?"

"They're all dead. I never knew them."

"I'm sorry."

"It's not your fault."

I watched an American game show on the flat screen for a few more minutes, then returned to my quarters to sleep. I gasped when I entered the bathroom. The wet towel on the bathtub was dripping broad, crimson streaks on the porcelain. I lifted it, wrung it out, and was filled with a fever of horror as a stream of dye painted a blood-red trail to the drain.

The following day, I toured more development-projects sites—a sanitation initiative and a women's cooperative, and witnessed these villages in the process of organizing themselves into thriving communities. At dinner in Musanze, a group of men sat at a table near us. They weren't menacing, but they were formidable, dressed like businessmen on casual Friday, with a confident air that indicated they knew—but didn't care—that they were the center of attention.

"Who are these men?" I asked the waiter.

"Security detail," he said. "The President is coming tomorrow."

As they shared their roasted chicken and cassava greens, I wondered whether they had been guerillas, fighting alongside the now-President in his rebel army, and wondered what they had seen, endured, and lost.

Back at the new guesthouse, I woke to one of Rwanda's shimmering mornings. My window perfectly framed the volcano Muhabura, crowned with clouds in the distance. We drove past brick colonial buildings to the staging area for the gorilla tour, where anticipation swirled palpably and the excitement verged on pandemonium. Walking stick in hand, I began my trek with seven other climbers, a tracker, and two guides armed and dressed like soldiers. One of the hikers, a German woman, told me that she had waited all her life to see these animals, and that she felt as if she were dreaming and was certain she would wake up any second in her bedroom in suburban Dusseldorf.

We strolled across a wet, green meadow flecked with pyrethrin flowers. The black skyline of the other nearby volcanoes hovered silently. Crisp air gave way to the heat of a dagger sun, then returned; it felt like the Swiss Alps in June. In front of us, a porter sliced away stinging nettles from the path so we could enter the bush. I caught my hiking shoes on vines and roots, and I slipped on stones while trying to leap across the streams. Worn from the workout about two hours in, I stripped off my fleece jacket before the final climb to see the gorilla family. The trackers had located them nesting in the jungle just over the stone wall that runs for 50 miles along the border between Uganda and the DRC, on the edges of which opposition Hutu factions have long been rumored to be hiding out. We scrambled along and soon found ourselves enclosed by foliage and silence.

We passed through a frustratingly opaque thicket for the final ten minutes, and at last I saw my first gorilla, a baby, and then its twin and its mother. I had the sense, however, that they were checking *us* out, and that they enjoyed (or at least tolerated) visiting hours as much as we did. I felt as if I had been allowed entry into a cage at the zoo. I tiptoed around the gorillas' living area, aiming my camera at them, transfixed by the infants' adorable faces and their nonchalance. We watched the 500-pound silverback scowl, his massive head as big as a ham. He glanced over at me, and his stare aroused twangs of giddiness and a full-body constriction of fear. I took more photos as the twins and several other babies crawled onto him, still outside the required ten yards' distance, but thrillingly close. He yanked a stalk of bamboo and shredded it in his mouth. The tracker made strange braying noises, apparently to communicate something friendly.

I was at the edge of our group when I saw the silverback rise and head straight in our direction. His arms were outstretched to his sides, swinging, and it was terrifyingly clear that I was standing in an intersection, in the path of a speeding truck. As he moved, he struck me, a solid roundhouse swipe to my right kidney. Our group had packed together so tightly in our rapid-flash panic that there was no room for me to go flying, so I teetered around, and one of the guides caught me mid-spin. He erupted with laughter.

"Well, nothing's broken," I said with tears of pain that poked through in spite of my efforts to thwart them, and which loosened the sunscreen from my face straight into my now-stinging eyes. After the shock came a ferocious trembling through my entire body, and I shivered as if I needed a blanket and a thermos of tea.

"He didn't hurt you, did he?" the guide asked.

"I'm fine."

"They're not aggressive," he said, though the throbbing welt on my side suggested otherwise.

I had done enough research to know that the gorillas were peaceful creatures, and I suppose I also understood that he was not targeting me specifically. He was just heading toward his family, his arms propelling him at a rapid clip, and I had simply gotten in the way.

"I think he wanted to cheer you up," said the guide.

"I think he wanted to show me who's in charge," I said, trying not to look as weak and scared as I felt.

There was a half hour left of our tour. I felt okay, if a little dinged up, and my seven co-travelers fussed over me, as if I had lost an arm. I put my camera away and watched these thirteen animals from the Hirwa family, including the toddler twins, caress each other, toss themselves around the forest floor, leap up trees and trampoline off their mothers' tummies. An adolescent male slicked back his pompadour and rested his chin in his hand like *The Thinker*. A toddler stumbled toward me, and I almost reached for her.

I snatched a few eucalyptus leaves off a tree, crumpled them, and held them under my nose to breathe in their medicinal scent. I stood in a white shaft of sun listening to the rustle of the animals, and tucked the leaves into my pocket. Soon we walked back to the vehicle, over ditches, through pastures filled with ox and acacia, and in spite of my protestations, the soldier helped me over the many rising brooks. "You will surely remember that gorilla," he said.

"I will surely remember this whole day," I said. "Thank you."

That afternoon, I drank tonic water and lime on the beach in Gisenyi and tanned myself next to the chilly water of Lake Kivu, which was as immense and infinite as an ocean. The promenade was lined with colonial-era houses, giving the appearance of a down-at-the-heels resort town. The crater of Mount Nyiragongo, just over the border in the DRC, bubbled electric orange. I strolled the palm-lined avenue to Goma, stopping for cold ginger tea at one of the old stone hotels. I knew there had been horror in Gisenyi seventeen years earlier, but for once I couldn't feel its reverberations, just the heat, the sun, and the silverback's handprint that burned the flesh around my middle, marking me for something.

On the way back to Kigali, we detoured for as many genocide memorials as we could locate. Most, like the one I saw in Gisenyi, were simple concrete tombs festooned with purple bunting, the sign of a country still mourning one fifth of its population.

"How many people are buried here?" I asked Anderson, the driver.

"Thousands, probably," he said.

"Did you know many people who died?" I asked.

"Thousands," he said again. I wonder whether he had been thinking, "Why should I even bother with this conversation?" He knew I could feel, but never understand.

Anderson and I were silent as he drove me back into Kigali, where he dropped me at yet a third place, a decent, if enormous, hotel. He and I made plans to meet the next morning.

At 9:00 A.M., he collected me, and we drove first to Ntarama, a small church forty-five minutes from the city center. No one was there to greet us, just a couple of armed guards who unlocked the door to let us in. I walked past the purple draping to the first enclosure, an open air shed. There were six white, reinforced bags on the left side of a shelf, a stack of mildewing books on the right.

"Are those..." I asked, pointing to the white sacks.

"Bones," the guard said. "Farmers still dig them up. So many were tossed into the rivers and in peoples' yards."

I picked up a decaying notebook, then a child's tablet. "This area was all Tutsi. The kids came here to do their homework." he said. "The Hutu threw grenades into the church."

There were exercise books of math problems, French-language workbooks, pads that contained what looked like writing samples, and piles of moth-eaten bibles. A young woman came to usher us around.

"Shouldn't these be under glass?" I asked her. "Preserved?"

"I don't know," she said.

Inside the church were clothes, glasses, identity cards, sandals, pens. There were skulls lined up on shelves, grimly demonstrating the three primary ways of murder: machete, blunt force, and gunshot. Anderson and the young woman showed me around the exhibit, wordlessly, and occasionally, when I had the stomach, I interjected a question.

We then drove to Nyamata, the church where five thousand Tutsi were murdered in the place they had sought protection. The below-ground crypts were piled top to bottom and end to end with human bones. Upstairs, the victims' clothes were draped on the pews. On the side of the church was a statue of Mary, looking helplessly down from her perch, covered in bird shit.

Every breath I drew that morning was tainted with sorrow. Purple petals from the jacaranda tree rained down on our car as we left Nyamata.

"Even the trees are in mourning," I said to Anderson.

"No," he said. "The trees are very much alive."

Within two days, I was back at the airport, my bag full of souvenirs: geranium oil, tea, bracelets, passion-fruit syrup and aka-banga—the hot pepper oil that comes in a bottle with an eyedropper, which people tote around in their pockets.

Anderson had been right. Rwanda *was* very much alive. I kept thinking of tragedy when the country wanted me to see its colors, put my toe in its waters, shake hands with its people, breathe its invigorating air, and taste its delicious bananas, passion fruit, and tree tomatoes. Despite, or maybe because of, my predisposition to let my conclusions get in the way of my own judiciousness, I was besotted with Rwanda, its red soil, its innumerable stately hills, and its survivors—who would not or could not talk about the past, at least not to me. I had to tell myself throughout my trip that experience is what matters, and that the heart can't quite know what the eyes haven't seen. Trauma is for those who suffered it, and the aftermath belongs to them too.

As I went through passport control, I saw President Kagame's half-smiling face one last time, with those eyes that had witnessed so much peering behind professorial glasses. Within those airport walls, I recalled the mothers I'd met, with the next generation of Rwandans at their breasts. I pictured the cheap towel that made me recoil in horror, but that dripped nothing but red dye. There was the cold tea I drank on Lake Kivu's sultry shore. Its tang shot relief through my body, making me ignore the hand-shaped bruise that was blossoming on my back. Maybe that gorilla *did* single me out, simply to knock some sense into me.

With dried mud still on my shoes, I went through security and slipped my arms back into my jacket. There was a little time to kill before my flight. Did I have any money left for coffee? I fished through my purse and then unzipped my jacket pocket. Inside was the clump of eucalyptus leaves, still pungent, still sweet.

Chapter 15

Twenty Years and Counting

Since 1784, Le Grand Véfour has stood at the northwest cor‑
ner of the Jardins du Palais‑Royal in Paris. The restaurant
seems forever married to the words "venerable institution"
because of the roster of luminaries who have warmed its velvet
banquettes over the years—Napoleon, Victor Hugo, George
Sand, Colette, Julia Child, Jean‑Paul Sartre….

And then there's me. One fall afternoon twenty years ago, I
had my wedding dinner there.

About that time, a young Savoyard chef named Guy Martin
was plucked from the Hotel Château de Divonne in the tiny Lake
Geneva spa town of Divonnes‑les‑Bains to lead Le Grand Véfour
into the twenty‑first century. Some eight weeks later, he served
his first dinner as chef de cuisine, and he remains there to this day.
I had never met Martin, but this year, at both of our two‑decade
marks, I wondered whether there might be parallels between the
life of a restaurant and the course of a marriage. So I returned to Le
Grand Véfour to raise a glass to history—France's, the restaurant's,
and my own.

I first ate there in the summer of 1984 with a sporty count
named Nicolas, who squired me around Paris in a Fiat Spider but

whose diminished circumstances became obvious when the bill arrived and he was a couple hundred francs short. What did I care about who paid the check? Champagne was careening through our veins, and the restaurant's red-velvet banquettes and gilded ceiling gave us the sensation that we were tucked inside a fancy chocolate box. Despite its age, Le Grand Véfour had the order and polish of something new and, for me, uncharted. Mirrored panels lined the dining room, along with portraits under glass of fleshy, bare-breasted goddesses bearing lilies, peaches, colored ices—paintings 200 years old, but with hues and sentiments as fresh as that July morning. All around me, the thrill of seduction mingled with the tranquility of permanence.

The scent of tarragon wafted up from my lamb chops, and cassis ice cream added another layer of pleasure, which—along with Nicolas' hand intermittently grazing my thigh under the table—heightened the anticipation in all my senses. The bubbles, his lips on my bare shoulder, a warm summer night—Le Grand Véfour was promise itself, the pure essence of Paris. I never forgot it.

Seven years later, I was back living in Paris and working as a journalist, traveling for stories in Eastern Europe and the Middle East. When I got engaged to Mark, there seemed no question that we would forgo the big to-do stateside and get married in the city we now called home. He had bought my engagement ring—a well-worn platinum, diamond, and sapphire band—at an upscale pawn shop on the Rue de Turenne for 1,200 francs, or about $200 at the time. Our rented apartment had a fancy Marais address, but I'd spent the better part of the previous year steaming off the stained, brown wallpaper that covered every inch of the place. I replaced the unshaded light bulbs on the ceiling with fixtures from the market at Clignancourt and hid the pockmarked, prewar linoleum under carpets that I bought at souks from Rabat to Istanbul.

In France, no one cared where we went to college or what our fathers did back home. We worked hard, scraped by, consorted with journalists and artists, and weren't on any regular family dole that propped up our lifestyle. Still, I was the youngest of four unmarried daughters, so my parents were eager to comply with whatever I chose for the fifty people we planned to invite—family, a few friends from the States and, mostly, those who were part of our life in France.

I had already lived in Paris long enough to dress the part. The city demanded a certain decorum, and so I obliged, eschewing comfort in favor of formalness, exchanging worn cords for tailored slacks. But some other things—like finding a wedding venue— remained difficult for a young American woman. I aimed high, but Paris was shutting me out. I inquired at what seemed like the city's entire varsity restaurant line-up: L'Orangerie and L'Amboiserie, Taillevent and Maison Blanche. In each dining room, the gate-keeper shook his head, topped it off with a puckered expression of Gallic scorn, and sent me packing. They seemed to be telling me what I suspected: a coarse Yankee such as I had no business getting married in such a refined place.

I hadn't considered approaching Le Grand Véfour; I consid-ered it a sanctum, impenetrable and holy. Yes, I had read that some people—snobbish Parisian food critics, mostly—saw it to be in decline since the recent death of its chef of thirty-six years. They said that it had grown stale and predictable, a quaint little relic with subpar food. And yet, all that gilt, all that grandeur, that singular backstory...I'd need to present a whole different persona in order to walk through those doors confidently, and one day, at a salon inside the Galerie Vivienne, not far from Le Grand Véfour, I inadvertently fell into one.

"Your hair looks very sad," my coiffeuse, Monique, told me flatly, referring to my brunette locks. Two hours later, I walked out as a blonde. Maybe it was the hair that gave me some guile; in any case, something marched me straight over there.

I stopped to read the placard in memory of Colette, who had lived upstairs and who, near the end of her life, was carried down in a modified palanquin each day for lunch at her lavish personal canteen. I turned the corner on the Rue de Beaujolais and walked inside, where I was greeted by an imposing woman with a chestnut bouffant and a spray of silk ruffles at her neck.

"Hello," I said. "I'm getting married on September 7th at the *mairie* of the 3rd arrondissement, and afterwards, I would like to have my dinner here."

To my astonishment, her face lit up.

"I'm Madame Ruggieri," she said. "Congratulations. We would be delighted to host your celebration."

When our wedding party arrived at Le Grand Véfour on an unusually balmy Saturday in September, waiters greeted us beneath the colonnade with flutes of pink Champagne on silver trays. At the time, the wine giant Taittinger owned the restaurant, which had been closed for a month—officially, this was the final day of its summer hiatus, during which it had been buffed, shined, and spruced up. The next day, it would open to the public again, but today it was ours.

With the sun pouring in and reflected off its many mirrors, the room shimmered. A lone cellist played a Bach suite as we trickled inside.

On the walls above the tables inside the dining room were small plaques in memoriam to those who occupied them. Mark and I sat side by side on Napoleon and Josephine's banquette, and I tried to imagine their passionate beginning rather than their disappointing end. The freesia and ranunculi that Madame Ruggieri and I had chosen for the tables were almost unnecessary, upstaged by the room itself.

Our lamb medallions were drizzled with basil sauce, and our wedding cake was topped with pulled-sugar roses, whose pattern matched the painted floral garlands on the ceiling. I was not hungry for much. Nothing heralds a change so completely as a wedding day, and as I transformed, my movements were tinged with an almost spectral lightness. The constant whir of emotions and people seemed to carry me like a blown petal from one guest to another, from one great froth of levity to another. I recall studying the lace cuff of my blouse, then observing my hand as it seemed to raise itself toward a goblet of water.

"I'm your wife," I whispered to Mark at some point during dinner. He reached around me on the banquette, grasped my hip, and pulled me toward him, sensing my incredulity at the pronouncement. I wasn't thinking about how long, or whether, we'd last. I simply needed to name what I had become, as if saying the word meant I had simultaneously transfigured into a more true and worthy soul. But I didn't feel the least bit changed. Instead, I sensed I had boarded the finest and sturdiest of ships but was terrified of water, and furthermore, it was too late for me to disembark.

"I guess that makes me your husband," he whispered.

"Forever," I said.

"That's the plan," he said. And as we toasted each other, he added, "you'll see."

The dining room was brightly illuminated, but white curtains covered the lower half of the windows, blocking the view. My husband, my family, my friends—we were safely contained on an island in the middle of Paris. All that was visible from my table was the sky, the green tops of linden trees, and the limestone columns that have framed the gardens since the Duc d'Orléans had them built in 1781.

A few weeks later, after our honeymoon, I was back in Paris, sorting through gifts of crystal and china, and I read in the paper about Guy Martin, the thirty-three-year-old chef who had just taken over at Le Grand Véfour. Such things made headlines in France.

Two decades passed, and while planning a trip to Paris to commemorate our anniversary, I remembered that news story. I was stunned to learn that Martin was not only still there, but also that, after weathering several vicissitudes endemic to his business—in 2000, he earned a coveted third Michelin star; in 2008, he lost it—he bought Le Grand Véfour outright in 2010. Whether it was fate or choice or some kind of compromise that had carried him to this point, Guy Martin—like me and Mark—had remained loyal to the decision he made all those years ago. I was intrigued. I wanted to meet him and hear what he might have to say on the subject; on tenacity and grit and endurance.

As I left for Paris, I was uncertain what awaited me. I suppose I wanted to recall the promise of my wedding day, to experience again the splendid room, and to peer back on my less-weary self with eyes that were now two decades older, and two decades more married. It was a sensation I sought, an assurance that longevity, whether in a restaurant or a relationship, does not have to equal decrepitude. I wondered whether my marriage had measured up to the place where it began, or vice-versa. I was simply following a map. I figured I could find what I was searching for if I took the old, familiar trail.

But Mark and I would have to celebrate that milestone later, at home. He was stuck stateside with a pressing deadline, and besides, we couldn't justify another ticket to France. But that was only part of the reason why I set off for Paris alone.

It had been barely two years since we were roughed up by the near fatal blow to our marriage, and though we were resolved to stay together, we were still figuring out *how* to stay together. Going back to the source and confronting our marriage at its origin might goose my growing state of optimism and help me formulate some ideas for our shared road ahead. Mark's presence might alter my state of detachment, or muddle up my powers of observation. Plus, rumination is best endured alone.

I was curious and excited, both to enter the transcendent realm of the restaurant and meal that awaited me, and for the fact-finding mission with Guy Martin that would accompany it.

The day before my reservation, I retraced the path I took on my wedding day. I visited the palatial *mairie* off the Rue de Bretagne where, after the ceremony, the mayor of the 3rd arrondissement handed us our official *livret de famille*, with blank pages for up to eight kids. Had the playground in the adjacent park been there on our wedding day? If so, I never noticed. Before I had children, now 14 and 17, a sandbox and jungle gym were invisible to me. Now I stood near the swing set trying to remember how Mark and I had traveled the meaningful distance from the *mairie* to the restaurant. Had a car taken us? How did my friends get there? I recall being possessed of a distinct lightheadedness, but not being a jittery bride. Still, I was surprised to have erased that detail.

This time, I took the metro to Bourse and walked over to the gardens, where I lingered over an alfresco breakfast of café crème and a brioche. It was an April day erupting with color and heat. Here, in almost the physical heart of Paris, the Palais-Royal was an enclave of calm. It felt almost rural, down to the low drone of bees in the beds of climbing roses. I tried to imagine how the courtyard must have appeared long ago at that time of year, from up above in Colette's salon. "The Palais-Royal stirs at once under the influence of humidity, of light filtered through soft clouds, of warmth," she wrote. "The green mist hanging over the elms is no longer a mist, it is tomorrow's foliage."

After my coffee and stroll, I took the long ride back to my hotel, in our old neighborhood near Père Lachaise Cemetery. At the front desk, I felt the ions shift in a blast of sensory memory; to my disbelief, standing beside me was one of my husband's dear friends, who had been a witness at our wedding. We were stunned into silence and then laughter. An Australian artist, he was living in Arles and had done the paintings in the hotel. I hadn't seen him in eight years, and his wife had recently passed away. Mark and I weren't able to attend her funeral service, and I still felt awful about it. We hugged, caught up on all our children, had a drink, and wondered where the time went.

The following day, in an upstairs office at Le Grand Véfour, I met Guy Martin and explained the strange coincidence to him—and how pleased I was that my friend would be joining me for lunch. He wasn't surprised.

"This is a magical place in a magical setting," Martin told me. "There's nowhere else in the world like it. When you do an important celebration here—no matter what happens down the line—it will always lead to exceptional things."

He walked me downstairs and, as it had the first time I entered, the restaurant enveloped me with a mysterious force. Twenty years seemed utterly insignificant—both the vestibule and dining room appeared untouched by the passing decades. But incredibly, nothing felt worn or neglected. It was all still there: that gleaming lightness that made me feel like I was swimming in a fizz of soda, and that heady sensation of being instantly transformed into someone of consequence. Inside the dining room, sunlight capsized onto the impeccable white table linens. It was the most beautiful room in all of Paris—of that I was certain. My shoulders drew back and I stood tall, shaking my head in wonder and speechless with emotion.

Although at first it seemed unchanged, upon closer inspection I noticed subtle nods to the present day—hidden LED fixtures brightened the female goddesses and their platters of glistening fruit painted on the wall, and the lace curtains that once ran along the perimeter had been replaced by etched frosted glass. But the soul of Le Grand Véfour was still there, preserved not only in the décor but also in the traditional recipes, which Martin was constantly reinterpreting and updating with new ingredients like Mediterranean sumac and Japanese yuzu. "What keeps it modern is what I put on the plates," he said.

The point, he said, was to allow for the inevitability of change. Nothing stays the same, he insisted, because nothing ever can. "I'm growing every day," he said. "I don't dress like I did 20 years ago. I don't drive the same cars. The same goes for my cooking. It's not a static thing. It is always in perpetual motion."

I pondered the wisdom to be gleaned here, and what I could extrapolate about life and marriage. I never imagined that I could one day be middle aged and scarred by an episode of doubt. Mark and I had survived, but I still sometimes wondered how I could wake up to the same person, every day, for the rest of my days here on earth. Martin said that in his case, the key was to remember the person he was back then, and to trust the impressions that had brought him there in the first place.

"When I came here from Savoie, the Palais-Royal gardens smelled like home," he said. "The first time I pushed in the door of the restaurant, I gasped. It was just like that." He snapped his fingers. "It was a *coup de coeur*, like when you meet someone—you aren't certain, but you know something happened. You just know. I knew I belonged here."

In other words, I needed to envision the young man I'd fallen in love with, and trust that I would feel the same way about him if I met him today. I needed to always remind myself why it was Mark I'd chosen to marry. And I needed to recall the much younger woman I had been—the one who was never going to settle—and believe that even if my tendencies were to be guided, somewhat, by passion, I also possessed good sense and abundant free will. I trusted both, and the sound decisions they allowed me to make.

"I never thought I'd be here for twenty years," he said. "Sometimes I'm still surprised. But as long as I feel good here, and as long as I have faith in what I do, I'll stay." Then, after a pause, he added: "Life is very short."

That, I realized, could also mean, why bother? Other adventures and other paths constantly tempt every man and woman in this life, forever posing the question of whether it takes more strength (or courage) to stay the course or to call it quits. After all, in marriage—and in food—twenty years is no small achievement.

This time, I sat in Jean Cocteau's banquette, with my old friend who was here with me and Mark on our wedding day. As I sank into the soft cushion, it was a strange thrill to feel my own history in this room. The chilled bottle of pink Champagne we drank was from the same cellar in Reims as the one Mrs. Ruggiero had served that September day, probably the same kind I'd shared with Nicolas, and the same I'll drink with my husband on our fortieth anniversary. Even the food managed to be revelatory: Martin's modern turn on the Grand Véfour's classic ravioli, now prepared with foie gras, seemed to prove that the best use of the past is to use it to chart the course ahead. A recognition of history does not have to weigh you down; it can propel you forward.

As guardian of Le Grand Véfour's culinary legacy, Martin persisted by leading it into the twenty-first century with the same perseverance and sense of loyalty that drives those too optimistic, or hopeful, to entertain the idea of failure. As with my marriage, hard work, flexibility, creativity, and love were a recipe for endurance. And for me, continuity—the strengthening force of the status quo—proved to be more motivating than cataclysmic change.

I missed Mark. He had alluded to his tenacity all those years ago, and because of it, I had something to celebrate. Forget about people moving apart, growing in opposite directions. For Mark, to fail would have been to acknowledge a twenty-year mistake, and he couldn't brook such a waste of his time and judgment. Plus, we had never stopped loving each other. We had survived what for many couples would have been insurmountable. And if I could learn anything from a restaurant that had withstood centuries of wars and misfortune, as well as Napoleon and Josephine's demise, and a chef who taught me that fidelity does not have to mean compromise, then we too would endure.

I knew that just outside in the gardens of the Palais-Royal, lovers kissed, children tumbled, and a work crew trimmed the lawn, releasing the cool smell of cut grass. I could see none of it above the newly etched windows, just the sky over Paris—eternal, faithful, delicious.

Chapter 16

Traveling Solo in the World's Most Romantic Country

One night last February, while sleet whipped my windshield as I drove through Normandy's early winter darkness into the port of Honfleur, my GPS sent me the wrong way down a one-way alley between two medieval walls. Alone, phone dead, with both side mirrors crushed like beer cans, I wanted to conjure up a companion, specifically my husband. For a moment, I longed for a simpler time, when he drove while I traced the route on a Michelin map from the passenger side and, out of the corner of my eye, spied a café where we might stop for a languorous lunch. The following day was Valentine's Day, and rattled from the scrape-up, I also felt a little sorry for myself. But this trip across the north of France was, like most of my recent travels, solo. And even here, wedged in a 15th-century cul-de-sac with no obvious way out but total demolition, I had to confess: I liked it that way.

Much as I love my family and crave the company of my friends, companionship on the road is often not worth the trouble. One of the great moments in travel literature takes place in *A Moveable Feast*, when Ernest Hemingway and F. Scott Fitzgerald meet up in Lyon, France and embark on a road trip to drive the latter's Renault back to Paris together. Hijinks ensue, naturally. Fitzgerald takes ill and believes he is dying from congestion of the lungs. Hemingway assures him that he is not, boosting him with plenty of white Mâcon wine and roasted chicken. Upon returning to his wife in Paris, Hemingway offers this assessment: "Never go on trips with anyone you do not love."

I tend to carry this advice even further. If possible, never go on a trip with anyone at all. It's easier to get absorbed in an unfamiliar landscape when solo, reliant on no one and vice versa. Alone, I can weave my way into other cultures and sceneries, explore without limits, find relevance, allow observations to morph into insights. Travel is stressful, and nothing is more conflict-prone than discussions around food, particularly dinner venues. My idea of bliss is to reach the end of a day and crack open a bottle of mini-bar Côtes du Rhône with a box of nuts in my hotel room, all by my sweet lonesome.

More and more frequently, these trips had become the scaffolding to my life as I began to construct the second half of it. Leave, stay, leave, stay—each time I settled into a comfortable space, at home or away, I looked around for the exit. When I left the cocoon of my house, I addressed the first question: what am I leaving? And each time I arrived somewhere I addressed the second: what will I discover that will lead me back home again? I could best find these answers alone. Company distracted me and threw things off course. But when I started to research my book on France, the foundation of my lone-warrior stance seemed to crumble like a stale macaron.

Even unaccompanied, France is the most romantic country in the world. Its sweeping vistas, buttery pastries, sultry beaches, ganache-filled chocolate hearts and history of love affairs that changed destiny stir—for both men and women—the deepest reaches of our sensual selves. For couples, France and its abundant beauty provide an ideal metaphoric backdrop for the newly love-struck or the long married. The country's light, architecture, and insistence on savoring life's comforts, both elemental and voluptuous, blow sweet oxygen into a relationship, imbue it with vitality and consequence. Memories, including mine, are created here, under bursts of stars and over Champagne brut. Twenty-five years ago, I moved to France with a man I loved; a couple of years later, I married him in Paris's 3rd arrondissement, and we stayed on for a few more. These were heady times in my young romantic life, and my own *histoire d'amour* lingers like a ghost on the quais of Paris and at tables in the sun along the Côte d'Azur.

I encountered some of these memories when I embarked on four extended solitary road trips, with my only partners a trusty fuel-efficient rental car and a fickle GPS. My first leg was along the Riviera, through Languedoc and then over to Bordeaux. In Mougins, a few miles inland from Cannes, I opened the door to a stunning hotel room that overlooked a valley and the gray-green maquis of Provence. Had I been with my husband, I would have grabbed him and tumbled onto the bed, for the sheer pleasure of crisp sheets under our road-weary selves. Instead, I explored the roomy closets, sampled the complimentary coffee, put on heels and went to dinner. The chef set up a table for one in the corner of the kitchen, and I feasted on foie gras, truffled vermicelli and scallops.

"This is incredible," I said again and again, and I wondered whether he thought it was strange for a woman to be by herself in such a glorious place. I smiled confidently to reassure him that yes, I'm unaccompanied and yes, I'm really all right. Okay, mostly all right. Few meals ever tasted better, yet it was strange to drink all that good wine—red, white, rosé, Champagne—and sink into that lovely, empty bed alone.

Pangs of loneliness stung me in Arles. At night, the Roman amphitheater glowed with the masculine swagger of imperial might, and I had to swallow my expressions of awe rather than gasp them to my husband. When I entered the dreamy courtyard of my hotel in Nîmes, again, I had to effuse in silence. But slowly the anonymity of my solitude was beginning to course through me, as agreeable a sensation as slow-melting sunshine on the back of the neck. It was distinctly comforting to feel free to contemplate and not to converse. Liberating to run a bath and pad around in the nude without the prospect—neither desire nor dread—of an exhausted but obligatory romp. At 53, there are darker things than a short spell in a sexual vacuum.

Later, as I took in Norman Foster's modern Carré d'Art, which mirrors the ancient Maison Carrée—an unsullied Roman temple—beside it, I knew my husband would have circled both buildings, multiple times, with the excitement of the artist he is, and photographed every perfect angle. He would have a history lesson hanging loosely in his head to impart, about first-century Augustinian architecture, or Thomas Jefferson, who admired the temple's beauty so much he modelled the Virginia State Capitol in Richmond after it. I respect my husband's curiosity and knowledge, and the image of him made me cognizant of the best qualities of this man, things that vanish in the hustle and drone of the day-to-day. This thought of him as a patient and curious voyager forced my hand, to delve deep, to read the plaques, to slow down and just gaze at the blinding white stone columns.

By the time I got to Bordeaux, the pangs had faded. This lightness began to invigorate me and urge me, unfettered, along the highways of southwestern France. It was the opposite of loneliness: this was freedom itself, that familiar sensation from my travels elsewhere when I became not a wife or companion, but a traveler, afraid of nothing, surprised by how capable and decisive I could be. In the morning, I enjoyed café au lait and croissants while getting ready for the day, all at my own pace. I was deliciously unrushed as I pulled on a sweater and swiped my mascara, and felt equally relieved not to be scrambling my husband out the door.

My choices counted because they were mine alone, and that included my mistakes and missteps. I got a bargain, last-minute rate at a four-star hotel that certainly looked dreamy. Sadly, my room was far from it—cold, dim, and too close to the kitchen vents. I wanted to convey my dismay to someone, just for the sake of complaining, but it was hard to deny the obvious: I had got what I paid for. So instead I moved on, celebrating my newfound mellowness with a box of *canelés* at Baillardran. Which I didn't have to share. I rented a bicycle near the Cathedral St André and whizzed along the Garonne River. My husband would have wanted to ride all day; a bracing one-hour spin was perfect for me.

It was winter when I returned to France again, and icy storms raged along the English Channel. I walked the seaside paths in Dinard, dined on buckwheat crêpes full of ham and cheese, and washed them down with cidre brut. I had seen the limestone cliffs at Étretat twice before, both times with my husband, under piercing summer sunshine. He loves this place, its chalky rock formations and the choppy sea that changes by the hour. But I savored my own vulnerability on the cliffs that were slick with rain, past the Notre Dame de la Garde chapel and down the ladder to the beach. It was ideal weather for intimacy, with the gusts, the torrents, and occasional glimpses of flinty light, but I was moving too fast, on my own timeline, detouring to small towns or a ruin or a lighthouse, no discussion needed. Normandy's atmosphere in winter is a blur of clouds and mist—in other words, romance, which does not necessarily have to equal passionate love.

There was a stirring of regret as I wandered among the vastness inside Reims Cathedral and shivered from the chill and a fever of emotions. There was no one with whom to marvel at the incredible story of Joan of Arc, who, by leading Charles VII to his coronation under this very soaring skeleton of arches, saved France from British rule in 1429. Onward I went to Veuve Clicquot for a tour of the house and limestone *crayères*, followed by lunch. A server in white gloves poured glass after glass until I seemed to be floating under a veil of frothy La Grande Dame. Loose and light with the near perfection of this day, I was also aware of its ironies. Here I was, immersed in this temple to Champagne, the thirst for which is so permanently fused with the concept of romantic love that it risks cliché. And yet the clarity was startling: I was travelling alone but not a single thing was missing. My lunch companion—my guide for the day—and I raised our glass to a new, fast friendship, to the astonishing Widow Clicquot, and finally to the singular beauty of a crystal flute of Champagne glowing like a lamp in the low winter sunlight. In every way, it was a celebration.

In all, I made four trips in one little car or another, crisscrossing 5,150km of France's roads and highways. I tooled along Brittany's temperamental coastline and headed east to the *bouchons* of Lyon, then through Basque Country, the Midi-Pyrénées, Picardy, Poitou-Charentes, and our old stomping grounds of Burgundy, the Var and the Vaucluse. I set my GPS and chugged away, left when I wanted, stopped when I could. I collected boxes of bistro matches that I would use to light my fireplace, in front of which my husband and I would sip the Armagnac I would carry home. I kept a master list, amassed napkins from restaurants I wanted to write about or just to remember, made notes of where we should return together, took photos to add depth to my retelling.

"Love is rather inhibiting in my view," said the travel writer Jan Morris about her preference for the solitary voyage. "We are always thinking about what each other wants to do." Sharing these trips only with myself gave me keen eyes and the clear head to see with them.

If all journeys lead to self-discovery, the alley in Honfleur proved that point. With no one to blame but myself, and nothing to do but gun it through the narrow portal, I did just that.

"God, oh God, oh God, oh God, oh God," I repeated, along with a string of profanities aimed at the alley, the walls, the blackness, the rain, the GPS, and mostly, myself. I could not see in reverse, so I took the only course that was proper: inhale, put it in drive, clutch the wheel, and give myself a rallying cry.

"AHHHHH!" I exhaled through clenched teeth.

But for the mirrors, my car made it through almost unscratched. When I got to my hotel, I must have looked distraught because the duty clerk offered me a snifter of Calvados and a fluffy towel. Chocolate hearts, wrapped in red foil, tempted me from a dish on the counter so I grabbed a few. Cozy in my room, I plunked on the bed, called my husband and related the tale of my wrong turn and daring escape.

"Honey, are you okay?" he asked.

"I'm great," I said. I unwrapped a chocolate, felt it melt for a moment, during which I sensed the briefest ache of longing for my own kitchen, the portrait-still tableau of snow outside the picture window, and him. Then I sunk into the silky European linens, savoring a toasty swallow of apple brandy, allowing the liquid to delight and warm my throat. "By the way," I said, "Happy Valentine's Day."

Chapter 17

Milk, Bread, Butter, Chocolate

*I*t was one of my more notable detours in a lifetime of imprac‑ tical diversions on the road.

Last summer, on the way from Lourdes to the airport in Biarritz, I made a hasty exit north off the A63 for Bayonne, a riverside city in the Pays Basque, just inland from the glittering beaches of the Atlantic coast. In truth, the whole route had been a detour. Good sense would have dictated that I fly out of Pau that day, which was much closer both to Lourdes and to where I had been staying for a week on the edge of the Pyrénées. Plus, I was not overly eager to pass through hordes of chi‑chi vacationers inching through airport traffic on a summer evening on the Côte Basque, of which Biarritz was the de facto capital. Although I risked being late for the 8 P.M. flight to Paris—the first leg of my trip back home—this was no ordinary pitstop. I could anticipate the constellation of sorrows and regrets that were all but certain to engulf me if, because of some airplane reservation, I lost my chance to pull over for Chocolat Toast at Cazenave.

I had finished my work in the Pyrénées, a story on a magnif‑ icent rare peach that harvests during a short week in July. I had gone to seek perfection and had found it, plucked pink and ready by the bushel in the Béarn. Not that I was dreading home exactly, but I was reluctant to pry myself away from southwestern France and the markets filled with lavender soaps and ripe summer fruit. No doubt I would miss the feathery lightness I experienced on the drives past fields of Jurançon grapes, and the acres of sunflowers that tinged with yellow the visible expanse of the horizon. Rather than watch my fortnight in France dribble away on the lackluster highway to the plane, I sought a resounding conclusion to it. A moment that would buttress me for the journey home and the work that awaited me.

Shifting gears in my little Citroën, I began to collate the chores by category, none of which I had thought about for even a moment since I had been away. The abrupt mental switch made both the car and my heart rate accelerate. A couple of appliances in disrepair, taxes to be filed, a broken attic window to be replaced. Did the outdoor spigot get fixed yet? Was there half and half for our coffee in the morning, indispensable for our treasured routine with oatmeal? Must fill the fridge. I visualized a vast leafy matrix of weeds obscuring the flowers in my garden, stunting their growth. In twenty-four hours, I would probably be down by the pond deploying my hedge trimmer, cutting back the wall of green brush that would certainly be marching toward my back porch.

This was the life that I cherished and accepted in full as mine, replete with duties domestic and otherwise. I was as efficient looking after the needs of my home as I was looking after my husband, children and dog. The demands of our overgrown world suited me, now that I had not lived in a city for well over a decade. Mark was deep into a big commission, and I was excited to learn the details of his progress—of his carving, hammering, slicing, fork-lifting. Our daughter was home for the summer and I longed for her company. It was time to sit down with my notes, and weave the many bits of string gathered for this story into a narrative. Yet I knew by now that the distance between sweet reentry and the urge for going could, sometimes, be perilously short. Above all, there was no telling when I would return to the Pays Basque.

Every great food city has its emblematic dish: Singapore has chili crab, New Orleans has beignets, Brussels has moules frites. The singular aspect of Chocolat Toast, though, is that this signature Bayonnais concoction is served only at one place in town, Cazenave, a third-generation family-owned shop on the Rue Port Neuf.

Its construction is simple: a cup of foamy hot chocolate as thick as Greek yogurt with a stalagmite of whipped cream on the side, two slices of buttered brioche toast and a generous pitcher of ice water (presumably to cut the blood fats swirling around after ingesting this achingly rich combination). Served at breakfast, at *l'heure du thé*, or right before closing time, the Chocolat Toast ritual is perhaps the sole obligation of the visitor to Bayonne. This may be an especially forceful coda for departing pilgrims, like I was: spent from praying for miracles at the Sanctuary of Our Lady of Lourdes, craving the earth's most heavenly comfort food.

"People often stop here because it's a tradition, which is both because of Cazenave itself and also because of the history of chocolate in Bayonne," owner Pantxoa Bimboire later told me. A child of the Basque country, his grandmother had been a waitress at the *salon de thé* in the rear of the chocolate shop. In 1930, she convinced her husband to sell his jewelry store and buy Cazenave. Even then, a tray laden with Chocolat Toast was the iconic specialty of this small city on the banks of the Nive and Adour rivers, the ancestral home of the cocoa bean in France, which had journeyed there from Mexico, via Spain and Portugal.

The Cazenave shop window is a rainbow of chocolate bars in gem-hued wrappings, arranged like boxes of Crayola crayons. Normally, I'd stop to swoon over the stylish packaging, but it was late that July afternoon, and I only had a two-hour window to return the Citroën and catch my plane. I half-raced through the store to the tea room. As a Bayonne landmark, it is ravishing.

Lined with smoky, century-old mirrors, the vestibule is suffused with Belle Époque glamour, the kind unfortunate restaurateurs in the New World try pathetically to mimic. To further the sensation of being ensconced in a jewel case, I seated myself under the milky white and gold stained-glass dome, installed in the 19th century. Not wanting to rush, I cast the briefest glance at my watch anyway.

As the server quietly placed a simple white tray before me, I imagined the fanfare that could—and maybe should—accompany this hallowed ritual. Instead, I rearranged the components, all of which, except the glass pitcher of water, were served on delicate, rose-speckled china. I spooned a heap of whipped cream as thick as butter onto the chocolate, and gently stirred. Gulping my first mouthful, I felt a stab of pleasure that rendered me motionless. An onlooker might have wondered about my beatific countenance, why my eyes closed and my lips curved upwards.

There is nothing terribly complicated about the recipe, mostly unchanged since long before my first time breakfasting and ruminating on Chocolat Toast thirty years ago. Yes, the chocolate tablets are now made from organic beans grown in Peru or Ecuador, but the hot milk poured over them is still from cows who pasture in the hilly Pays Basque, as is the cream for the thick chantilly. The brioche toast is sliced from a special golden loaf, created by a local baker only for Cazenave. Most unusually, the foam that provides a tantalizing lid to the hot chocolate is still whipped by hand using a wooded *mousseuse*—beater—fashioned from boxwood. "It will always be the same," says Bimboire, "because this is the heritage of Bayonne."

And, I decided, it is somehow my heritage too. Almost half a lifetime ago, I took a train to Bayonne, in search of a cheaper hotel than the one I had booked near the beach in Biarritz. What I found there was some kind of culinary perfection, and a dish I have, since then, now and again, physically craved. This time, I was drawn to this gilded refuge not simply for the fat and sugar, cream and cocoa, ice and water convened on a tray in sheer gustatory harmony. Indeed, it is almost mathematically pure. Sweet chocolate compliments savory toast, chilled water tempers steaming cocoa, whose creamy smoothness is startled by the crunch of buttered brioche. No, it was something else. Here one simply encounters the most elusive, essential, and even miraculous of virtues: balance.

Often, when I traveled, I pondered which of the beautiful but imperfect of my two existences—the home one or the away one—was real and which was the response to it. At this moment, I was suspended in that anticipatory space between both of them, making a beeline for what will sustain me and fortify my journey back to the people I love. On this summer day, in this tea room, I was not merely satisfied. I was also, for the briefest moment, still.

Chapter 18

The After Season

*I*t's the middle of October and the throngs have gone home. A clear breeze blows through the land, as if the roads themselves can breathe now that they are relieved of the traffic and congestion that gums up the corniches throughout the high season.

The Côte d'Azur is still awash in money. Russian billionaires, software titans, and oil potentates are rebuilding the stone mansions that dot the coast and roost in the hills, turning them into fortresses. It's unlikely that many artists can afford to chill in the sizzling Riviera as many of the greats used to do. Cocteau, Matisse, Picasso—they all made homes here and left their mark in chapels and museums and homes they inhabited (or stayed in indefinitely as guests). I am told there is now a house in Cap Ferrat on the market for 400 million euros. Another person tells me the real price is 500. Whatever the sticker, this place holds among the most expensive real estate in the world.

But this time of year, the glamour is understated, muted like the sun on the beaches there—simmering, not scorching. At the African Queen, which sits on the port at Beaulieu-sur-Mer, I am met with a lunchtime cocktail of Aperol and Champagne. There is no question in these parts of refusing the fizzy, pink concoction. The restaurant is full but the atmosphere is pleasing rather than chaotic. The owner chats as cheerily with the regulars as with one-timers like me, but I am a journalist and so am given the gift of a cookbook. Skimming through the pages, I see a photograph of the gazpacho I am eating now.

Who are the people here? It's a Thursday. Most of the crowd speaks French. Everyone's table is domineered by a bottle of white wine on ice.

Every time I go to France, I'm reminded how, sometimes, I forget to live. When we moved there, my husband and I felt as though we spent too much time eating and not enough time working. But today, I have the sense of letting too many days tick by at home in Connecticut, in the quiet of rural sequestration. It seems a shame not to be sharing this meal with Mark, my kids, a warm cluster of close friends.

At home I'd be eating a tub of yogurt in my kitchen, standing up.

Six courses and a short car ride later, I am hoofing it to my room at La Chèvre d'Or in Èze, which looks clear down to the sea, almost a straight shot down, as if I could leap beyond the rail into the pale Mediterranean. The tourist crowds from summertime are absent in the winding medieval city. I climb up to the botanical gardens full of cacti and succulents and the sun gets hotter on my head. I take a wrong turn but eventually the sign of the Chèvre d'Or swings back into view. Soon, I'll be napping on the terrace of my room, gaining back my strength and appetite for dinner.

Early the next morning, I descend the steep hill down to the sea via the mule path named for Friedrich Nietzsche, the German philosopher who ensconced himself along this coast during the 1880s. At the time, he was enduring the oncoming torments of blindness and madness. "When he had reached the top of the mountain-ridge, behold, there lay the other sea spread out before him: and he stood still and was long silent," he wrote in "The Wanderer," Part III of *Thus Spoke Zarathustra*, which he conceived on the trail that now bears his name.

The following day is devoted to Le Corbusier (his hideaway, Le Cabanon), Coco Chanel (her house, La Pausa) and finally to Jean Cocteau (his den of creativity, Villa Santo Sospir). Every corner of the latter is painted with Cocteau's line drawings of satyrs, sirens and *fougasse*—the soft flatbread of the region. At last, I say goodbye to the sea and drive inland to Mougins, down the olive-tree-lined drive to my hotel. It is a white stone *bastide* (the provençal word for a country house) that has been renovated to a state of entirely appropriate luxury. The grounds are peaceful, and my guess is that, in the busy season, it would feel exactly the same way.

In my room, there is a plate of *gateaux* encrusted with small bits of chocolate. There is a carafe of port. There is a Nespresso maker. There is a terrace that has a view of the neighboring hill town of Grasse. I relish all the scents: of cypress trees, geranium blooms, lemon groves and rosemary shrubs, wafting over from the town made famous for its perfumes. The muscles in my body slacken, as if relinquishing their strength to this array of sensory offerings. I wonder why it is, when I feel most alive, that I need to remind myself to live—*live*—fully and assiduously the rest of the time. I'm still alone but if I weren't, I would stay here forever, if only for that reminder.

Chapter 19

Headlights

ebruary is not the ideal time for a road trip to northern France, but the moodiness of the sea, wind, and sky appeals to a certain breed of loner like me, drawn to the echoing voids of the off-season. Coastal Normandy is famous for its dramatic weather, and in winter, it grows wilder still, with thrashing winds and squalls of frozen sleet that churn up from the English Channel. The region is a sweep of battlegrounds and fortified castles, stone-cold Norman abbeys, and craggy ports that have hosted centuries of departing and returning soldiers. Here, God and war forge their strange alliance, as they often do, and the backdrop of tempests, tides, and occasional shards of sunlight render it fertile ground for ghosts and their keepers.

I had endeavored to Mont St. Michel to seek some perfect solitude. One night was all I could spare for a brief reconciliation between me and my universe, an instant quelling of the racing brain. I had always wanted to spend a night in the small village beneath the monastery, and the dead of winter seemed the ideal time to do it—with the theatrical weather but without other visitors filing into the one narrow street. My hope was to experience, just for a spell, the abbey as the pilgrims had, in this place that brings such wonder to the eye that only heavenly devotion and fear of hell could have conceived it. Over a thousand years ago, men had achieved the near impossible and raised a church atop a 276-foot granite rock in the middle of a bay, slashed by monster tides and some of the fiercest currents on earth. They built it to endure long past their fragile lives, and as an achievement it declares unequivocally: God is powerful and nature unforgiving, but under their sway, it is man that is unyielding.

To get there, let alone ferry construction materials on their backs, meant to brave quicksand, wind, fog, and the bounding sea. Later, pilgrims were obliged to wait for low tide to cross over to Mont St. Michel, but even then, there was risk, one only the faithful were willing to take. By the time they arrived to commune in silence with the resident monks, they had already weeded themselves out and proven their piety along with their mettle.

I suppose I was seeking some clue of the divine here as well. In France, I often venture into the dusky wombs of cathedrals, basilicas, rural parishes. While inside these limestone temples, I look for proof of the almighty (signs anyway) and the wisdom of saints. In Europe, crosses loom over every village, admonishing me with very little subtlety of what I can never really abandon. I'm a committed former Catholic, but the church I was born into and raised in still whispers to me daily. It is a firm, plaintive voice that offers one truth: *This is who you are*.

I'm not brave enough to have renounced my religion outright; I could only chuck it aside. Sunday school did an excellent job of teaching me everything and everyone I was meant to fear. But not long after my confirmation, I began to crave adventure with boys which cast me as an irredeemable sinner. I began to understand that women were outcasts in the church, something the pope was okay with. Eventually, I learned of the criminal priests in my native Boston. I slipped away, stopped going to mass, but all that I absorbed from catechism—guilt, sin, purgatory, mercy, the promise of heaven and intense dread of the alternative—still unwittingly shapes my life.

Most of the time when I enter a church, once I cross myself at the holy water font, the outline of faith emerges, as if this gesture tracing out a crucifix on my head and chest offers entry not just to a place of worship, but also, to comfort and certainty. When I'm in a pew, the sacred space above me intuits my secrets, and forgives them all. For what if not salvation would the ancients construct these elaborate structures, and embellish them with statuary and stories told in colored glass? It is safer to believe, and in church, I do. And then, it dissipates as soon as I exit the sanctuary into the light of day.

These bursts of affinity with something elemental and vast bring not exactly euphoria, but calm. They are reminders that we mortals are not the most important force in the universe, so I can get over myself, already (at least for a spell). Maybe, at Mont St. Michel, with its near miraculous back-story, I'd again find that holy, ephemeral sunbeam I never stop chasing. All I needed was a few minutes inside.

Days earlier, I had passed through the Normandy battlefields under a wintry sky that, one moment, was softly glazed with pink and the next, blackened from a wall of sleet. It's the least I could do: hike through spiky gorse, cross the beach, and imagine the final heartbeats of all the living boys who had died exactly where I stood. I drove to cemeteries and gravesites and to the great Tapestry of Bayeux, the thousand-year-old strip of linen on which unfolds the story of William the Conqueror, the local bastard turned king. In one scene, Harold, the eventual usurper (at least from the point of view of the French) rescues two soldiers from the quicksand of Mont St. Michel. Even then, the perils of this forbidden place were fabled and feared.

I steered my car among the flooded roads and highways, until, at last, I rounded onto the coast and, from a cliff in Champeaux, looked south into the bay. And there it was, rising on the horizon like a volcano in fog. The sight of Mont St. Michel is perhaps most sublime when emerging from night or sinking into twilight—now gold, now white, now black, now white again—but at 2 P.M. on a somber day, it still exerted an astonishing, almost terrifying, grandiosity.

A while later, I parked my car in the lot and waited for the bus.

I was last here one July, two decades ago. Then, I wore a tank top, and a water bottle sloshed around in my purse. The heat had been severe, and I trekked barefoot across the tidal flats, with the sun baking my back, flip-flops in hand. It was suffocatingly, grotesquely crowded with tourists, who gazed up hopefully at the monastery, as if vying for a heavenly sign—or a gulp of oxygen. I recall the grip of wonder and awe when I looked up myself and saw him for the first time: Archangel Michael, the prince of them all, commander of God's army, Catholicism's literal angel of death, who descends in our final hour to escort the faithful to heaven. His gold figure crowns the spire of Mont St. Michel, 511-feet above the sea. It was he, during a visitation in 706, who told the local bishop to "build here and build high." On that sunny day, his raised sword seemed to throw sparks into the sky.

This time, I was on a bus, inching through rain along the causeway. I was surprised when the driver stopped in the middle of a mudflat, and instructed me to hop off, leaving me a fair distance from the bottom of the hill and the village. Buses were supposed to stop right at the foot of town. He advised me to walk the rest of the way, for the approach was a massive construction zone, and the stormy February weather had also made a mess of things. Bulldozers and Bobcats were scattered beside the path, as were orange plastic ribbons that formed makeshift do-not-cross fences. It was, I learned, the home stretch for the colossal reclamation project that would return the sea to the bay of Mont St. Michel, which had been partially silted over by centuries of agricultural development. This silting had inhibited the regular sluicing of water to and from the Couesnon River into the bay, so the Mont was no longer the true island it had been when the monks built the church.

The currents, though, were unchanged: still erratic, still deadly. High tide can rise up to forty-five feet, and water sweeps in at an astonishing 200 feet per minute. Occasionally a video pops up on YouTube of fools who try to beat the sea and, instead, have to get rescued by helicopter. And periodically, some deluded danger junkie wanders into the quicksand on a lark, and must be pulled to safety.

Every bit of me was drenched and spattered as I traipsed toward the village, and when I reached the hotel, the desk attendant dispatched me to my room. Steam erupted off my clothes when I draped them on the drying rack. As I filled the bathtub, the radiator crackled with heat, and the room filled with the musky whiff of wet wool. Rainwater coated the panes of the leaded windows, through which was a view of the bay, now the color of boiling milk. My body nearly ached with comfort in the bath, and I struggled not to doze off.

When I ventured out later that day, the narrow street that strained to accommodate half a million tourists a year was deserted. The biscuit stands were open, though, and the columns of primary-colored tins of *galettes* and *sablés* painted a picture of optimism. I climbed to the abbey and walked around the monastery and the Merveille—the church—stopping at the cloister that was lined with boxwoods and tidy colonnaded *allées*—a green respite on this grim day. Through an opening here, I could see faraway stretches of the Norman and Breton coasts, and against them, the sea—gray and thick as wet cement.

I wandered through the chambers and chapels, the vacant assembly rooms and grand halls that bore no reminders of their bustling pasts. I stood at altars and under crosses, friezes and sea-water-green stained-glass windows. I glanced up at Gothic choirs, vaults, and across to fireplaces, crucifixes, and the gold-cloaked fig-ure of Notre-Dame du Mont-Tombe, the Black Madonna, holding her child, who wore a shiny crown. But I struggled to feel the pres-ence of a deity in these rooms. The best I could do was reflect on the ingenuity of the men who believed so strongly in one, they car-ried boulders across this distant, forbidding terrain, hoisted them up, and erected a masterwork in tribute. I yearned to experience this strength of conviction, this defiance, but all I could do was admire theirs. Here, in the emptiness of a medieval abbey, I felt strangely empty, too. I couldn't even summon a prayer to murmur.

After dinner, darkness crept into the village while the rain dissipated into drizzle, then mist, and at last a cold, clear night. Spotlights replaced daylight and the building was transformed. From a mottled edifice coated with lichen, tarnish, and rain, it turned pale and fortress-like, stained by shadows thrown from sconces affixed to the façade. The turrets, covered in charcoal slate, had receded into blackness. I descended to the bottom of town so I could look up at the structure again.

There, perched on the tip of the great spire, with his gold wings spread and sword drawn against the night sky, was Saint Michael the Archangel, so airborne he seemed to have just touched down. Behind and above him, clouds darted across the disk of what was almost a full moon, which radiated white light onto the figure, making it glow. Warmth seeped honey-like over me. I stared and stared. It—he—was spectacular: so high, so permanent, and some-how so powerful. I only looked away when my neck started to ache.

Here, from below, I understood that on this island, faith was proportional to distance. Its power was in the ever-fluid move-ment of sky over weather over water over stone. The pilgrims must have shared my wonder, exhausted their supply of adjectives and exclamations, even if many met a merciless end on their way.

They arrived at this desolate place with a belief so vast, only isolation could accommodate it. Here, now, was the moment I had come for, the elusive crucible of trust and awe and relief. *This is who you are.* And right then I believed. The simplicity of my certitude caught in my throat.

At 4:00 the next morning, I gathered my clothes from the heating rack and woke the desk clerk to confirm with her the special off-hours bus I'd ordered to take me to the parking lot. I had a meeting in Burgundy at 2 P.M., and it was easily an eight-hour drive. "It is waiting for you," she said.

The rain had returned, hammering, and the structure on the hill that had choked me up hours earlier soon slipped behind the gloom. My epiphany about the divine, too, got stuffed back in my travel bag. There was one lonely sound above the wind: my rubber boots clomping on the path down to the landing area, which was vacant. No bus was waiting for me. But given that the day before I had had to get off and walk a couple hundred yards to the village, I assumed that today I'd have to do the same in reverse. I stepped off the road, switched on my iPhone flashlight, and took what I believed was the walkway I'd come on yesterday.

I walked with speed and purpose, anticipating the relief I would feel when I reached the bus and then, my car. Grit scraped the wheels of my bag, splashing mud on me as I proceeded. All at once, the trek seemed too far and too long. There was no bus, no turnaround, no clearing. There were no Bobcats or bulldozers. Only wind, sleet, and desolation. And suddenly, there was a proliferation of warning signs: "It is **extremely dangerous** to venture *alone into the bay, including immediately close to Mont-Saint-Michel.*" Minute by minute, my optimism left me. My parka had absorbed many times its weight in rain, and it pressed upon my shoulders. The iPhone cast only a wan pool of light before me. I could not discern how close I might be to the water, the tides, blackout. On the plus side, my rubber boots, high and heavy, clutched and warmed everything south of my knees as if they were sentient beings. They seemed to be sacrificing their lives for the integrity of my ankles and feet, and I loved them with all my might.

"Good boots," I cooed as if they might answer back.

But they were leading me nowhere. I stopped and dialed the hotel.

"Where's the bus?" I asked. Panic scraped my windpipe.

"It's right at the bottom," she said.

"But it wasn't there!"

"He probably turned around when he didn't see you."

"I took a wrong turn," I said. The call cut off with an echo of sheer hopelessness.

It seemed absurd to be lost only yards from the third most popular tourist attraction in France. I walked and walked, sloshing through a thin blanket of mud on what seemed like a solid path, disconsolate and captive on the road that had no visible beginning or end, composing my obituary. *Mother of two*, it would read, *vanished in the quicksand of Mont St. Michel.* Not embarrassing, exactly. Like a snakebite or a failed ripcord, it was an adventurer's demise. But I was a traveler, not a daredevil. Exploring is great, but danger is for fools.

Fools like me.

It didn't seem appropriate to appeal to the almighty, whose existence I'd doubted not six hours earlier. I looked for Archangel Michael on the spire, but he was invisible, shrouded under the veil of winter and night. Maybe that was a good thing. God's avenger was also the angel of death.

It was so frighteningly dark. As I set forth again, I heard the lapping of water amongst the drone of rainfall. The wind swept around me, forming icy walls that I walked right through, emerging colder and wetter than before. There was little chance I was near the bay, because the feared high tide was three days away, after the full moon. But the sea was unpredictable, and I also wondered, when I put my foot in a deeper batch of clay, if this could be quicksand. It could be anywhere. Relief when I kept my stride, but for my level of certainty, I may have been walking in circles. I pictured my husband, my children, our universe that was miniscule compared to this pitiless place. I craved the sanity of my morning routine: coffee, toast. Life.

And then, lights. Small, low ones seeping through the pearly curtain of vapor to form an incandescent glow. They approached from straight ahead, and declared to my satisfaction that I was traveling along a real road and not the soggy clay barrens. The car pulled up and someone reached across to open the door.

I never saw him clearly. Blue eyes or brown, pale complexion or ruddy—years later, I still haven't a clue. But I remember the grayish spikes of his hair and the sharp contours of his profile. Both his face and head were outlined in the glare of his car's head-lights, which froze on the wall of rain, and bounced back through the windshield with the potency of a ten-watt bulb. I also recall the flash of relief, an audible release from my lungs, as I accepted the invitation, more like a command, to enter the stranger's car. Swiftly, reassuringly this man would deliver me to the bus, but not without conveying his concern and discontent. His voice was soothing, with a touch of morning scratch, not quite caffeinated, but full of annoyance. It must have been alarming to see my drenched figure shuffling in the inky pre-dawn and then, for this wretched human to take a seat in his car.

"What in God's name are you doing out here?" he said.

"I'm lost…"

"*Au nom de Dieu.*"

"I couldn't find the bus," I sniffed.

"Didn't you see the signs?" he asked. He shook his head again and again.

We crawled along a firm, mud-coated road, probably carved out by landscaping crews to ease the wholesale re-shaping of the tidal flats. I never asked if the danger he kept pointing out referred to my general foolishness—the weather, the hour of day, my exposure, or my solitude. My hunch is that his admonishments alluded to something more ominous. That I had wandered into a truly perilous place where I risked misfortune from construction debris, or more likely, from nature's force, against which we all—saint, sinner, reverent, skeptic—are powerless. Mont St. Michel was never a place for the weak.

"You are very lucky, Madame," he said, and as he spoke his voice shifted from reproachful to kind.

He drove to a well-lit turnaround and stopped the car. I should have passed directly through this clearing an hour earlier, but somehow, inexplicably, I had diverged. The bus was there, idling.

"Be careful," he said. "*Soyez sage.*"

"Thank you," I said to his nodding profile. "Thank you." He brightened with a fraction of a smile, which caused his cheeks to shift upward. The dark swallowed his car instantaneously, as if it had never existed.

I have no idea who he was. I was too cold, distraught, and embarrassed to ask. Maybe he was a worker finishing up the night shift. Perhaps he was a cop on security detail. The site foreman surveying the periphery. I will never know how he found me roaming around this treacherous place in the middle of an ice storm, just when I was ready to call it quits and give myself over to quicksand or dawn, whichever came first.

What is certain is that ten minutes later, I warmed up my car just as daylight glided into place to reveal another soaked winter day in Normandy. As I rounded the highway, I gasped at the distant sight of Mont St. Michel, its jagged black form stark against the soft gray of the sky. How elegant the spire seemed that morning as Archangel Michael emerged, gleaming, from behind the clouds. How worthy of a prayer.

Chapter 20

Connie Britton's Hair

"How much longer?" I asked Eugene.

"A very long way," he said. "Also, it gets much steeper."

In our short acquaintance, I already knew our guide wasn't one for sweetening the news. In fact, he seemed to relish his role as grim realist, the battlefield reporter with the cold hard facts. It's difficult to say which half of his response filled me with greater dread.

"Like another hour?" I asked, alarm leaking into my voice. "Steeper than this?"

With an upraised palm like a hostess at a car show, I indicated the vertical swath of mud looming above me.

It was not yet 9:00 A.M., but an hour since we started up Mount Bisoke, a dormant volcano in the Virunga range, which straddles northwest Rwanda, southern Uganda, and the eastern reaches of the Democratic Republic of the Congo. I had no idea for whom or what I was traipsing upstream of a landslide. My legs were trembling, periodically forcing me to lurch off the wet, shiny stones into clusters of stinging nettles and pools of black magmic sludge.

There were seven other climbers, and the Greek one wouldn't shut up. Between his white noise and the realization that my body was already failing me, I knew I needed to make quick work of this mountain. The woman who booked my excursion assured me I'd be back at the hotel in time for lunch. The idea that I'd be alive by then was implicit. I already felt the heat of a fresh bruise spreading across the upper quadrant of my right thigh after one humiliating tumble. And I kind of wanted to get back to *Nashville* and Connie Britton's hair.

When I arrived at the park earlier that morning, I registered and filled a mug with coffee. Pierre, my driver and companion for the week, directed me to our guide, Eugene, who was all business, laconic and unsmiling. From the outset, I tried to charm my way through his bluntness—a cry for reassurance, the obvious ploy of the terminally insecure.

"I hear this is a snap," I said, my voice larded with cheer. "Couple hours up and back?"

"Oh no," he said, "not during the rainy season"—which we were smack in the middle of. "It is a strenuous climb. You must be very fit."

I scoped out the other climbers. Demetrius the Greek, already chattering pointlessly, was no David Beckham, nor were the Russians exactly Olympic decathletes. The rest I surmised were roughly on par with me. Only Monica from Holland looked to be in fighting shape, but she was about twenty and, well, Dutch.

I took a spin class once in a while. I'd manage.

The air was laced with the smell of eucalyptus at the clearing beyond the entrance of Volcanoes National Park, the staging area for the day's excursions. The other tourists, most of whom were preparing (or at least hoping) to see gorillas, milled around under a large gazebo, sipping coffee and tea to ward off the chilly morning.

I rolled my eyes at the safari folk tricked out in gadgetry and pricey adventure wear—gaiters, air-permeable layers, and high-performance hiking boots. I was awfully confident in my trail-running shoes and my teenage daughter's surf hoodie.

Sunlight shot across the mountains and fields, rapidly erasing the shadows from the landscape. It was a gorgeous morning for a trek, much like the one I'd enjoyed a year before when I set off with seven other people and two guides in search of gorillas. We'd been unusually lucky that morning; our group had just broken a sweat when we got word that "our" family of primates, which included a set of newborn twins, was about to swing into view. On that trip—my first to Rwanda—I'd been captivated by the sight of the gorillas, but also by the vision of five volcanoes that formed a sensuous but formidable ridge cradling the forest. It didn't occur to me that I'd be back a year later to climb one.

I'm not much of a nature girl. But because I come from hardy immigrant stock—ship captains and quarrymen on one side, farmers and campesinos on the other—I'm a bit ashamed of my predilection for pure cotton sheets and finely-tooled Italian pumps. It's always struck me as a weakness, a trait I should at least resist, if not someday overcome. When I was young, although I'd have preferred to spend summers perfecting my country club backhand, I nevertheless marched off to Girl Scout camp in Vermont every year with my three older sisters to sleep in a tent for four weeks, outfitted in flame-retardant shorts and rubber boots that even then offended my fashion standards. I was certain (as was my mother, probably) that if I could rough it, even briefly, I would be a better and more selfless person. There were no bubble baths or downy pillows on the Flume Slide Trail of Mount Washington, but the stew we slung up in our mess kits was tasty and the hardship negligible (and temporary). I didn't exactly love the cold nights I spent shivering in my sleeping bag on a floor covered with grit and spiders and eleven other girls, but I did appreciate the camaraderie and esprit de corps—at least in retrospect.

Many years later, when I could make the choice, I almost settled down with an Argentinian clotheshorse, but instead married the reincarnation of Ernest Shackleton—an outdoorsman who has bestowed his love of adventure and fresh air upon our children. And I appreciate this, because it takes the heat off me.

While my family sets out on summer mornings before dawn on twenty-mile hikes through the Adirondacks, I sleep in. Long after the sun comes up, I enjoy the view of the mountains from my perch across the lake over slices of buttered toast. I have taken on the role of princess in our family narrative, and my children and husband play along, coddling me, but also needling me about my preference for the languorous lie-in over physical exertion of any kind. They fall short of calling me "lazy" but their knowing euphemisms—"Just hang out and relax," they say—speak their own truth.

After a hip replacement at forty-five (it was trashed by high school sports and faulty anatomy), I finally had the excuse I needed to basically never go outside again. But now, a few years later and a few years older, I was beginning to feel a creeping regret over my adventure phobia. When my family pushes off with their water bottles and trail mix, I still wave goodbye cheerfully, but with the nagging sense that I'm missing yet another seminal moment, the gorgeously-lit future memories that would, if I could only bring myself to participate, flood my mind toward my life's end. My son running up ahead on antelope legs, or extending a hand to my daughter over a steep patch of trail as determination floods her being.

And there's something else. Not since my summers trudging up the White Mountains had I experienced the singular do-or-die obstinacy it takes to make it up and down a tricky slope, heart and legs begging for mercy. Lately I've begun to envy the accomplishment my family feels after a day's climb and how rightfully they earned their fatigue. Several months ago, with a reporting trip to Rwanda on the calendar, I decided it sounded like the perfect opportunity to tackle a mountain. And after some online research, I determined that Bisoke—"the easy one"—was the one for me.

Which is how, with the clock running out on opportunities to conquer things, I found myself inching up the side of this particular volcano.

I live for these respites: eating meals alone, keeping my own counsel. It's only after hours, in the extreme quiet of my room, while the single glass of wine I drank with dinner delivers a drop of sleepiness, that I get twinges of loneliness. I wonder where my kids are and begin to question what issue can be so bewildering, that I need to escape to solve it.

I've found that the best distraction from the torture of my misgivings and the attendant insomnia is entertainment. Nights on international assignments, therefore, have turned into an excuse to watch whatever TV series I've missed that everyone insists I should see. And this time, here in Rwanda, it's *Nashville*—not the film, but the more modern nighttime drama which also happens to be about generational rivalry in country music, this one with gorgeous tunes sung by Connie Britton.

She plays Rayna James, a woman roughly my age, give or take a couple years (okay, ten), a beloved country singer facing challenges from an ambitious up-and-comer. I'm hooked after three episodes, and all because of her. It isn't just the pitch the actress strikes perfectly, portraying both celebrity and suburban hausfrau—it's her character's take on middle age. She never lapses into self-pity—there's too much going on to dwell on the inevitable downsides of aging. Instead, she keeps evolving by working harder than anyone else. And in so doing, she spares us the usual

"Forty and Fabulous" bromides and cougar manifestos endemic in pop culture.

It helps that—with wavy strawberry-blond hair coiffed with curling irons and volumizer, and a wardrobe that changes in the course of fifty minutes from jeans to a sheath dress to spangles and back again (along with her nail polish: navy blue, then aubergine, ending with flannel gray)—she is endlessly fascinating to watch. She is groomed and rich and desired by men of every age, and never wears the same pair of Louboutins twice.

And I confess, as I look down at my legs trudging up Mount Bisoke in these god-awful hiking pants, I hate her for all of it. I also admire—and even envy—her. "Time is precious," her actions insist, as she braves one creative leap after another. Unlike me, the woman is afraid of nothing.

What I have never told my family, what they don't know, is that I am averse to nature because, in fact, it terrifies me. I fear insects and unseen branches that could draw blood from my neck. As for mountains, I fear I won't make it up them, and even more that I won't make it back down. What didn't scare me were the four soldiers from the Rwandan Armed Forces with AK-47s strapped to their torsos who accompanied us on our climb. As far as I was concerned, that was security. We were spitting distance from the DRC, where a brutal war was in full swing and refugees and soldiers were rumored to be seeking cover in the dense forest. I didn't care if some hopped-up Congolese rebel interrupted our peace; I was not even afraid of the wild buffalo known to pose an even greater threat to tourists. I was only afraid of confronting my own helplessness.

But at least I had the good sense this morning to hire Foster. Since I'd convinced myself the hike would be a snap, at first I balked at the idea of someone helping me with my cargo.

"Do I look like I need a porter?" I asked Eugene after the orientation.

He didn't laugh. As they had done on the gorilla trek, young men in green uniforms lined up at the trailhead to be enlisted for the day. I caught Foster's eye and handed over my backpack filled with three bottles of water, some cashews, a Milka bar, and a raincoat. He smiled broadly, and later I wondered whether he was just happy to be hired or if he knew he'd be saving my life that day.

There was little to see on the way up, and after two hours I stopped looking. Eugene, Dr. Doom, kept bearing bad news, but I asked for it, appealing desperately for a heartening update, one that would tell me we were almost there. We weren't. We didn't even bother to veer off for the mile-long walk to Dian Fossey's grave. We still had, by my calculations, two miles until the crater lake at the top. It was treacherous going, and the temperature was dropping.

"If it rains," he said, "we will have a problem."

The sun toasted my bare shoulders. I was drenched with sweat. There did not appear to be a cloud anywhere on the African continent or within a thousand miles.

"It's not going to rain," I said.

"It will," Eugene said.

"You need to work on your delivery," I told him.

There were three things on this hike. There was the ground in all its viney chaos, studded by rocks glazed with mud. There were the Greek guy's dire prognostications, delivered on a continuous loop but somewhat mirthfully. ("One of us is going to slide off this mountain!" Demetrios offered. "And our friends with the Kalashnikovs are not here to scare buffalo.") And lastly, there was Foster's hand. I have friends who, when I am in a crisis, know what I need better than I do. This was Foster: pure instinct, pure empathy. Sometimes when Foster reached for me, I waved him off. "It's okay, Fos, I'm fine," I said, and lost my footing anyway—it was a game of millimeters—while his hand appeared from the ether to lock into mine and right me standing.

He read my body, pointing to a spot in the mud where he pre-dicted I could safely place my shoe so it would not veer sideways in the other direction of the rest of me. If he thought I was com-pletely idiotic to be on this march, he never let on.

"Very good, very good," he said after sparing me from spinning off a boulder, or untangling me from the brush with one deft tug. Other than "thank you," they were the only words he knew in English. If Foster were to ask me to help him hold up the Bank of England today, in any language, I would dutifully follow.

As I climbed, I prayed not to God but to Dr. Schutzer, the surgeon who installed a titanium rod where my hip bone had been. Even my good joints were giving out, my legs quaked from exertion, and my lungs were tight and breath halting from the elevation: the climb began at 8,200-feet, but were ascending to over 12,000 feet.

I was appalled that as I bushwhacked, vertically, through this supposed war zone, I was not contemplating lofty geopoliti-cal concerns, the kind I went to graduate school in international relations to ponder. No, as I slogged ahead, I was thinking about Connie Britton, and extrapolating life lessons from ABC prime-time entertainment. Take risks, her character told me—but be true to yourself. It was all kind of boilerplate self-help stuff. But maybe boilerplate is what one needs when one has no business trying to summit a Rwandan volcano in tennis shoes during the rainy season.

Just above the treeline, I heard a text message jingle inside my bag. I knew the man who drove me here, Pierre, was likely wor-ried about me, his charge. I had already been climbing for hours and was meant to be back by now. Foster turned to let me fish the phone from my backpack, and as my hand clutched it, I fell backwards into the basin of mud and roots that we'd just labored across. My skull grazed a stone that jutted from the swamp like the head of a shark, and my knee smashed against another rock. Nausea pooled in my stomach. Foster grabbed my other hand and as he pulled me up, I fell against him and wept.

"Very good," he said.

I pushed the button with a mud-soaked finger. "Vodafone welcomes you to the DRC!" it said.

"I will not make it down," I sniffled. "There is no way I will make it down." As I uttered the words, a horizontal wind slashed my face, ushering an onslaught of sleet that painted the sky dark gray.

"We are really fucked now," said the Greek guy.

"Could you lighten up?"

"Do you think they could send a helicopter?" he said in response, turning and laughing. Maybe he wasn't so bad.

An hour later, we summitted. The crater lake sat under the weight of heavy clouds, with only narrow slivers of anthracite gray water visible below the mist. As we stood together looking at absolutely nothing, hailstones the size of gumballs started pelting us, making hollow conking noises as they bounced off our heads and shoulders. Demetrios had no raincoat and I worried for him. With a flourish, he yanked an umbrella out of his pack.

"Come seek refuge from the elements," he said.

I crouched with some of the others in a huddle. Even Monica, the strapping Dutchwoman, looked wretched. Demetrios' extremities were still bare, now pink from the wind and chill. I reached for his free arm and tried fruitlessly to warm it between my two ice-cold hands.

"Are you okay?" I asked.

"Of course," he said. "Never better." Somehow, I believe him.

The hail continued to pound us. Eugene sheltered under a ficus tree with Foster, the soldiers, and the other porters. After a while he approached our group.

"We'd better head down." He looked miserable too—or maybe just grave.

"How long have you been climbing this mountain?"

"Thirteen years."

"Will we make it down?"

"Of course," he said.

My fingers were frozen into claws. I thought of the cocktail ring Connie Britton twirled on her index finger in the episode last night. I thought of her manicured nails and smooth hair, no doubt scented with Parisian styling crème, the kind I might have been massaging into my own waves if I weren't on this damned mountain. I thought of my children, this insane endeavor, and my self-inflicted misery. When I recount the details to them, they will surely assume I am exaggerating. I contemplated my need to triumph over something, anything, if only because I was afraid that time was running out and if not now, when. And I thought about how exhausting it was to do battle with your own character and how trivial it can feel when you try too hard to be someone you are not.

As sleet slipped behind my neck, drawing rivers of ice down my back, I considered an entirely new option: maybe I didn't need to be ashamed of wanting to be safe and warm and out of harm's way. What if I was not fearful and lazy, but rather cautious and observant? What if I just had a preference to stand apart from adventure and observe it from a distance, rather than be in the thick of it? My kids weren't keen on changing me, so why should I be?

It took three hours to get back down the mountain. Demetrios kept me company on the descent, and I appreciated his optimism. Whenever he fell silent, I worried that he was as frightened as I was.

"Hey Dima," I yelled, "how ya doing?"

"Good thing I know how to snowboard!" I watched him skid down the mud, now a foot deep.

The storm sluiced cascades where the path used to be, and the trail was now a waterfall flowing with icy sludge. Foster kept a permanent grip on my hand; if I asked to be carried, he would surely toss me over his back like a sack of potatoes. For a moment I considered this option. I was helpless—we all were—in the downpour. I fell hard and often, sometimes bringing Foster down on top of me, and I laughed to show I was still conscious and to prove that there was something comical in almost-tragedy. By the very end, I'd begun to enjoy myself a little. But only—maybe—because I was still alive and almost off this mountain.

When we said goodbye, Demetrios and I exchanged kisses but not email addresses. I knew he would remember me with a certain tenderness, as I would him.

"Murakoze," I said to Foster, hoping the Kinyarwanda word for "thank you" might also mean "I love you." I gave him and Eugene all the money I had, and it was not nearly enough.

I spotted Pierre in the parking lot, and he did not recognize me as I approached. My hair, shoes, arms, raincoat, body were laminated with a thickening crust of mud. My pants were torn and bloody at the knee. I collapsed in his arms. "It was scary," I said. "There was hail."

Eugene caught a ride with us back to the staging area.

"You did it," he said to me, grinning for the first time all day.

"I felt very safe with you," I admitted. "Was today an unusually tough climb?"

"It was normal," he said. I gave him a look. "A little tougher."

"Were you scared?" I asked.

"It's a mountain," he said. "It makes its own rules. It's nice to climb them, but maybe sometimes we shouldn't."

We headed back to the hotel, where the staff scraped Rwandan dirt off my walking shoes and washed them clean. I un-caked the mud from my body in a warm bath, and my fingers defrosted with the help of South African brandy. I dug out a few Advil, which I hoped would prevent me from crouching in pain in the morning. Later, an attendant appeared out of the darkness to light a fire inside my bungalow.

"How was your climb?" he asked, rearranging the pile of logs. I handed him some kindling. I caught my reflection in the window, and saw dirt still smeared on my face.

"It was hard." I was sore and bruised and a tiny bit lonely.

"It's a big mountain," he laughed. "You must be very strong."

The flames grew in the fireplace and the room filled with the smell of burning eucalyptus wood. Was it strength that brought me up that mountain? Or weakness? If I'd remained true to myself, I would have stayed on terra firma.

I considered what the always-candid and ever-direct Eugene had said in the car. He was right. Maybe, I thought, *maybe* not every mountain needs to be climbed.

After the man left, I inched into the big bed and felt my body unclench from the day's strain. From my jaw muscles to the pads at the bottom of my feet, each part of me flared one by one, as if momentarily shined-on by a small heat lamp. The strain in my thighs still scalded but less so, and I rubbed the tops of my legs vigorously.

I felt alright. Actually, better than alright. In the bath, I had cleaned up the gash on my knee, and it was safe under a bandage. Other small cuts—on my hands, wrists, and cheek—now just looked like scratches. Most of all, my central nervous system had checked out of stress mode into a state of physical quiet.

I relieved my loneliness by watching a nighttime soap opera from Nashville, from Hollywood via iTunes. Naturally, Connie Britton had a glorious head of hair throughout the episode, and in one scene she sported killer chocolate brown eyeshadow with an intriguing dash of shimmer.

I didn't envy her tonight, though. I finally understood for myself what her character already seemed to know. Time might be unstoppable, but so am I. And the message was clear, or so I thought. I don't have to summit a volcano or battle my own self to prove anything—not to anyone else, and especially not to myself.

But as I plunged into a deepening exhaustion that grew sweeter and more euphoric, I wondered whether Rayna James might be suggesting the exact opposite.

Chapter 21

The Offer that Refused Me

nce, a man I will call Sam wanted to buy me. Actually, he wanted to purchase my occasional services, on retainer. He proposed securing an apartment for our assignations, which would take place whenever he desired, however rarely or frequently he came to Paris, where I was living at the time. In French, they referred to such a place by the word *garconnière*, which in English meant, roughly, *"fuck pad."* I imagined myself enlisting the talents of some Parisian decorator, with whom I could wade through oceans of fabric swatches.

I tried to envision a parallel existence that would be invisible to the one I was leading. In that life, my artist boyfriend and I lived in a dank apartment which was rendered more so by dog-brown wallpaper which the landlord, Monsieur Cadiou, had finally allowed me to scrape off. I combed the weekend flea markets for bargains, gathering—candlestick by candlestick, mirror by mirror—the narrative for my future with the man I was soon to marry.

A week earlier, on my flight to the Persian Gulf, the pilot pointed out the oil fields that burned black, thick, and everywhere as our plane flew high over Kuwait, a few months after President George

H.W. Bush had declared victory over Saddam Hussein. I was on my way to the same hotel in the same country where I had been stationed since before the war, only this time I was not going with a broadcast television network, but as a freelance producer researching a news documentary.

I had about a week in which to secure the right person who would agree to participate in a story about business in the Gulf states. Within a day, the one who had been on board had dropped out, and shortly after that, a second one bailed. I met another candidate and made my pitch over tea in his office, but he politely declined.

All of my journalist friends and colleagues had long since gone home or headed for new adventures in Riyadh or Baghdad or Johannesburg. I only had a handful of local contacts, one of whom suggested Sam for our segment. So I began to pursue him. It became the focus of the next days: get Sam to meet me so I could bring my request to him personally, to get him to appear on camera.

I waited by the phone in my room. Order after order of hummus came to my door—laced with cumin, a stream of dark green olive oil running over the top. I had grown addicted to it when I had been there during the war. I missed my friends, how we woke up and hopped an airplane to Qatar or Dhahran and came home at the end of the day, swapped stories, and got hammered by the rooftop pool. This time, I smoked and watched CNN. And sat.

At last, the call came in. Sam's assistant had arranged a meeting. Within an hour, the driver I hired for $25 a day delivered me to a glass tower that sprang from the desert. I could see it from a distance, a megalith surrounded by miles of brown dust. The region would soon develop into billionaires' playpen, but the boom was a couple of years away yet, and the few Jetson-inspired skyscrapers that erupted from the landscape looked freakish and random. Inside, the air conditioning was so cold the skin beneath my fingernails turned violet.

Sam was in his late fifties, good looking and elegant. He wore darkly-tinted professorial glasses and a *dishdasha*, the long white robe that is the traditional male dress in the region. I fell all over myself thanking him for the meeting, and he responded with a brisk up-down twitch of the head. His office was empty except for a waiter who padded in and out silently, due to his cloth slippers. Ringing phones tinkled somewhere in the background, so I assumed there was employee life elsewhere on the floor.

We sat in a cavernous space strewn with carpets, and faced each other on leather couches, a table between us. Outside, beyond the glass panes, there was only sky and heat—120 degrees worth. The visit was cordial enough, but he barely acknowledged my interview request. I talked, flattered and flattered him some more while the waiter brought more tea and switched up the delectables tray, from which I sampled cakes and dried fruit.

"We would be remiss if you were not included in our piece," I said as I reached for a dried date, and held it between my thumb and forefinger, an inch from my lips. "You are too important for us to do the story without you." I popped the dried fruit into my mouth.

Sam alternated a nibble of his sugar cube with a sip of tea, and repeated this gesture throughout. At last he thanked me, declared the meeting over, and invited me the following day to his beach club for lunch. "You have a bikini?" he asked. He sensed my desperation and lack of negotiating power, and had already begun to lay out the terms of his deal.

"I do hope you will seriously consider my request," I said.

"I will see you at the beach," he repeated.

The next day I suited up in my hotel room, deliberately flouting the country's strict laws, which I presumed were neutralized at resorts filled with expats. I had packed an old blue bikini, faded from the neighborhood pool in Paris, where I regularly swam laps. My sandals had higher heels than were necessary, and I looked in the mirror and saw the unmistakable contrivance, the beauty contest sleaziness of pairing dressy sandals with a bathing suit. I felt like I was in an old episode of *Charlie's Angels*.

Hastily, I fastened my linen cover-up, and as I did, felt the discomfort of crossing a line, the twin surge of panic and unease one feels when venturing on purpose into a risky neighborhood after dark.

I wore it all to meet Sam. A careful stain of crimson mouth, a dress unbuttoned just enough, and underneath, the abdomen-baring attire he requested. I hoped that he would be pleased enough to agree to an interview. As a freelancer, I could not bear the thought of calling my boss to tell him I'd failed to find anyone to go on camera for this story. I needed the seven hundred bucks a week and I needed not to tank my career as a journalist. So if a little degradation could get me hired on another project, I could live with it, as well as the accompanying nausea that was bubbling up inside of me.

Sam did not invite me to join him at lunch, so I sat distract-edly on the beach and tried to read, getting more ticked off and disgusted with myself each minute at the progress of this twisted pursuit. The heat was thick, so I dipped into the waveless Persian Gulf waters, and strolled along the white sand. At last, he sum-moned me to his table and as I approached the patio, I fastened a wrap around my hips.

"We need to fatten you up," Sam said and guffawed at his joke.

"Then I need to eat," I said firmly. Time was running out. "Are you considering the interview? Because if not, I need to find someone else, quickly."

"Of course," he said.

"Of course, what?" I asked.

"Of course I am considering it."

He shrugged.

With his right hand, he scraped the corner of a sugar cube on his lower teeth. His left hand held the tea glass.

"Meet me for dinner tonight," he said.

"I have a fiancé," I said.

"Don't worry," he said. "You are not my type. I will pick you up at seven."

At dinner, Sam got very revved up about lobster. The menu arrived and, without opening it, he ordered for me.

"I'm from Boston," I protested. "I only like Maine lobster."

(In fact, I did not like lobster then or now.)

He held forth grandly. "The best in the world is from Oman. Caught off the island of Masirah. In the South Arabian Sea."

I dutifully ate his Omani offerings, ripping off the claws the same way I would at a summer clambake in Gloucester, Massachusetts. The flesh was not white, but deep orange, almost red.

That night he dropped me off at the hotel and as he did, he said, "You are very sweet. I like you."

"I like you too," I said, hating myself.

"I will do your interview. But you must have another lobster with me tomorrow night."

I pecked him on the cheek. "Thank you," I said. "But I really don't like it."

Sam busted up again at that one. "You will find in life that you end up liking some things that you think you don't like."

Back in my room, I ran a bath, and as I began to undress, I heard a knock. I opened the door to see the concierge, who handed me a bag. Inside was a square blue jewelry box. Though I was alone, I instinctively looked around before I opened it. It wasn't exactly a watch; it was more like a cathedral in a box— diamonds, gold, a choir of angels.

I stared at it, no longer hearing the rush of the bathwater or the chattering anchormen on CNN. And then, with no idea of what else to do, I put it in the safe with my passport and cash, watching the red lights blink as I shut the door.

The next night, over dinner, Sam was unusually forthcoming. We discussed his adopted country, whose hotels crawled with mercenaries and U.S. government contractors since the war had ended. If there was a wife, she never came up. I told him about my artist fiancé, and my hopes for my career.

"I don't know what to say about your gift," I finally said.

"I am very insulted," he said, grinning broadly. "Why didn't you wear it?"

Before I could stumble through an answer, he'd begun his proposal. I would like to make an arrangement, he said, in so many words. You will be available to me, although I am rarely in Paris. It will be mutually beneficial. He knew how to hook me: between the lines, the promise blinked in neon: *Think of your artist.* I lived in Paris, so the concept of "mistress" was hardly taboo; I just never thought it would be me. Moreover, it was a subject that seemed to invite little debate, suggesting that he had done this before. For him this was just a simple transaction, a contract that required my signature. Money never came up, but the generosity was implicit.

He seemed genuinely confused when I balked, mostly because I could neither speak nor quite comprehend. "Why ever not?" he asked.

Indeed, why ever not? I wasn't prudish, but I was traditional. Sex usually came with love, or else with an unbearably close friendship for one secret night. I had been in love several times, but it was only with my fiancé that the constant need to find the next one seemed to end for good. I was done with dabbling and discovery. I knew I wanted to marry him. And now I was entertaining a massive betrayal so I could comfortably afford our road ahead? I felt despicable, and yet, strangely intrigued. The temptation was in the freedom the offer paradoxically represented—an antidote to the difficult path I was already, willingly, on.

My destiny was choosing me, and it was not shaping up to be too cushy. Life as a journalist would never be secure and would probably not make me rich. I suspected I lacked both the political acumen and the steel spine that might be required to soldier up through the ranks to television moguldom. My dream job offer at the London bureau of a news network had fallen through at the last minute, and in Paris, I was too far from the mother ship to matter. So I took freelance jobs around Europe, and had a few loyal friends in New York who hired me regularly. But I wanted to stay in Paris and I was in love with an artist, the best and bravest man I had ever known, who might never be secure or rich either.

I was not sure how I would stomach the vicissitudes of the art market, or tolerate fickle dealers, or the desperate feeling when wealthy collectors cancelled commissions with no explanation, or struck bargain-basement deals with the artists they claimed to support. I had already seen frequent and undeserved humiliations at his expense. But giving him up was unthinkable, even though we already seemed perched on a precipice of financial uncertainty. And then there was our apartment, dank and boggy, filled with greasy cooking fumes from the neighbor who skinned her own rabbits for dinner, then breaded and fried them. Monsieur Cadiou stopped by whenever he pleased, to remind us of the incredibly low rent he charged which for us, nevertheless, was no bargain.

Sam did not seem pressed for an answer when he dropped me off after dinner. Because I was slightly flattered, and too surprised to be properly humiliated, I thanked him for his kind offer. After saying, "Good night" at the hotel entrance, I went upstairs to stare at my watch. I slipped it on my wrist and studied the ungroomed nails on my same old hands, one of whose fingers held my engagement ring that I had worn for all of three months.

The next morning, I ordered a giant breakfast as if I was already on somebody's expense account. Cappuccino, eggs, sliced mango, waffles—sixty dollars' worth of food arrived on a tray, complete with a vase of yellow roses. Then, I called the concierge and rented one of the hotel cars. The highway was almost devoid of traffic. With no speed limit, I barely noticed when my black Toyota approached the border of Oman. The frontier guard was perplexed by my almost entering his country without reason, so with a menacing wave of his American-made weapon, he sent me back in the same direction I'd come from. I drove aimlessly, accompanied by pirated cassettes I had bought at the souk, the familiar music—Tom Petty, Bonnie Raitt, George Benson, Womack & Womack—that usually filled up my Paris apartment. I stopped to swim at a wadi I knew from the year before, and sunned myself on a bed of smooth stone.

I had debated it with, upon retrospect, remarkably little disgust. The "timepiece" incentive Sam had sent to my hotel room was not a factor, though its wattage crushed the somber watch I wore, a gift from a prior, more subtle suitor. My boyfriend, soon to be my husband, would never need to know if I let Sam buy a tiny share of me. And I trusted Sam to keep his side of the bargain: not to interfere, ever, in my life. I tried to imagine myself on a mattress lying beneath him, wondered what fantasy I would need to conjure to sidestep my shame and disgust. I wondered whether I would even be able to weigh this plot against my Catholic-girl nature. I was no virgin, of course, but so far, I never had been much of a cheater, either.

After dinner that last night, I braved a kiss with him. We were in the parking lot of the hotel. I'd drunk too much wine but felt none of the stirrings shellfish were supposed to induce. I accepted his lips, felt the strange nearness of an unknown mouth and his rough moustache. I closed my eyes and attempted to push my brain out of the way. I was aghast from my hope that I might feel something from this dry, perfunctory kiss, and even more ashamed at my disappointment that I did not. Poor guy. Poor *me*.

I was resolved to end the game right then. For a nice girl from suburban Boston, these waters were too deep. Relationships should have secrets. They are soulless without them. But I would have broken under the weight of such a permanent transgression. It would not, could not work.

I would be boarding a plane home in the morning.

"I'm still considering," I lied, and continued. "I'm pretty sure I can't," I said.

"I am an optimistic man," he said brightly. He stroked my hair, pushed it behind my ears. "But not a very patient one."

Nor—given his excellent mood—did he seem like a heart-broken one.

"I'm sorry," I stammered, "I'm flattered…" I inexplicably grabbed his hands.

"My dear," he said. "Business is business."

I felt no relief, but I did feel stung. I had mistaken his attention for attraction, and been timid to reject him, concerned for his feelings as if he cared at all. I drew a breath and leaned in to kiss him, flat and square, on his mouth—a consolation prize, a no-hard-feelings clincher. But Sam didn't want me anymore. The deal was off. With unabated cheer, he had already moved on. He would not let someone he might sleep with once in a while get the best of him. He was a busy man.

We said goodbye and we teased each other, probably about crustaceans, Maine vs. Oman, a truly exhausted joke. Inside the hotel, I saw Corey, a friend from the war, and we drank Stoli and tonic at the bar, one after the other, squeezing hunks of lime. He was a photographer and old Gulf hand who landed in his baili-wick to sniff out the next big story. Mercenaries. Terrorists. The construction boom. He would be there when it all began to blow. We talked about mutual friends, and the fun we had craning our necks out of airplanes, getting shots of aircraft carriers that cruised the Gulf waters. He had lost his purpose, and was desperate for another conflict. After more vodka than I needed, he offered to take me to the airport the next day.

Upstairs, I climbed onto bed, and lay still with the lights out, sniffling away the mildew smell from the overactive air conditioning I had encountered too frequently the year before. Under the blankets, I swished my feet to generate some heat. The room was chilly, an enclosed chamber never penetrated by the soft desert air outside. Beyond my window, there were a few twinkles in the distance—cars, planes, random lights of an adolescent city. Voices passed my room in the corridor, followed by a trace of cigarette smoke that drifted through the crack below the door. Then I picked up the phone to tell my boss I had struck out, but that I had a few leads and I would follow them up from Paris. Lame, cowardly, pathetic, ineffective—whatever I was besides a bad journalist, I did not get the story done.

After checking out in the morning, I met Corey for coffee and could tell that he had stayed too long at the cocktail lounge.

"I almost fucked a guy for a story," I said.

"Please," he said. "Happens every day."

"Could you do me a huge favor?" I held forth the bag with the watch inside, along with a sheet of paper with the address of Sam's office tower. I had also enclosed a letter. I asked my friend to drop it off when he could.

A week later back in Paris, Sam called.

"Is your artist selling any sculptures?" he asked.

"He is," I replied. "Why don't you buy some?"

"Your friend came by today," he said.

"I'm glad I could trust him with such a treasure," I said.

"It was yours, dear."

"It was very generous of you," I said.

"But you are very sweet. And hard working. I will be happy to do your interview, any time. I do mean that. I always keep my word."

"I believe you," I said. "Thank you, though. We've sorted it out."

We had, in fact, found a great character for our story, with no conditions, and my boss was returning shortly to film the segment.

"Why did you include your phone number in your little note?" he asked.

"You tell me," I answered.

It got to me, I suppose, that what he desired was not me. He wanted guaranteed sex with a nice, practical New England girl. That's easy to explain, the part of the story I laughed about for a while with my fiancé, now my husband of twenty years. As if I never debated it on the highway to Oman, land of the lobster. As if I didn't feel that, in this warped scenario, I had somehow failed. I'm thankful that the combination of chemistry and morality swooped in to save me from a certain, regrettable prison. But I wish I'd kept the watch. Right about now, I would sell it.

Chapter 22

The Stories They Tell

*I*t started with the gold. A cluster of unremarkable rings from a guy who could never get it right. A cheap Hand of Fatima from the souk in Istanbul. A smashed bangle I'd bought with babysitting money forty years earlier. Tangled chains and a charm bracelet bearing a chalice from my First Communion, and a Sweet Sixteen disc, complete with a white rose. I hauled the icons and amulets from my childhood, travels, milestones and romances to the "We Buy Gold" on a busy three-lane highway in Oakville, Connecticut.

Not long ago, my possessions—stashed in satin-lined boxes inside cabinets, or tucked into felt pouches—began to overwhelm me. For the most part, they sat idle, representing the tactile promise of a life I was once poised to live. Accumulation had at one time been thrilling and even obligatory, before a lifetime of bills—of health insurance and copays, roof repairs and orthodontists—would render the concept of sentimental value almost meaningless, and before dust or oxidation or time would obscure the usefulness of an object.

It seemed logical, even urgent, to pare down. Classic middle-aged move, perhaps. There was no noble purpose behind my big sell-off, no implied or declared goal of living a less materialistic life. Nor was this a trendy makeover, at least a deliberate one, to declutter my space and by extension, my spirit. No, I just wanted some money, something to burn a hole in the shabby wallet I needed to replace. A too-expensive dinner, an extra pair of jeans. With a burgeoning career as a travel writer, I had accumulated the first significant credit card debt of my adulthood. As I filled out my kids' school financial aid forms and put off car payments, I determined that some of the better stuff on the shelves could be excellent wolf repellent. In a two-artist family, it seemed ridiculous to hoard the shiny things of my distant past. I needed to make room, but for what, I had no idea.

I parked in front of the pawnshop and looked around, afraid another mother from school would see me skulking around. Even inside, I worried. I wanted the man behind the counter not to think I was feeding a drug habit, so I babbled.

"I didn't make a lot of money this year," I told him.

"This is a service we provide," he said without looking up. He tested and weighed the chains and three gold hoop earrings, whose mates were long gone. He snipped the rose off the Sweet Sixteen charm with wire cutters and handed it to me. I remembered that November day in 1976, when I went for my learner's permit in Medford, Massachusetts. Document in hand, I drove myself back to school with my mother in the passenger seat. On the way, we stopped at Friendly's for lunch. She was younger than I was now, wearing a smart navy cardigan with her hair freshly clipped. She daintily parceled her cheeseburger into sections like a pie, with a knife and fork. She was so calm—yet all the while she was planning a surprise party for me, which would take place that night at home.

"Would you like the pearl?" he asked. This time, it was the wafer above the chalice in the first communion charm. The shame that had blazed on my face had begun to subside. This man was unlocking something and it stirred me.

"That's from second grade," I said. I saw myself, a newly minted but eventually lapsed Catholic in a white crinoline minidress and child-sized bridal veil. My mother again. I could almost feel her hands as they arranged the white lace around my shoulders. "Saint Mary's Church," I said. Silence. "Boston."

"The sapphire is negligible," he said, holding out a gold ring with a small blue stone. The band was etched with a fussy pattern. I'd never worn it, not once.

"I think this came from Damascus," I said. "The gold is different, right?"

"24-carat," he said.

"Keep the sapphire," I said.

It was from Greg, from 1988. He crashed through the door, his sandy hair flapping, after weeks on assignment in the Middle East. I pretended I loved the present, but I didn't love it and I didn't love him. When he got his own apartment two weeks later, he refused to take it back.

It seemed proper to keep the charm of the state of Arizona, from my first plane trip to my father's native state when I saw the Grand Canyon, the summer of my sixth year. And also the cross from my baptism. They would go back into a drawer. I staggered out with them and my pile of cash, giddy from this sudden flushness but reeling from wave after wave of sepia-toned childhood.

A few days later I got an eBay account, for which I chose as a username the street in Paris we once lived on. Many of our wedding guests had expensive tastes and, apparently, I did too; optimistic ones, anyway. We had received Baccarat crystal, Limoges china, and sterling place settings, all of which I believed was required for newlyweds starting a life together in France. Soon we were kitted out for a château, surrounded by vineyards, possibly our own vintage. We were given ivory-handled fish forks, a pair of silver plate water pitchers, and nineteenth-century asparagus tongs. None of which I ever used, let alone polished, and all of which I could certainly live without. We never made it to the château, but my marriage had lasted twenty-five years already, and none of this stuff had anything to do with its strength and durability. My husband, unattached to things like crystal stemware said, "Sure, go ahead."

So I sold the glasses, the jelly spoons, the Victorian grape shears that filled my cabinets but not my life.

A person named Andy bought the Baccarat fluted tumblers. I wiped away the dust and packed them tenderly in rolls and rolls of bubble wrap. It had been years since I'd seen the friend who gave them as a wedding gift. She had a merry, cackling laugh and deployed it often, even during her double mastectomy a decade ago. I felt a stab of remorse shipping them off.

My eBay seller email was in honor of the song "Sitting Here in Limbo." It seemed appropriate for someone in middle age, on the cusp of something. After I sent the tumblers, Andy wrote to thank me. "P.S.," he—or she—asked. "Where is Limbo?"

I wasn't sure what to say. Everywhere?

"Connecticut," I finally answered. "I used to live in Paris," I typed with a shrug, the meaning of which was clear only to myself.

This was not what I expected when I resolved to lighten my material load. But simultaneously facing the landmarks and heartbreaks in my past was starting to overwhelm me, as was the self-reproach about taking gifts chosen by people I love or loved and turning them into cash. It's the memory, not the thing, I kept telling myself, but these dormant images were elucidating something I had failed to anticipate. I wasn't selling my possessions. I was getting paid for high-resolution snapshots from my emotional archives.

But still, I kept going.

Next, a vintage chronometer watch that had sat in darkness for decades. The glass was scratched, but I soon learned it was rare and coveted.

One bidder asked how I got such a treasure.

"A gift," I answered.

"Nice gift," he responded.

"Someone left it on the dresser when he left the country," I wrote.

"I hope the parting was mutual," he responded.

It wasn't. I remembered his call from the airport, and his unequivocal, permanent goodbye. Afterwards, I walked around Manhattan like a madwoman, my incinerated heart spilling embers all over the sidewalk.

Next, an elegant clock, still aglow in its box. I had tried to love it, but it made too heavy a statement on our decidedly informal mantle, loaded up with my daughter's ceramic witch and son's clay vessel. I had all the paperwork. A French couple had given it to us along with a vintage lamp from a store near the Madeleine in Paris. The husband was old, with a chronic illness. We knew them through my parents, and though we saw them often in Paris, we did not keep in touch when we moved back. A few years ago, he took his own life. I had the clearest memory of his strange smoky cologne, a smell delivered to my own two cheeks during our routine double-kiss greeting on the Rue de Castiglione.

I took the spoils and got caught up, putting the rest to work in the bank for the next emergency or plane ticket. Neither my husband nor I felt any sense of loss, but we did notice the breathing room, the space that was not a void, the perfect liberation of the empty cabinet.

We still, undeniably, have too much. There will be enough left for my two children when I am gone—the few rings I do wear, my grandmother's Ironstone china, and the flatware (should they care to buff it regularly), and the remaining silver pitcher from Paris that gives a hint of the château-that-never-was to our dinners—held around a table my husband made—in rural New England. I hope they won't fight over that, or any of it, when I'm gone. Actually, I hope they jettison it all to finance their own travels, or pay a bill, or help someone, or get them out of a debt they might not have predicted. I wish for them to travel light.

Meanwhile, pieces of my history are somewhere else, intact, in someone else's hands. I don't need to know if my gold charms were sold off again and heated into molten metal to make bullion. Getting rid of it all made my memories burn vibrantly, and I was as enriched by my confessionals with strangers as I was by their money—and their curiosity.

"Wow," wrote the person who bought the fancy clock. "It's in perfect shape."

"One of those wedding presents I never used," I wrote.

"Hope everything's okay," the person wrote.

"All good," I messaged back and began to type, "We're still together after…" Forget it, I thought, and deleted the sentence. It *was* all good, and at that point, better left alone.

Chapter 23

Dog Walk

bout a mile into my usual dog walk, there comes a clearing that opens across a valley with no name, just a normal up-down flow of trees and meadow. There are a million such vistas across rural New England, but this happens to be the one I think of as mine. As the birch and maple part to my left, as I come upon the sight of the white house wedged into the hillside above the pond, there is always the same surge of anticipation, a spike in the heart rate and the chemicals that cause that. It's as though I'm at the airport to pick up one of my children.

The house appears to be a patient dwelling and indeed the windows seem to resemble watchful eyes that gaze over the ridgeline, suspicious or protective. It is my home, in a sense. And yet when it appears this way, beyond the last thicket, the woman walking her dog seems to detach from the woman who resides in that distant house. I know her story, but I wonder about it anyway. What burdens live behind those walls? In my mind, I always seek the darkness first, but eventually I think to wonder as well how brilliantly the light shines through, and how reliably.

The house is framed by fields and sky, resting as still as a portrait. In that place across the ravine, I am growing old and restless and, to my astonishment, content. That big white house, shrunken by distance, is the repository of my small existence, my reveries and insistent dreams. Thanksgiving dinners and school nights, how many hundreds of them? Locks of my children's hair folded in tissues. A formidable shoe collection. Stacks of unopened bills.

Behind one window is the probably-unmade bed I retreated to for almost two years, draped with clean sheets, Arctic white. The bed is cheerful. It remembers nothing, forgives everything. Whatever secrets I have are safe under the pitched roof that, from here, shows no hint of damage from the latest destructive winter, but from up close, reveals gaps where shingles had spun off into a hurricane last fall. This remote rural idyll, tucked among pastures and oak glades, is the place where experience is making its final bend toward wisdom—that dreaded word that at one time was synonymous with "old." This house contains almost all of me. All, except for the part that disappears from time to time, though maybe that's in there too.

Then I turn and walk on. The house vanishes behind a wall of leaves. A woman, her dog, heading toward a home whose attic—under that roof that needs patching—holds an empty suitcase. Brownish gray, it has been catapulted onto luggage belts, tossed in taxicabs, wheeled for miles around airports, hoisted and jammed and crammed to bursting. One day soon, I will detach from my routine and the people I love. I will pack only what I need into it and shut the door behind me. We will be on our way.

Chapter 24

Falling

The air is weighted with cook smoke and heat when my flight arrives on a Friday afternoon in Siem Reap. I'm so drowsy that my head no longer feels like it's attached to my neck, but hovering above it. The sensation makes my heart beat with a staccato rhythm that verges on panic. I hail a tuk-tuk and dash up the avenue to my hotel.

In the room, picture windows overlook somewhat manicured gardens framed by a steeply pitched red Khmer-style roof. It's a clean and simple hotel, not one of the new luxury offerings whose spas are lovingly depicted in glossy pages and websites. On the bed, three pillows perch invitingly on the bleached white sheets. It seems a cruel tease given the terminal case of insomnia that has tormented me since arriving in Asia five days ago.

Downstairs, I grab another tuk-tuk to the Foreign Correspondents' Club, a handsome vintage watering hole, where I order a vodka & tonic. A paddle fan chirrs, accentuating the emptiness of the bar. Besides myself, there appear to be no correspondents, foreign or otherwise, stopping by the club at cocktail hour. The view outside is of the sky, which glides from cobalt to starless black. I sip my drink and suck on the lumpy rind of the kaffir lime wedge. The waitress brings me a bowl of peanuts. It's only seven o'clock, so when I'm done, I return to the hotel to figure out dinner. I'm here on a weekend break from a project in Singapore, and have already noted a few restaurants that look intriguing. But within minutes, I burrow under the bedding like a pine vole and tumble into a dark, impenetrable sleep—my first in days.

At 11 P.M. I jolt awake, change into pajamas, return to the warm envelope of my bed. My head is constricted by hunger, thirst, fatigue. But I can't fall back asleep. I'm spinning, spiraling, frustrated to tears in my longing for the plunge.

Since an Ambien mishap in Tokyo a few years ago, I'm unable to take sleeping pills.

Before leaving for Japan on a high-pressure project, I'd had a quartet of tablets prescribed to me "just in case" by my doctor to mitigate the fourteen-hour time difference. I nibbled a crumb when I went to bed, another when I woke up three hours later, and so on. By the third day, I spent a morning in meetings, taking meticulous notes at each of them. I remembered none of it when I startled awake in the car on the way to lunch. I had been sleep-walking through the government conference rooms of Tokyo. My notebooks were gibberish, neatly transcribed lines of letters forming non-words, a chronicle of a brain gripped by madness.

So now when I travel, my body is left to its own faltering powers. Jet-lag has turned, at times, into a chronic illness. The sensation is almost one of derangement. The brain whirls. No thought can be isolated to be spoken or considered. My mind is a slurried mash of fragments.

With the ruse that I am rested, I begin my day. At 3:30, I'm dressed. The in-room brew coffee isn't half bad. A caffeine vice grips my head in almost-pain. Lucidity, or something like it, descends.

I had not planned to see the sunrise at Angkor Wat at all. I needed to catch up on sleep. A dayside visit would do me fine. But a hand reaches through my brain fog and pulls me out the door. I hire a tuk-tuk for the morning. It costs $10. First, we stop to get my temple pass. The instant photo on my ID shows not me but a maniac with ashy semi-circles under each eye. A few minutes down the avenue, my driver drops me at the entrance, where he will wait for me. His name is Leap, and the canopy on his tuk-tuk is neon green. I tear a page from my small memo book and write the phonetics of my name for him: "Mar-sha." It is 4:30 A.M.

I ramble along the rocks, tripping on roots, stumbling on stones. Fluid shapes of people and temple shards are rendered ghostlier still in the light of my iPhone. The crowd is sparse. I find an attendant, who points me in another moonless direction. I arrive at a body of water. My toes graze the edge. It must be the famous reflecting pool, but I have no perception inside this pitch-black vacuum. Within minutes, I sense a mob begin to swell behind me, increasing by tens, hundreds, thousands. A man with a long-lens camera and a lit cigarette almost shoves me into the water. This is why I did not wish to see the sunrise at Angkor Wat. I dig my heels into the dirt.

The air smells of sweat, tobacco, earth. At last, I discern the famous outline, with its pair of symmetrical towers and central conical peak coming into high relief. There is just enough dim wattage from the coming day to rouse the mosquitoes to dart and buzz. My arms are so huddled against other peoples' limbs that I can barely lift them high enough to swat away the pests.

"Would you like some bug spray?" the young woman beside me asks.

"Thank you," I say.

She opens her pack and removes a bottle of Off, which I try to spritz on my hair, neck, arms, wrists. Alcohol and lemongrass.

The Asian heat emulsifies the night with the dawn. Sweat pools in the caverns of my collarbone, behind my ears. I sigh. It must be 80 degrees already.

"I have an extra water," my neighbor says, fishing out an unopened plastic bottle. "Want one?"

"I can't believe I forgot water," I say.

Usually, I'm the one armed with all the required stuff. I'm a mother and have traveled to sixty countries. I know better, but I was too tired to be embarrassed by my lack of preparedness.

I drink, and we chat a bit. She's from Toronto, just quit her job, is traveling solo, as I am. Flew in from Chiang Mai.

Day breaks. Above me, shafts of violet and iron gray wrap around strands of dainty clouds. There, at last, is Angkor Wat. On the left stands the great lollipop palm tree. The crowd clicks away on cameras while I gaze and gape at this structure rising majestically out of the night. A curtain of warmth begins to ascend from my chest and then up my face, which is glazed with cool sweat. My heart is drumming out a rapid patter. I'm so tired. I yawn and crumple against my neighbor from Toronto.

I fainted once in the Hall of Mirrors in Versailles. It is called Stendhal Syndrome, and it can happen, albeit rarely, when overcome by something of staggering beauty. But today, maybe it's the heat or because I stood for so long the blood could not reach my heart. Might be my empty belly, the cocktail last night with no dinner, the sweat from other peoples' bodies rubbing off on mine. Most likely, sleeplessness blitzed my circuits and knocked me out.

When I come to, the woman from Toronto is pouring water over my face. I was out only a few seconds, she says. "I have a tarp, if you want to sit." She brandishes a folded plastic sheet from her pack, but there is no room in the crush to rest. She helps yank me up and once again, I reclaim my same narrow upright cylinder of space. Perspiration has fastened my loose white blouse to my ribcage. All I see is snow, like bad reception on an old TV.

"I haven't slept for days," I say. "Literally days." My hands shake. I blink and blink. Within a few moments, the outlines of two temples—the real one and its mirror image in the pond—come back to focus. "What else is in that pack?" I ask.

"I have these," she says, brandishing a clear bag stuffed with balls the size of grapes, each wrapped in yellow cellophane. "Tamarind candy. From Thailand."

I rustle loose the sticky brown glob. It is sweet, sour, spicy, salty. It is everything and for the moment, it is also too much. I try to look nonchalant as I spit it into my hand.

The sky flares into full-on daytime. Behind me swarms a massive and terrifying crowd. Gillette Stadium parking lot after a Patriots game comes to mind.

The woman from Toronto says, "I'm heading back before it gets too nuts."

I follow, afraid to be without her in this place. But before we leave, I turn my head one last time. It's a struggle to imagine that what I'm seeing is real and not a page from a compendium of wonders. I have felt this elsewhere. The Grand Canyon. St. Basil's. The Northern Lights. It is an odd thing to be confronted with the unfathomable.

We bolt from the mass of bodies and return the way we came, across the same stones, past the figures that earlier seemed to float shapelessly in the blackness. There are hundreds of tuk-tuks. She peels off to try to find hers.

"Thank you!" I call after her. Her arm raises in brisk acknowledgment, while her pack gently sways on her shoulders.

"Get some sleep!" she calls back.

I turn my head and see an electric-green awning on a tuk-tuk not far from the entrance gate. A man sleeps inside the carriage, hunched on the seat.

"Leap?" I call.

He springs out to greet me. "Mar-sha!" he says brightly. I am relieved and reassured.

It is 6:38 A.M.

Back at the hotel, I wash the tamarind residue off my hands. I kick off my sneakers, streaked with mud and sand. Later, I will eat some spicy amok in town and return to Angkor Wat. My feet will carry me up its crumbling stairs and my fingers will graze sandstone bas-reliefs. I will ponder the devotion that inspired it, the hands that built it, and the stories of the sacred mountains it depicts. But now, I can no longer feel the ground I'm standing on.

The sight of the bed scares me. It is enemy territory. I slide in anyway. I soar up against a brightening sky when my body becomes heavy as a boulder. I am crashing to the floor, through the ceiling, splashing into the groundwater and descending to the boiling center of the earth.

Chapter 25

Seven Drafts of Coffee

1. From Delhi to Kigali

With no idea what day it was on the Gregorian calendar, or for that matter the Roman, Julian, Chinese or Persian ones, I awoke to the pilot announcing the imminent descent to Bole International Airport in Addis Ababa. I had been traveling for hours, maybe days. First the car from the hotel in the mountains outside of Rishikesh, lunch in Haridwar, a horribly, wonderfully crowded train to Delhi. (When the pandemic arrived and my family and I were locked down and marooned, I would long for the misery of the packed compartment on that four-hour trip.) How delicious was the dal makhana, the soggy circle of naan, the fluorescent light, the human race cheek-by-jowl.

Overnight, I had crossed the Arabian Sea and met morning on the African continent.

The landing delineated a fracture, maybe more like a crease, between two halves. My India story had ended and a new one in Rwanda was soon to begin. At the moment, I had four hours in Ethiopia, a mental deep-clean of a layover. Behind me, the Ganges would forever flow through the plains to nourish and irrigate all of India. In front of me were the green fields and soft-shouldered Rwandan hills.

The elements of yesterday's story are comfortably in my bag, waiting to be unveiled in the stillness of my home. Every stop, every step, every café, every ticket stub, every receipt jammed into a large envelope or the bound pages of a promotional brochure. Calling cards, phone numbers and emails, home and business. Trinkets, too. A scarf I bought in Agra, a mala necklace made of rudraksha seeds that was a gift from one of the hotel managers in Uttarakhand. Notebooks upon notebooks upon notebooks, one containing a clump of dried curry leaves, another a smashed red hibiscus blossom. These things will dislodge something in my heart, and sometimes a narrative can then form around them.

I imagine that once, the Addis airport was a humble sort of thoroughfare, but today it is a sunny enclosure of floor-to-ceiling picture windows and a mosaic of coffee bars. Dozens of coffee bars. The whole airport bears the bitter, toasted smell of roasting and brewing. My pulse begins to race and my throat to expand in anticipation of the first swallow, a ritual that ushers in morning, every morning. We are all globalized man and globalized woman, and a latte is a latte everywhere. So the young barista steams me one, this drink that means "milk" in my Italian grandparents' native tongue. Arabica beans that grew, I read on the sign, in the highlands of Ethiopia, the southwestern rainforest. Drinking it is a blood connection with the place I am passing through this morning. A froth of milk tickles my nose and up close, yeah sure, I smell the cocoa, the strawberry, the cinnamon "notes" indicated on the blackboard. Morning here seems like morning elsewhere, except it never really is, because I have never had a cup of coffee as perfect as this one.

I seat myself in the far, far corner of a great hall, fifty-eight-year-old me checking my emails, wondering if anyone knows or cares where I am. And not feeling bad about that sentiment at all. The comfort of having one story behind me gives way to something else: raw, unbridled excitement. The horizon fills with clouds. In three hours, I will fly into Kigali in a sky full of rain.

2. Under the Arch

It is 7 A.M. in downtown St. Louis, and I'm swilling a cup of room service coffee. Delivered with kindness, technically before the dining room opened, it arrived in a silver-plate pot, and tasted metallic even after I poured in billows of heavy cream. But it's hot and plentiful, and it's morning and I need to think.

Sometimes, I need to situate myself and on this late August day, I wonder: where am I? I have been to many places so far this year: Morocco, Paris, California, New Jersey, Singapore, Cambodia, Chicago, and Pittsburgh. At times, only coffee reminds me that I am the same person, roughly, everywhere I wake up.

My king-with-a-view discount special, dimmed by night the prior evening, turns out to face the side of a pristine brick building so high I can't see the top of it and I'm on the 16th floor. It must be another hotel because the curtains—rows and rows of them, fixed and unbreathing—are identically drawn. The windows appear to be locked shut, as mine is, much as I'd love a draft of air, even the thick, syrupy kind stewing this close to the Mississippi River. When I crane my neck to the side, I'm surprised by a thin shard of blue sky so tall and spindly I could perch a fedora on top and spin it. The strip of daylight must be a talisman of some sort, which I'll accept for the cheap metaphor it is and allow it to offer me a sliver of promise.

I pour more coffee, and the slightly charred scent is invigorating. It triggers a sensory memory, of overnight stays in bad hotels when I worked in television. But I love it, and how it wakes me up, snaps open the day, leads me out of my ruminations, makes me remember.

Yesterday, I dropped my youngest child off at her dorm room. Mark arrives later today, and we will all have orientation together, and then there is an evening planned with the purveyor of St. Louis's most famous frozen custard. I geared every moment of mothering toward this morning, graced as always with the hot coffee that fuels my life. And for a moment I allow myself to feel as if I have fallen into an empty well with no water, no ladder, not even a 5-watt bulb to light my way. My sweet beautiful girl, born happy, comforting her graying mother. "It will be okay, Mom," she says.

And she's right. St. Louis itself will accompany me out of melancholy because I am also here to write about this still-mighty city, home of the National Blues Museum. I consider all I have to gather. I know what will happen. The city's architecture and history will make me stop mooning for my own recent past. Will deliver me to the great Gateway Arch, through its wondrous parks and museums. This is where my daughter lives now, and I am delighted to make its acquaintance. I have no choice but to trust it.

3. La Quinta Hotel, Flagstaff

With a three-hour wait until my daughter's flight arrived from St. Louis, I drove from Flagstaff airport and headed south past the still snowy mountains and broad sweeps of Ponderosa pines into the Coconino National Forest. It is composed of a couple million acres, but my mission was a quick and straightforward one, and that was to take a picture of the brown, retro-shaped sign at the entrance of the park. I was certain that it was not the same one from 1946, when my father and a T-shirted male crew posed in front of it wearing big, postwar grins.

"We all came up here from Tucson to work, every summer," he told me the last time we had been together in Arizona, his home state. "We cleared brush and chopped down trees."

"Where did you live?" I asked.

"In cabins," he said. "There was a mess hall. No girls at all. We made fifty cents an hour. It was great."

The past is an unruly place to visit, let alone to live. But I'm writing a memoir and Arizona offers clusters of old but vibrant images, and I enjoy wading into that translucent pool of memory. The state was emerging as a broader character in my book-in-progress than I had anticipated. It was my father's boyhood home, and though he had boarded a cross-country train for medical school in New England and stayed there forever, his time in the desert ineluctably shaped him and in turn, his wife and four daughters. We visited the southwest every summer of my childhood. When Mark and I had children, we introduced them as babies to Arizona.

And I was returning again—this time, with my daughter, over her spring break. My instinct was to mark the trip's beginning with homage to my father's youthful self at Coconino (he had just turned 85) before I picked her up and headed east toward Arizona's delirious moonscapes. Of all the places I travel, the metaphors that surface in the desert are the most on the nose, and here at Coconino, I sought the most glaring one.

In the morning, Ava was enjoying the sleep of a bone-weary college freshman. How many hours I have spent watching the rise and fall of her belly as she slept, witnessing the surefire reliability of the human breath, with love blasting warm and sweet through my body? On this morning, I felt what I always felt. Clouds darkening the moment, heaving shadow on perfect contentment. The pull of caution from loving someone too much.

Breaking my reverie, I deduced that the mini-Mr. Coffee maker in the room was not going to cut it. The contraption smelled like mildew and rust. I'd have to find another source to marshal me through my first hour of the morning. I needed to switch the rental car and its scary squeaky brakes, since I had about 1200 miles to drive over the next week. Dressing quickly, I kissed Ava on the cheek, and conjured up the forces to hurl myself into this very moment, this day, this trip. I had scheduled many stops that day on the way across the state to Chinle—Meteor Crater, Walnut Canyon, the Petrified Forest—and I felt the familiar neck grip I knew so well as a travel writer. Too much everything, except hours.

Relax, I told myself. *You're off the hook.* Nothing was due, no editor was waiting for my words. *You're with Ava, the antidote to all, the darling and easy companion.*

Downstairs, the lobby smelled of coffee. Without putting too fine a point on it, it was the smell of rebirth and it unleashed a flood of epinephrine.

"Good morning," I said to the desk clerk. "Can you point me to the coffee?"

"Oh, it's run out," he said. "Lots of early flights this morning. Where are you headed?"

"Is there anywhere to stop for coffee on the way to the airport?"

"Your best bet is to get coffee there. Or wait for a fresh pot here."

"No problem," I lied.

4. Paris Solo

Day 4:

I stop at the St. Regis on the Île Saint Louis, a gleaming island in the Seine. It is a gorgeous bistro, with white tiles and well-patinaed wooden banquettes. "Only me," I tell the waitress. "Of course, Madame," she says, and seats me at a corner table. I tuck into a *salade de chèvre chaud* and a *crème brûlée*. Finally, over one noisette (an espresso with a drop of milk) and then another, I open, half-heartedly, my book, *Earthly Paradise* by Colette, who wrote passionately about the sky over Paris. The book was already worn when I bought it almost forty years earlier from a *bouquiniste* on the Quai de la Tournelle. This city is skilled at punctuating each part of each day with rituals such as midday dessert, multiple coffees and lunches that stretch long into the afternoon.

Afterwards, I cross the Seine to the Marais toward the Place de la République and the Canal St. Martin, the urban waterway ordered in 1802 by Napoléon, who realized he needed more fresh water for the city's growing population. It took twenty-three years to make, and was paid for by a tax on wine. It is Paris's trendiest neighborhood, but the energy is less electric than bucolic. Plane and chestnut trees line the waterway and cast a reflection below on the glassine canal. I think of Amélie, the title character of the quintessentially Parisian film, kneeling on one of the bridges in a red dress, skipping stones into the water.

I beeline for Du Pain et Des Idées, a temple to patisserie excellence, nibble on a fresh apple turnover, and then to Centre Commerciale, a store full of sunlight and chunky wool coats. My feet move purposefully, boots clacking on cobblestones, but I'm in no rush. This is what a person does in Paris. She moves, she wanders, she has a point, maybe, but jettisons it constantly.

At home, when alone, I'm lonely. When I travel alone, I'm free.

Especially in Paris. Engaged with my surroundings, loose, all senses on, I am absolved from all constraints or negotiations over where to visit or eat dinner. I traverse the city on my own steam, with spontaneity instead of an itinerary.

Life is truly lived in Paris's cafes. Sometimes it feels as if the whole population is outside: flirting, discussing, cocooned in intimate tête-à-têtes over strong coffee and vin de table. Back in Colette's neighborhood of the Palais-Royal, I park myself outdoors at venerable old Café Le Nemours before a stroll through the gardens. One cup later—I know, it's gauche to order café au lait in the afternoon, but the server is used to such lapses—I'm fortified for a show at the Théâtre du Palais-Royal, luxurious and unchanged on rue de Montpensier since 1784, the year Thomas Jefferson arrived in Paris, five years before the French Revolution.

5. Tambacounda

The morning after the festival, my last in Tambacounda, I met Mamadou Alassane Sem, known everywhere in Senegal as Neggadou, at his house. A rich haze of roasting onions and chunks of pumpkin filled the courtyard. The women were preparing that day's *thieboudienne*, which we would eat from a common vessel between rows of kale, tomatoes and peppers in his urban garden. "Did you see the hundreds of young people last night?" he asks, pinching a piece of chicken with his thumb and forefinger. "They will follow my example and stay here. Migration to Europe is a sure path to an early death."

I believed, as he did, that youth in the most economically strapped section of an already impoverished country would pay heed to one of its most celebrated rappers. "He speaks for us," Guelel Diop, age 15, told me last night at the festival. The sky above the crowd, drums and music was pink and full of promise, casting hope onto Neggadou and everyone around him—his friends, brothers, and now, his allies in government. "Small farms are the future of Senegal," he said, followed by cheers, drums, the pounding of feet. I was reluctant to depart this far-flung corner of the African continent, Neggadou, and his beautiful plans.

A few hours into the eight-hour drive back to Dakar, we detoured for a quick rest and a coffee in Kaolack, a different place than the one we stopped in while heading east to Tambacounda five days earlier. Strong, spicy, of this exact corner of earth, the coffee was served in a shot glass-sized paper cup. I left my colleagues at the bar, walked onto the road and half thought, why not? I have my wallet, a baseball cap and this here coffee. But my story is not finished. No story is ever finished. I had a plane to catch, a home of my own, children to love and an article to write with whatever I had gathered. I hoped it would be enough.

6. Home

I station myself in a quiet corner of the house and spread the spoils on the carpet next to my desk. Business cards bearing the contact details of those I interviewed: hotel managers, restaurant chefs, tour operators, government officials. Amassed to help me remember. A scholar in colonial history in Ouro Preto. The man who owns the little gem shop in Rishikesh. The mango farmer in Haiti. The head re-enactment guy at Little Bighorn Battlefield. The spa manager in Santa Fe. (Must call her with the question I forgot to ask. Always the one answer I need is the one sliver of curiosity that eluded me when we were face-to-face.) My notebooks are jammed with the stuff of travel, placed there deliberately to jog a memory. The plucked flowers, now squashed, or a napkin from a restaurant, the one in Tiradentes that had ice cream made from jaboticaba fruit—the kinds of things I once taped to the pages of my high school scrapbook—stuck inside.

Every story ends up in an envelope. My cabinets hold many such packets, little time capsules that I carried home and opened up like a Christmas stocking on the morning the writing began. Once I put them in their resting place, they tend to stay there.

An unfortunate truth: the writing takes much, much longer than the trip. Gloriously loose in the exterior world, I now cement myself to a chair, in the taut act of funneling the earth and the sky into 1500 words. I'll start with an anecdote. Then scrap it, and try another.

Maybe I open with the welcoming sunrise from the plane as I greeted the day from above, desperate to extricate myself from the middle seat in coach, the crumbs and cracked plastic glasses? There's one editor who likes stories that start on day seven and circle back to the beginning. Make a knockout lede. Writing is a life of disquietude and doubt, but in stories about place, I always carry the certainty that a story will rise as clear and defined as a diver emerging from the surf.

I sit down with my coffee.

Chapter 26

Petra or Bust

The day I arrived in Amman, a taxi delivered me atop a high hill to the Citadel to saunter around the Temple of Hercules, weave through the remains of the Umayyad Palace, and look upon the Roman amphitheater, a perfect clamshell tucked into the jagged geometry of Jordan's capital. It was springtime, and I dressed the way you'd think to dress for a trip to the desert. But when the rain began to come down, then sleet, and the temperature plummeted, I knew my windbreaker was not going to cut it for my impending hike through Jordan's barren wilderness. Soaking wet, I took refuge in an outdoor store on Abdoun Circle, where the owners laid out waterproof gear and fleece turtlenecks. Armed with a few extra layers, I left the next morning for the Dana Biosphere Reserve, a national park in Jordan's far west that nudges the Great Rift Valley.

Although sleeping in a tent is not my preferred way to overnight and the word "camping" fills me with dread, I've recently been swayed by the unattributed code of great travelers throughout history: the best way to know a place is to walk across it. Jordan made this irresistible by inaugurating a path linking the south of the country to the north. Over four days, I would cover the 33-mile section of it named by *National Geographic* as one of the best trails in the world, which afforded me the rare opportunity to enter Petra through the back entrance. My journey would finish at the red-sand expanse of Wadi Rum, a small but quintessentially Levantine desert known for its sandstone mesas, natural arches, and dramatic, ethereal light.

The small group of adventurers, strangers all from seven countries, was led by an excellent guide named Ayman Abd Alkareem, who possesses an encyclopedic knowledge of botany, Middle Eastern history, and, I would come to learn, the psychology of reluctant outdoorswomen. On a crystalline and chilly morning, we set forth, immediately skirting and descending a wide gorge. "This is a virgin trail, made by shepherds, donkeys, camels, and goats," said Ayman. The strain on my muscles became a chronic discomfort to overcome, not unlike how I feel in spin class when my body collides with my will and the latter somehow prevails. My boots ambled on hypnotically, adding my footprints to the dust.

A great heart beats in Amman, but Jordan's soul is in the desert. So is mine, though it might seem strange for a woman born, raised, living in tree-covered New England. But the desert was in my blood after annual vacations there with my family as I grew up. From my first visit when I was five years old, I believed myself airborne—as if the sky was the land, the land was the sky, and the whole earth was joined by threads of sunlight. The desert clears the cobwebs in my brain, and more frequently as my body pushes sixty, so does walking. The first spontaneous steps I took as a toddler have transformed into something deliberate and momentous. A simple act loaded with significance, walking connects me to the earth and when I need them, people, and marks with a percussive beat the seconds that remain.

Once a week without fail, and sometimes twice, my friends at home and I meet for our walk. Usually, we take a trail that begins in the rough midpoint between all of our houses, and ascend to a lookout above a suspension bridge over the Shepaug River. Some days we confess our own or our children's frailties, and other days we parse the relative merits of our vacuum cleaners. Some of our bodies are, to varying degrees, starting to crack, and a lot of our conversations are about the time and effort we spend trying to patch them up. My joints are troublesome, one friend's heart needs attention, and another friend's breast cancer has returned.

We walk all summer and throughout the winter, two short hours of a day quickly erased in camaraderie and movement through the fresh air that, more and more, we require. We stride through the weeks and years, and walk each other through the tender work of growing older. Our feet pound out a pleasant rhythm and for the most part, we are patient with our dogs. We move, always ahead and always together, which is a silent expression of the love that this commitment to our walks implies.

I have grown dependent on the idea of forward motion, the physical rendering of time passing. I have fallen in love with our path for the qualities that surprise me. Certain sections are blanketed with pine needles, and branches get strewn about during autumn storms. At times the river is frosted with whitecaps, and releases a threatening roar. Other times, the water dips too low, and even the great blue heron fixed midstream on a boulder seems worried. On our trail, the ground underfoot switches from ice to mud to hard soil and the cycle continues, another year escapes. We are forever planning a walking trip—Maine? The coast of England?—but so far it has not come to pass. Here in Jordan, I was taking notes not just for the article I had to write, but also to suggest to my friends that one day, we might return here together.

There are stories to write and stories to tell. I pondered both as I advanced through the desert.

The path opened up at the bottom, giving way to a labyrinth of dried river beds known as wadis, which led to iron-rich canyons. Tamarix, cypress, and jujube trees painted patches of green along the path, and artemisia—or wormwood, the active ingredient in absinthe—blew floral scent. The only sounds were the hum of wind and the scrape of feet over stone. Loose pebbles crunched under our soles, and on smooth outcrops, our treads made a thump. White sandstone formations reminded me of southern Utah, but here, the canal system was made by Ottomans and fed by the Sea of Galilee.

The wind began to blow skeins of chill straight to my bones, and it seemed that a coating of frost had spread beneath my skin. I quickly learned the necessity of my new down wardrobe, plus the indispensability of blister bandages. I had stashed a few bags of M&M's in my brand-new pack, but it was hard to beat Ayman's mix of cumin-seasoned almonds, pistachios and cashews. We stopped often along the way to rest and snack.

This stretch of Jordan is home to dozens of Bedouin communities, who have roamed this land—their land—for thousands of years. At day's end, we passed through a tent village and a young girl rode up on her donkey to greet us. A bright crimson blanket draped over her saddle and the tawny head of a baby goat poked out of her pouch. "Her foot is injured," she said. Straight ahead was the rest of the herd, and they nudged our knees with their sweet faces.

Just beyond, the mud-brick of our ecolodge seemed to rise organically from the sand. After a dinner of cabbage soup, hummus, and four spicy vegetables dishes, I repaired to my room, which, like the entire hotel, was lit only by candles. The sheets were crisp Egyptian cotton, and, to-the-core exhausted, I wrapped up tightly in them.

Leg muscles tight and sore, I limped to breakfast and after a Bedouin fortified us with grainy coffee in his tent, our trek began again. There was a spray of raindrops, but it was history that engulfed me most. This was the same trade route trodden by the Nabateans—merchants who settled here in the sixth century BC, transporting spices, copper, and sugar. At lunchtime in a stone clearing, the hilltop tomb of Moses' brother Aaron was visible across the ridge. Soon, we threaded ourselves through a narrow opening into Little Petra, a Silk Road village carved into red sandstone walls. Here, one's gaze tilts up, at the ingenious dwellings, at a ceiling fresco of grapevines, at the ribbon of sky above.

At the next campsite, my feet, calves and hamstrings were too spent to care about much besides comfort, so I shed my hiking boots and peeled off my socks with a gratified sigh. Dinner was prepared zarb style, Bedouin barbecue—chicken and vegetables roasted in an underground fire pit. Soon, I melted onto my mattress in my zero-star Coleman tent, fully dressed in tomorrow's clothes. No sooner had I fallen into a thick, dreamless sleep when the flaps of my tent levitated, followed by a crash. With the incessant drone of the high-desert wind, like a low E-flat from a bassoon, the whole flimsy structure had uprooted and collapsed on top of me. Ayman arrived with a flashlight and together we reconstructed my shelter, this time driving the stakes deeper into the sandy earth.

While most tourists are bussed to Bab-el-Siq and enter through a slot canyon at the front, in the morning we approached the city backwards. After a 3.5 mile walk, battered by frigid winds, we saw the outline of an urn emerge over a hill. Soon the monastery appeared, a massive façade carved into a mountainside, and we descended 850 stairs into Petra proper. Donkeys, camels, and merchants vied for my attention, but I focused on the niches, temples, monuments, tombs, and colonnaded streets where 30,000 people once lived, gathered, and died. Up and down stairs and into cut-rock passages bearing the imprimaturs of thousands of inhabitants and wanderers before me, whose spirits hovered through this so-called lost city.

I wound through caves and the strikingly colorful tombs sculpted into rose-pink sandstone cliffs. Some of them had later been transformed into Byzantine churches. Sun blazed overhead, turning the edifices and chasms shades of orange marmalade. Sometimes it was difficult to see where the built environment ended and nature began.

At the end of the day, we reached the Treasury, Petra's greatest showpiece, believed also to be a Nabataean royal tomb. I had worried that this stock travel brochure sight would be almost too familiar, and that I would have to muffle a world-weary shrug due to overexposure to its likeness. My camera clicked away as if fulfilling some kind of obligation.

But I had not anticipated its majesty, or how indelibly it would seep into my marrow. There I stood, unexpectedly thunderstruck. It is a tender feeling when cynicism is undercut by awe, and I wanted to hold fast to this hour. Finally, we passed through the Siq, the great winding gorge flanked by towering cliff faces. I kept turning around, hoping the Treasury would peek through the canyon walls and manifest its power or telegraph some secret to me. It had been so brief, and I longed for another day.

Three days, thirty-three miles, and the Jordan Trail was behind me. Through stillness, landscape, and time, my sturdy but aging legs carried me forward, the only direction life ever promised to move. With each metronomic step another second vanished, relegated to the past and to memory. I wondered with regret if I had been too tired or too focused on the finish line to mark each moment with the farewell salute it deserved. And then I asked myself, isn't it always that way?

We still had to climb Jabal Umm ad Dami, which, at 6000 feet, is the country's highest mountain. The guides advertised an easy hike, but it was, in fact, a near vertical scramble over loose rocks and boulders that threatened to detach and roll down the slope. Depleted but emboldened, I stumbled to the summit, where a heavy drizzle cooled us off and there was a panoramic view of Saudi Arabia and the Red Sea. Though Jordan is known to be secure and is conflict-free, the vista gave a sense of the crowded and fraught neighborhood of the Middle East it inhabits.

We drove by pickup to Wadi Rum, and though I was worn out from the hike, the looming shapes and haunting desolation jolted me, indicating that something here was beyond my reach, even my comprehension. An aura of eternity seemed to linger in the landscape that was, at once, pillowy soft and coldly forbidding. The late King Hussein used to bring his children for camping trips here, and his son King Abdullah II still calls it, "his favorite place in all of Jordan." T. E. Lawrence launched his forces from here for two years during the Arab Revolt against the Ottomans and its loveliness rendered him speechless. "Rum(m) inhibited excitement by its serene beauty," he observed in *Seven Pillars of Wisdom*, describing it as "vast, echoing and God-like."

The name means "Valley of the Moon," and though it is arguably lunar, it is definitely extraplanetary: Hollywood has long used it as a stand-in for Mars. *Lawrence of Arabia* was filmed here, and as I looked in the distance, I imagined the ghost of David Lean, setting up a tracking shot of Peter O'Toole on camelback.

Also on my immediate horizon were the rusty remains of the Hejaz Railway that once connected Damascus to Medina, and which, in 1916, was partly blown up by Lawrence, among others, in the uprising against the Turks. The circumstances surrounding the destruction of the train and symbol of the Ottoman Empire was fictionalized in Naji Abu Nowar's cinematic masterpiece *Theeb*, a harrowing story of survival in the desert during wartime. No film has showcased Wadi Rum's native people, harsh weather, and starkness, along with its chasms and cliff faces, quite as forcefully as this film made a century after the events it dramatizes.

Most of the year, the pink-red sand broils under summer heat, but not this time. Instead, there was a churn of snowflakes and clatter of hailstones. Inside the main tent at Milky Way Camp, the room grew smoky from a fire kindled with olive, apricot, and pine logs. My friends and I huddled beside it, eating platefuls of hummus with *za'atar*, a mix of herbs and spices that includes sesame seeds, cumin, and sumac. The temperature sank below freezing and I was shivering, too chilled to go outside, dreading the trip to the frozen communal bathroom or to the tent that I was sharing with two other women. Reeking of campfire, I riffled through my bag for extra pants, sweaters, a turtleneck, even dirty socks to layer, then slipped under a thick slab of blankets.

At 4:30 A.M., I affixed my headlamp and ventured out for sunrise, to wander around in the silence. Stars washed across the sky and eerie outlines of rocks resembled their own shadows under the white spiral of the Milky Way. Slowly night dissolved into dawn. I stood in terror when a dozen or so camels announced their presence with a loud racket and passed with bendy struts, close enough for me to see their eyelashes above their haughty stares. Heads held high in the direction of the rising sun, they marched over waves of pink and orange sand toward the steep oxidized cliffs. I was between worlds, the sleeping and the wakeful. The transcendence and the view funneled a promise to my core, and I had the sudden thought: If I die here, I will die delighted.

Ayman told me that Wadi Rum sand carries a healing electrical charge. As daylight lifted the dark cover from the dunes around me, I removed my shoes and socks, dug my feet into the damp red earth. They were a patchwork of bandages and mole-skin. All the camp still slept and I was alone in the desert with the animals. I walked toward the sunrise, right foot, left, toward Saudi Arabia, toward Baghdad, Iran, India, China, the Pacific Ocean, toward home. This is what human legs are built to do. Move across the ground and force electrostatic charging between grains of sand into the limbs of a camel, or a woman, so they might stride lightly into another day.

Inside the main tent, it smelled of cinnamon, cardamom, and sage, the stuff of Bedouin tea. A man stoked the fire. He looked at my bare feet, grinned, and raised the kettle.

Chapter 27

The Stick

At the tail end of March, leaf muck coated the still-brown yard. Branches were strewn about, gathered by the wind into random piles. A length of fence unfettered itself and wrapped around a tree during one of this season's forty-seven snowstorms. Last October, after growing season, I did not bother to yank the dead tomato plants from the raised beds, and the withered spindles reminded me of my apathy, when, at the onset of fall, I was fed up with planting and pulling, entirely done with yard work for the season.

It was a time of pacing around, waiting: for the phone to ring, for a response, for answers, a scintilla of an idea that might take form in my head and emerge on a page. For one of my stories, sitting in various stages of the assembly line, to be finished or accepted or edited or published. I got lots of emails, naturally. Goody, the hair accessory manufacturer, kept in very close touch with me, as did National Car Rental's Emerald Club, and Priceline certainly had lots of good deals on resorts in Mexico. And then Facebook. Unlike me, my writer friends seemed to be prolific.

In most ways, the empty house was a thing of beauty. My duties, if anything, were larger and more profound with my now-older children: the day-in, day-out, the preemptive talks about dating and drugs and the future, were over. My husband and I lived alone now and more simply, and we had the space to concentrate on our work, which often took us away from home and never at the same time. But sometimes I rattled around the house with an addled brain, wishing for the schedule we used to complain about, when work had its place around other priorities.

Now, with acres of time before me, I could worry all day about my next meeting with the accountant, and the world my kids inhabited. I could also fritter away time weighing my options: essays, fiction, whether to pause the exhaustive pitching of stories to overworked editors and make way for the big idea. I pondered my many missteps and the moves I was scared to take. I grew confused. I waited. I wrote a few sentences.

Lately, there was too much time alone. This is why, today, the 100th day of the year, I busted out. I packed the tea I carted home from Nyungwe, Rwanda in January. I brought the lip balm I snapped up in Stockholm. I put on the surf jacket my friend "lent" me in Hermosa Beach a month ago. And I got in the car, drove an hour north to the Berkshires, and checked into a little motel.

At the entrance, I was welcomed by an illuminated profile of a bear, another animal that hibernates during winter and eventually emerges all disheveled in order to regain her strength or purpose. I asked the owner if there was somewhere nearby safe for me to walk by myself. He gestured across Highway 7, about 100 yards down, to Monument Mountain. I jogged across the road and found the trail entrance.

I travel to hide in plain sight, to immerse myself in elsewhere but emphatically not to push myself into danger. Yet, even in the Berkshires on this tiny mountain, I knew it was unwise to hike alone. The leaves were slippery and there's always the outside chance of a coyote on the loose, a mama bear keeping vigil on her newborn cubs. I veered off the trail slightly to look for a potential club. On a heap of decomposing pine needles, I found a broken-off branch that spoke to me, wedged between two rocks, one covered with lichen and the other with moss. It had a long handle and one end split into a V for Victory, a slingshot, an upside-down peace sign. This was no ordinary walking stick, and when I picked it up, I was surprised by its heft and sturdiness.

I was wearing the wrong shoes (the story of my life)—leather sneakers which looked new because I never wore them hiking. I followed the powder blue painted blazes up the trail and the first roadblock came: a fallen tree. I doubled back and took another path. Soon there was a second fallen tree—this time a birch, around which I veered in a wide semi-circle. Then a third fallen tree, too high to climb over, almost too low to shimmy under. First, I lay down my stick and then, as if it were a saddle blanket, my jacket. I sat for a minute. Change course, negotiate, and tackle: me versus the obstacles. Tree trunks. Decisions. Forward movement. Action. I slid my body beneath the tree, its bark snagging my parka.

Soon, I came to a grand stone staircase, like the one in the ballroom of the Titanic, and I was truly confused: left or right? I opted for neither and changed course again. Some challenges, I just ignored. I came across a waterfall that gushed like springtime, crashing onto well-worn schist and granite boulders. Cracks in the rocks shone from the winter's last snow. There were tiny icicles deep in the crevasses. They would melt in no time.

When I returned to the bottom of the mountain, I placed my stick in a bed of leaves to the side of the path. I planned to do the same walk, bad shoes and all, before I headed home the next day.

After breakfast, I crossed the highway once more, toward the mountain. I looked around the trail entrance, wondering if my stick might have survived the cold night. And there it was, almost in the same spot, but now resting upright against a tree, tenderly placed there by someone else's hands.

Chapter 28

Into the Cold

"This is one of the deepest lakes in Sweden," said Joachim, gesturing toward me and the passenger window. It hardly seemed like a body of water, but rather like a boundless prairie blanketed with snow. "Many people have drowned here on snowmobiles. They completely disappear under the ice." We were driving along the shore of Lake Malgomaj on a February day and the tire studs scraped beneath our Subaru wagon, clashing with the Jennifer Lopez and Pitbull duet thumping on the radio. The horizon was a rainbow of grays—dove to steel to charcoal—like a Benjamin Moore paint strip. Several fishermen were planted in cleared-out spaces on the surface. They were bundled under ear flaps and bulk and their poles stuck out from holes drilled into the ice.

"How deep is it?" I asked. The nightclub music made it difficult to give the icy gravesite its due. Joachim tapped off the power button and silence inflated inside the car. "How deep is it?" I repeated.

"One hundred seventeen meters," he said. "And 45 kilometers long."

Thirty minutes ago, Joachim collected me at Vilhelmina Airport, a one-room outpost in Southern Lapland. He was the only person in the "arrivals" corner of the enclosure. The whole scenario might have made me wary and for a moment, my head entered the Scandi-Noir rabbit hole: I, a lone woman, piled herself and her bags into a stranger's car, whereupon he told me of frozen bodies that floated somewhere under the lake just a guardrail away, and proceeded to drive 80 miles with him on a snow-packed road to the hotel he manages. Right.

But I knew my instincts well enough to trust them and with few exceptions, those I encounter when I travel alone. Besides, I was elated to be in the opening moments of a brief disappearing act. Joachim had no idea that he was in collusion with me as I faded into the recesses of Lapland's forlorn geology for a few days on my own, with no plans for anything except to be out of reach.

I'd come to Sweden to do a roundup on spas for a glossy monthly, and had spent the last four days in Stockholm getting rubbed and pummeled, kneaded and oiled with extracts of birch, lingonberry, and seaweed. I couldn't lie, it was a peach of an assignment but while there I still inhabited my own familiar skin—artist's wife, preoccupied mother, magazine scribe for hire under constant harassment from a smartphone. My friend told me of an interesting hotel up north, so I decided to decamp from Stockholm and all that cosseting, and withdraw for a quiet long weekend.

Until I moved to a wooded corner of New England, I had spent my adult life in New York and Paris, or on the road roaming Fez's bazaars or the alleyways of Phnom Penh. But lately it was the remote I sought, the far-flung mirror of my rural existence, total sequester to erase the static and stagnation. The more I wandered the world's most crowded places, the harder it was to shake the burdens that had become a part of me: of middle age, of ailing parents and growing children, of regrets, of financial uncertainty and professional precariousness and, perhaps most unbearable of all, technological overload. It was a time of life that required contemplation, which I could achieve neither in the context of my home, where I stewed and spun domestic wheels, nor in a nervous urban swarm of bodies racing to get somewhere. A conundrum began to emerge on repeat: I sought to remedy isolation with greater isolation.

It bears mentioning that striking distance from the Arctic Circle would not be my chosen paradise. I loathe the winter, which, in northwest Connecticut, lasts from mid-November to the end of April. At the moment, though, a beach was a hemisphere away, so I planned to stay indoors and wrap myself in reindeer skins for a few idle days. My lackluster appetite for outdoor adventure, or for being outdoors at all in such glacial temperatures, clearly bewildered Joachim and I found myself a touch embarrassed by it.

"You don't want to ski?" he asked, incredulous.

"I never learned how."

"What about the snowmobile?"

"I don't think so, thank you," I replied, by which I meant, *You're kidding me, right?*

Joachim tried not to look confused. "We can take you in the Caterpillar up to Mount Klöverfjället, or you can go in the helicopter. That would be very nice, to ride in a helicopter. It's very beautiful to see the mountain from the top."

How many more ways could I politely say no? He was the owner of a winter resort and his new charge was a complete dud. I wanted him to believe that I was happy, and that my sense of adventure, however paltry to the naked eye, was already satisfied by this excursion north. I did not need to chase powder on a Snowcat, courting avalanches and frostbite. No one except a friend in Stockholm knew my whereabouts. I did not require much more.

"Does the hotel offer massages?" I was not sure my muscles could withstand another beating but at least it was an activity.

Joachim lit up. "Yes! In fact, we have a new person starting today," he said.

"That's great."

And then, after a moment, he added, "You can also go for walks."

It was mid-week, so, Joachim told me, hotel guests were sparse. There was a fireplace that I could curl up next to and stoke for the next three days. "You will be very happy in the restaurant," he said. "We have a nice wine list and we carry a small-batch local gin which is wonderful."

"Now you're talking," I said.

Eventually, Joachim exited toward Borgafjäll, and into an expansive flash of neon white even more intense than the landscape we'd just traversed for the past three hours. He pointed to two distant peaks that were the town landmarks. "That›s Klöverfjället," he said. "Locals call them 'The Tits,' or more often, 'Anita Ekberg.'" Clouds obscured one of them, the right breast perhaps, but they were wispy ones, like linen curtains on a spring day, and the sky otherwise was sapphire blue. It was not yet 11 A.M. and the sun was low on the horizon.

"This is good for tonight," he said. "You can see the Northern Lights only when the sky is clear."

"What are the chances of seeing them?" I asked. It was the middle of February and because the air tends to be less moist than earlier in the winter, it was, in fact, the optimal viewing time—and we were sixty miles from the Arctic Circle. The Aurora Borealis occurs when electrically charged solar particles collide with atmospheric gases as they are drawn to the North Pole. In fact, I learned, the 11-year cycle of solar activity was predicted to peak in what is dubbed the "Solar Maximum" this winter—so the auroral activity, according to Joachim, had been in full disco throttle. But he knew better than to promise a guest a show, lest nature fail to deliver. I looked warily at the sky.

Hotel Borgafjäll was a low-slung yellow structure built by a famous English architect, Ralph Erskine. Inside, there was a pleasing mid-century vibe, and a skylit seating area around a mod white wood stove, the angled kind you see in books about Scandinavian country houses. As Joachim's wife Gertrud led me to my room, we passed a vitrine where stuffed wildlife from the area was on display in a wintery diorama: an Arctic fox as pale as powder, a snarling lynx, and a snowy owl with a disturbing gaze that was both cross-eyed and direct.

I had heard there were some modern rooms but I didn't get one. Perhaps I overstressed my limited budget in my correspondence with Joachim. It would be fine for sleeping but it was awkward in a kind of vertical way—very tall, very narrow, and very small, with the bed shoehorned into an upper loft space. I navigated back to the aesthetically fascinating main part of the building, across the dorm-like upper floor where my room was located and past the woodland taxidermy. There was a funky, suspended staircase and painted white I-beams that bisected the rooms and ceilings, which jutted and angled in no particular direction. I found my home: the dining room, as welcoming as my little quarters were not.

Gertrud, who also worked in the kitchen, obviously got the skinny from Joachim on their boring new guest.

"You would not like to go to the slopes today?"

She placed warm bread and butter—both made locally, she said—on the table. The fire sparked invitingly.

"Actually, I have a lot of work to do," I said, a blatant lie. Another woman approached the table and introduced herself.

"I'm Johanna," she said. "We have horses. Would you like to go riding in the forest?"

"That's so generous of you," I said, shellacking a smile on my face. By now my apathy had insulted them, their hotel, and in fact the entirety of Lapland if not all of northern Sweden.

"Actually, I don't know how to ride horses."

I've been on a horse exactly once—the same number of times I've been on skis. I began to wonder if there was anything I actually did know how to do besides languish my days away in a state of indolence.

"The horses are very nice and gentle," Johanna said.

"Old and out to pasture would be better," I said.

They laughed. "Tomorrow then."

There was no point in any further refusals. "Maybe a short ride."

The afternoon passed slowly so I ventured outside for a quick walk, in mittens, hat, and the boots I carried overseas for Stockholm's snowy sidewalks. Still, the cold dealt me a body slam when I opened the entrance door, as if it was something tactile and in need of wrangling. At first, the air felt brittle as cut glass, so pure I burst into loud hacks at each inhale, the city expunging itself from my lungs. I sped up to generate warmth. The drifts were higher than I was and my footsteps made a sound like creaking floorboards. There was a tinge of daylight, dim and transparent. I passed by a small church designed by the same architect as the hotel and peered inside. My face grew numb while the brief stroll turned into two hours, then three. My body was moving, heated, forcing me ahead as if I rode a conveyor belt, farther from the hotel. My head was undcluttered and thoughts almost blank. I did not pass a soul on the road.

There was little to see but a bleached-looking landscape embellished in parts by a green-black tree line somewhere, two, or maybe two hundred, miles away. It was difficult to gauge distance at all. Though the vista was uniform, every new angle from every corner startled me just the same. Sweat prickled my stomach and between my shoulder blades and pooled in the waistband of my jeans when I veered toward foreign territory: the ski area.

It was strange to grow up in New England and never learn to schuss down a mountain. My father was an Italian from Tucson, first of all, and second, he worked every weekend of my childhood. While my friends hauled off for Vermont on Friday afternoons, I stayed home and baked Toll House cookies all winter. Skiing wasn't in his, or subsequently our, vernacular. So when my husband and I moved to the countryside, I was determined that my kids should tackle what I never had. For a few years, I dragged them on Wednesdays and Sundays to the mountain near our house and had them kitted out for lessons. At one time, I thought I'd join them, but instead, opted to toast my bones in the lodge by an ancient fireplace, at tables carved with initials and encrusted with ketchup and French fry grease. I always fretted until I saw their little bodies at the bottom of the run. Such adventure sports involving speed and risk and ice were not among the range of hobbies knitted into my DNA.

Inside the lodge was a shop, and the surroundings were familiar from those times with my children, as was the welcome warmth. Skis lined up in colored stripes against the walls, kids with pink faces trudged in boots. I even recognized the wet smell of the worn carpet underfoot. Behind the equipment rental room was a snack bar, with antler chandeliers poised above tables full of skiers exuding the hale flush of exhaustion. I wished for a fraction of their spent physicality. My lips unfroze to sip hot tea and chew a few forkfuls of chocolate cake. Passing back through the store, I turned and headed for the counter, where a man bent over a metal contraption, waxing skis.

"Do you offer lessons for cross country?" I asked.

"Yes, but our teacher is away for the week," he said.

"Is it hard?"

"Once you get used to it, it's like walking but you'll need to practice."

"Can I reserve a pair of skis for tomorrow?" I asked.

I filled out a form, leaving my name and a deposit of SEK 100, and departed the lodge with a written commitment to teach myself to cross country ski the next day. I assumed I would cancel, but I was no longer brooding when I got back to the hotel, or dreading interactions with Gertrud et al. There were only a few of us at dinner, including the new massage guy whom I had booked for the following day. The meal was magnificent—even the sliced reindeer. I was ashamed to tell these nice people that for the moment I was not eating meat, either, so I swallowed all of it, as well as Arctic Char from Malgomaj, the death lake. It had been an entire day since I'd checked my emails or my credit card balance. No texts from the kids far away at school. Exhausted, I sauntered to my room to get ready for bed.

Just before switching off the light, I remembered the Northern Lights and Joachim's prediction that the conditions were ideal. I was warm, deliciously at peace, but I forced myself down the ladder and back into my boots. The hotel bar was hopping, and I prayed no one would glance outside to see the woman with a down coat thrown over her nightclothes looking up at the sky.

I walked around, inhaling the cut crystal air, seduced by the thought of the warm bed I just abandoned. I jogged to the road to battle my apathy, promising myself a deep slumber if I could be patient for once, to persist in this bitter cold a few more minutes. After scanning the sky for flashes of celestial energy, looking one way and then the other, I went inside and slid into bed.

A few minutes later, unable to sleep, I lurched out of bed again and piled the layers back on. The wine had leached from my body and now I was colder and emptier. I half-ran out to the road once more, where I spun around and observed the waif of a new moon and the stars, chrome studs shimmering against a violet sky. The chill lodged in my joints and my ears tingled from the sharp, windless air. I waved my arms to keep the blood flowing.

I know, the Aurora Borealis is a crapshoot, like spotting a pod of whales in a boat off Cabo. I could not fight my fatigue anymore so I wandered back to the front door, buying a little time with slow, deliberate steps. My neck ached from craning it skyward.

The air crackled so softly it almost hissed, and I turned to the source of the noise. To the north, above the hotel apartments, I saw a corner of the heavens illuminated with a swoosh of ghostly green light. The colors seemed to brush against my face as they swirled against the black stretch of horizon. I heard a murmur of people exiting the bar to watch the spectacle. We stood silently, then cried in pleasure at the shifts in this great supernal tableau. The sky flared and unleashed a rolling arc, watery flashes of electric green and blue. The lights contracted from a wide stripe to a thin yellow-green band. When it disappeared, I finally exhaled. I had not dared to breathe.

The next morning, Johanna insisted on taking me for a horseback ride. I tried to refuse, mentioning my upcoming ski excursion, but there was a softness about her insistence and frankly, I was somewhat worn down. The lethargy I desired looked like a problem to them, a petulance or perhaps a defect that needed rectifying with bucking up, Swedish optimism, and even more suggestions. As she drove me to the stables, Johanna confirmed it was a banner season for Northern Lights. "It was a small one last night," she said, "but I never get tired of seeing it."

The wind puffed in long crescendos, yesterday's sun had vanished, and I was about to mount a horse for the second time ever. The barn had the universally sour and fresh smell of hay, which many people apparently love, and the animals, of the Northern Swedish breed, were enormous. She introduced me to my ride and I astonished myself and my frozen heart by loving him immediately, despite the fact that he was a giant and seemed in very hale health. I did not reveal to Johanna my next piece of bad news: that I'm allergic to horses. I did have an urge to ride, once, when my daughter started taking lessons in a stable on our street (about the same time I enrolled her in ski classes) but I suppose I chickened out and bagged that, too, what with my allergies and congenital fear of everything.

"See how kind he is?" she said. "His name is Besten, which means Beast."

"Not encouraging, by the way," I said.

"It also means "the best." She smiled.

Johanna stroked him and whispered both to me and to him. "You'll be fine, I promise." She handed me a brush and showed me how to groom his coat, and where to scratch him. I dutifully obliged, careful not to inhale too deeply and start wheezing. I caught him squarely in the eyes. "Friends, okay?"

Johanna draped a saddle over Besten, then mounted her horse with ease, and riding bareback. I donned a helmet that was too tight over my wool cap, and we headed into the woods. Though I was surely terrified, I was also exhilarated. The horse trotted too quickly over deep snow but soon my thigh muscles relaxed enough to tighten properly and I settled into his pace. We crossed over rocks and brooks, past thickets of birch and rows of giant spruce that seemed to close in on us like encroaching spiked walls. We sauntered up and down a few steep hills, and when my body lurched parallel to the ground, Besten made a split-second recalibration, helped me reposition, and kept me from tumbling off. We had ridden a few miles when Johanna led us into a pine glade for lunch, where we tied up the horses. She unwrapped cheese sandwiches and a thermos of coffee and we settled on a blanket into a snowbank. The sky was nearly as dark as the treeline, a looming barricade of evergreens that resembled a strip of pitch-black spears. I thought of nothing but what I was: far, far away, and what I was not: miserable.

I envied Johanna's ease with the horses and the forbidding terrain. I envied her competence and knowledge and clear-eyed purpose and positivity. She bought a house in Borgafjall with her husband, who ran the ski area and simply loved this magnificent place.

"So why did *you* decide to come here?" she asked.

"You mean, and not ski?" I asked. We laughed. "Just for a break."

"Life is very complex," she said as we fixed our eyes on the frozen horizon and prepared for the hour's ride back to the stables.

Back at the hotel, I was exhausted and a little wired from the exertion. The muscles inside my thighs had fashioned a clamp around Besten and now they burned like fire. I reluctantly ate elk sausage for lunch and felt my stomach churn in the aftermath. At last, I wandered outside in my usual cold weather get-up and my feet led me in the direction of the ski lodge. My acquaintance in the shop welcomed me with my rented equipment, unfortunately freshly waxed, which I carted over my shoulder back to the hotel. I dialed my husband.

"Hi, I'm in Lapland," I said.

"You're what?"

"In Lapland. I just rented cross country skis." Mark skied almost every morning on the trails near our house. "Can you give me some pointers?"

"Wow!" He'd never once convinced me to join him, despite asking me daily. He had only reluctantly accepted the fact that, even if I was from New England, I disliked being outside in winter, especially if it involved breaking a sweat.

"It's cold but for some reason, it's not bothering me," I said. "So I figured, why not?"

"Way to go!" he said. "Lift the heel of the back foot as you push forward on the front leg. The poles are key."

"Here goes nothing."

Gertrud directed me to the trails right behind the hotel. Shortly, I was winded, dripping perspiration, crawling, sliding, struggling to keep my legs parallel and loose. Strapping Swedes with gaunt cheeks and high-tech outdoor gear whizzed past me. The route sloped downward and I accelerated for about 200 yards before I lost control and pitched headfirst into the snow.

Awkwardly and with great difficulty, I got to my knees and then to standing, and clicked my skis back into place. Before long, though, I was spent. It was strange to see my feet in ski boots as they trod across the whiteness toward the lodge. In them, I was a different person, all legs and athleticism and heartbeat, without a thought except to walk steady and not slip. I saw my breath but no longer felt the cold.

Back at the hotel, I met up with Johanna, who confirmed my massage the next day. "You are okay?" she asked.

At dinner, four snowmobilers on a guys' getaway invited me to their table and offered to share their fine Bordeaux.

"You have never been on a snowmobile?" one of them, an executive for a mountaineering equipment firm, asked me. He was incredulous, but I replied that what he thought I was missing, I actually wasn't.

"You have to come with us tomorrow," another said. "We are going 25 miles to Saxnos."

We debated it after dinner by the fireplace, over cognac and the local gin. Too dangerous, I maintained. Nonsense, they replied. It's the Nordic way of life!

At breakfast, they were all there, my drinking buddies, in swell outdoor attire—tangerine Gore-Tex and chartreuse Microfiber shells. "You can still change your mind," one of them cried across the room.

I laughed. "Thanks anyway."

Gertrud was sitting at the next table, and she informed me that the new masseuse had quit after one day. "Lapland is very far," she said, nodding, then fixing me with a now familiar stare. "Joachim and I are going out on the snowmobile to put some restaurant flyers on the trail." My stomach gripped tightly. Oh brother. I knew what was coming next. "Why don't you come?"

I was not getting any thinking done, nor had I been able to submerge myself in a pool of thoughts. But the night before, I had barely touched the pillow when my pleasant dreams began, arising, no doubt, out of my extreme well-being. I could no longer deny that the Arctic air up here in the north was clearing my head. I was healthier than I was when I arrived two days ago and I had her persistence in large part to thank.

"As long as it's safe," I said, thinking of Lake Malgomaj and the reckless adventurers. "Please, will you go slow?"

I held onto Gertrud while Joachim sped up ahead. The acrid odor of exhaust wafted around us, and I worried about befouling the virginal air, but not as much as I feared calamity and my own vulnerability on this contraption. "Slow" for her was still too fast for me, and I tightly squeezed her waist. When she took a sharp corner, we dipped toward the ground like a listing ship. I imagined the motor slicing into my frozen neck. But always, she righted the machine, as Besten had done with his body. "We're fine, don't worry," she reassured me, sailing nimbly and rapidly into a field of pure, solid white.

We parked the snowmobiles and climbed to a cluster of round wooden huts, built by the reindeer-herding and often nomadic Sami, the indigenous groups of far northern Scandinavia and Russia. The crumbling structures were buried under caps of snow and inside, remains of fires blackened the walls. They were long abandoned. We clambered from one to the other and peered behind the disintegrating doors and soon resumed our trek.

Gertrud zoomed, allowing me to firm my grasp as we rose higher on the mountain. Joachim hammered stakes near the snowmobile tracks, and affixed flyers to them, which advertised restaurant specials for the following weekend. They were expecting a full house and, he told me, these same trails will be packed. Today, they were empty.

When we stopped, the cold, which had already lodged into the creases of my cheeks, nose and lips, wended its way under my coat, even under the ski pants Johanna lent me, even beneath the layer of thermal fabric closest to my skin. The couple had stopped for fika—the Swedish ritual of drinking coffee. We were in a clearing, in full view of the majestic white tits of Anita Ekberg, under a sky so blue and so loaded with atmospheric gases that this night, we might see the whole horizon transform again into a halo of lime-green liquid light.

Gertrud splashed a drop of milk into my cup. The hot drink tempered the Arctic air that engulfed us in every direction. The cookies, too, warmed me, the sensation of sugar against tongue, the comfort of sustenance. None of us rushed to finish our coffee but soon I climbed astride the snowmobile and clutched Gertrud. The elements were relentless, just as they are under a Caribbean sun from which, eventually, you need to seek shade.

As we rode back, the sky clouded over until it was a gray fluff of a coverlet poised just above the contrasting whiteness of the ground. There would be no Northern Lights tonight, but I was certain there would be something else to stumble upon and surprise me. I don't quite recognize the person these hardy Swedes had turned me into over the last days but I was getting fond of her. In fact, I might like to spend a little more time with her, engaged in anything, actually, but contemplation.

Chapter 29

Winter (with apologies to Colette)

*S*hut the door! It's freezing outside. I haven't been warm since November—or was it October?—when I first removed my fur-lined boots from where they were stored in the back of the front hall closet, and brushed the dust off them. My house is cold, my car is cold, my bathrobe is cold. I'm cold.

It's been winter forever. Icicles hang from the eaves and a few of them touch the ground. Some won't even budge from the force of Mark's 30-pound sledgehammer. When I come inside, I leave my jacket on, and sometimes my hat. I've been rotating through the same fleece sweatpants, the same thermal turtlenecks, for months.

Right now, I don't care about lipstick or high heels or present-able hair. Or trousers that flatter. I want to be warm. We are living on top of a glacier. The house is drafty and icy air daggers between the window sashes, too warped to properly close. To help, I build a fire. I go out to the porch to collect wood from the pile. I neglected to fetch my gloves for the chore, and logs give me splinters which I can't feel until my hands thaw. I should have waited for Mark to get back up from the studio. The cold has made me impatient.

Somewhere under the tundra are my sage plant, my raised vegetable beds, and my orange princess tulips that will experience some kind of sensory memory and reappear in April. By then, I might have forgotten this frigid winter. By then, the chill that has commandeered my bloodstream may have vanished and passed out of memory.

I'm cold. The dog is cold. He won't go outside, and when he does, he comes in and licks the pads of his paws, which must sting. Then, he sits on my lap, or on Mark's, and the heat from his fur seeps through to our thighs. I assume that we heat him up, too. Everybody's content.

I see the pear, the lilac, the peach trees. I don't know if they will survive these days and nights of being encased in ice. The peonies are buried, but not the memory of their blushing heads that burnish June evenings with color and scent. The magnolia tree has gotten bashed around each time the plow has come. The dune of snow keeps growing beside it, and several branches have cracked off. I don't know if it's dead or alive. I love the week in spring when it blooms stark white. The petals drop to the ground almost as soon as the blossoms appear and the tree starts to look empty—plain and green—again. For now, the shovel is lodged in the snow bank around the tree's broken limbs. I chip some ice off the steps and walk inside. "Let's make a fire, honey," I call out to Mark. "I'm so cold."

I carry the groceries and my daughter who is 13, follows me with her backpack. "I'm so cold!" she cries. Without unzipping my coat, I put some milk on the stove and stir in some cocoa. My hands are rough and chapped and I see that my daughter's are too. We drink hot chocolate together and don't say much. I pour a few drops of heavy cream into her mug. She smiles and I do too.

I'm too cold to work. Not Mark, who is outside all winter. But this year, he's spent more time than usual de-icing rather than carving his sculptures, which he has to do each day before he can work on them again. I abandon my computer and walk to the window. From the house, the yard looks vast and there are almost no markings in the sheet of ice that covers it. If my children were still small, I would not let them sled down that frozen hill. Once, Ray's head smacked a mound of ice while sliding, and we took him to the hospital with a concussion. He had been miffed that I made him strap on a helmet. The helmet saved his life, the doctor said.

I picture them on a steamy summer night out back, with Mark at the grill in a faded gray tee-shirt. The air fills with the smell of hamburgers and cut grass. The lawn freshly mown, my hands rough from digging weeds. The periphery of the yard is strewn with daisies, and my neck is damp with sweat. After dinner, we go out for ice cream. Mint chocolate chip for me, with hot fudge sauce.

At night the wind groans as it drags itself across the fields of snow. We hear something bang and crash, and Mark goes downstairs to make sure the roofs and walls are intact from the weight of ice. All clear. We wait to be lulled to sleep by the ceaseless baritone of the wind.

I am afraid the post-apocalyptic ice planet I inhabit of late is beginning to sap me of sanity. The whiteness is making me wonder if my eyes can process color anymore. The arctic landscape is unchanging by the day, and the weather report says there's going to be more of the same.

In the morning, I go outside and start the car. The cold catches in my throat and makes me cough. I see what was making all the clatter last night: our Christmas tree, which had been dumped way out back down the hill, blew its way back up and around to the front steps, as if wanting to be invited back inside. The dashboard thermometer reads 9 degrees.

Two hours later, after a blissful drive with my heat blasting, I open the car door onto West 16th Street in New York City. It's freezing. I forgot to bring my hat and the wind whips across the avenues, slices up my coat sleeve and smashes into my face. When

I meet an editor for lunch, I can barely speak since my mouth is nearly frozen shut. How do people live here? How did I live here once? How did I stroll two babies along blocks of skyscrapers on streets sluiced with bitter wind? I really don't know. It is freezing at home, but it is colder here as my feet, numb as stumps, thump the sidewalks between city's canyon walls. I imagine my blood frozen into delicate snowflake patterns.

On the way back, my car is a rolling furnace of pleasure, a tropical paradise. I peg the heat to 86 degrees—the highest it will go. Back at home, Mark has stoked the fire and all of downstairs is incandescent from the glow that jumps from the walls to the floors. I sink into a couch and bask in the warmth. After dinner, I draw a bath and put some oil in it to make me think of July. Rose and lavender, geranium and rosemary. From outside the bathroom, Mark asks what smells so good. Later, I make us some tea and crawl under two down comforters. "I have never been so cold," I say. The ice in my bones begins to crack and melt, and as I thaw, I begin to shiver under the blankets.

"In forty days, it will be April," says Mark.

Chapter 30

Time or the Sahara Wind

There's a photograph from my first visit to Morocco in which I appear as if on the floor of a canyon. Behind me is a cinematic backdrop: a towering pomegranate-red clay mountainside speckled with clusters of trees. I'm standing on a wide-open restaurant terrace, wearing white Capri pants and a black tank top, sneakers with socks. The wind blows my hair into chaos but one hand pushes the bangs off my face. In the corner, over my shoulder, there is a sliver of Matisse-blue sky. I am twenty-four years old.

A few hours from Marrakech, I arrived at this place, wherever it was, to the staggering sight of the mountains opening up beyond the valley. Then, I heard my mother's voice. "I'm just out of words," she said as her narrow foot swung lightly out of the car into the sunshine. "Isn't it something?"

My mother documented that trip to Morocco as she did everything in her life. Perfectly. Painstakingly. With the observant eye of a woman who was born an artist, but in a time and place where it would never have occurred to her actually to be one. Me stroking a carpet or chatting with a merchant at the souk, my sandaled foot in the stirrup of each camel I rode (there were, I'm afraid, more than one), the cluster of mimosa branches that riffled beyond the hotel window—it was all preserved on film. Back at home, my mother's deft hands slid the photographs into the pages of albums, which were left untouched for decades like forgotten or overlooked monuments.

The photos seem to be brushed with a brownish glaze. Maybe it's the passage of time, but perhaps it was the grit from the *chergui*, the wind from the Sahara that blows west across the Atlas Mountains and through Marrakech, Meknès, Ouarzazate, carrying fine particles of rust-colored sand. It was ferocious that year in the fall of 1985. The dust hung and thickened the air but it was also invisible, and may have left a film on the lens of my mother's camera, giving the snapshots a tawny cast that dimmed the brights of morning and churned the milkiness of the clouds.

The fine orange coating on my skin made it erupt with tiny hives upon arriving in Marrakech; some memories of the trip now seem as if they were filtered through a pleasant Benadryl haze. Even the novel I was reading poolside at the Hotel Mamounia— *The Mists of Avalon*—bears remnants of this dry desert wind. The paperback stands in my bookshelf, smudged with fingerprints the color of dried blood on pages stippled from pool water that dripped from my hair and dried in the heat. My mother photographed that, too. Her youngest daughter, asleep in her bikini, stretched out on a chaise under the prickly sun with a book resting on her stomach.

There are no photos of my mother from that trip. This is the fate of many mothers, who are so busy capturing memories for the family archives that their existence is obscured behind the camera. But even if she is invisible, her presence is everywhere in the sheets of these two albums, collections of moments she created, assembled and enshrined. In each picture, she is there, reflected in my own eyes that faced both her and her camera. Back then, on the green lenses of her sunglasses, I saw the moving pinprick that was me looking at her. Her arms, legs and face were browned, and her short hair tousled from the stifling wind that rolled across the terrace. She grasped the camera and when the shutter snapped, her engagement ring, and the other one with a row of tiny rubies, flashed white in the sun.

This is the version of my mother that passes through me when I am half awake. I want not to forget the image of her as she was, vitality intact. Thirty years have passed and today her mind is a vacant chamber, her voice often a profusion of unrelated syllables. Occasionally she can muster up decipherable language, but rarely context for the words that emerge. In Morocco, with her suntan and the skin still tight across her cheekbones, her eyes were almost sapphire dark. Today, her hair is a tangle of white semi-waves that the staff at her memory care home frequently grooms back into place. That, plus the pale skin on her face render her eyes a vibrant, almost pastel, blue. I have looked at them forever but only really notice them now. Her gaze is direct but tinged with opacity, and I cannot know what it sees. Though she is alive, her life is behind her. So I seek her out by studying photographs not of her, but of me. It is in this gathering of images, through the negative space she dominates completely in every frame, that I understand, miss, and grasp most urgently for the woman she once was.

I don't think my mother was searching for much when she first inhaled the sweet, orange-flower air in Marrakech, but Morocco was where she found herself. It was a midlife bloom, the triumphant gift of the empty nest. My father, a cardiologist, was asked to look after King Hassan II's heart and occasionally made a house call to Rabat, Casablanca, Marrakech—wherever the monarch was in residence at the time—with my mother always by his side. They traveled in style on these brief jaunts to North Africa, but that was the least of it. My mother was from humble New England stock, an academic wife and a far cry from a social climber. She was pretty but plain, barely wore makeup and certainly never colored her gray-streaked, short-cropped hair. In Boston, it was undignified to make pains to turn back the clock. Maybe it was the suntan, or the sudden swoosh of plum lipstick, or the muscular legs taken out of their suburban context that descended from her light summer dresses, but in Morocco she blossomed like a teenager into a beauty.

The extra-big seat on the plane pleased her, as did the little dopp kit with Hermès perfume, and once in Morocco, the official car and driver who ferried her to the souks, to other cities and across the streams and valleys of the countryside. In Boston, my father was known and beloved for his dedication to his patients, his medical school students, to medicine—to being a physician and healing—writ large. But his success had a price. He also worked 18-hour days, seven days a week, leaving my mother to raise four daughters essentially alone. I can't imagine her exhaustion when she packed me, the youngest, off to college. Sometimes I wish I had asked her how she celebrated that first night in an empty house. If she celebrated. Perhaps she wept, now that the second half of her life sprawled before her and there was no grand plan, and her husband still left her alone each day before dawn toward the work that fulfilled him.

Like most women married in 1955, she had given up her own work as a nurse to be a wife and mother. It's still not clear to me if it made her happy or if she ever stopped to consider what she was sacrificing. Sometimes, I saw resentment simmer beneath her unadorned exterior. Her husband was a well-known physician, which in a city like Boston was a distinct kind of celebrity. She was only his wife. I don't know what my mother questioned, if she ever questioned anything. I never asked her that either. I knew she loved us and that was all.

After her first trip to Morocco, it was clear that the country filled the great gaps that had opened in her life. She lunched with new friends. She devoured tagines swimming with candied lemon peel and tart black olives. She gazed up at the ramrod-straight palm trees crowned with sprays of leaves splayed like feather dusters. She reclined by the pool in the prickly sun, halted her steps to savor the dry breeze that blew across her face at nightfall, and loved to divert for a spontaneous meal of fresh fish and chilled wine on the beach in Essaouira. She trod her sandals over the green tiles and past the bougainvillea that grew in thickets along ramparts. She marveled at the oversized crowns of roses, two feet high and two feet wide, that His Majesty left in my parents' hotel room on each visit. She was dazzled by the mottled ochre walls and the lyrical disarray of the souks.

She was delighted that she, that daughter of a quarryman with an eighth-grade education, could visit the palace of the king she was invited by; but her real exhilaration came from how effortlessly she could transpose herself onto this strange and beautiful place, and freely seek refuge there. Sometimes, she stayed on after my father's medical work was done, even for a few days, unscheduled and on her own. She was entirely and happily liberated for the first time in her life and hungry to explore the country where she felt embraced and at ease. She was still my father's spouse there, but more than that too. She was unfettered, and did not have to look around her empty house and wonder where her four daughters had gone. Morocco dictated the flowing words of her second chapter.

And she wanted to share this new passion with me. As the youngest of the girls (though not the favorite by any stretch), I was often the lucky beneficiary of my parent's newly free spirits. I was the last one at home, suddenly an only child, so during those two years after my next-oldest sister left, I cleaned up on travel. My parents took me along when they could: to London, to Greece, to California to visit my father's parents, to the Soviet Union and elsewhere. Maybe also they felt guilty about all the hand-me-down clothes I had to wear, the incessant teasing, or the shorn pixie haircut my mother, weary after three older girls in braids, inflicted on me.

That year, in 1985, while I stewed over changes both professional and in love, I was invited to join them in Morocco. When I arrived, I swooned at the dusky interior light, the fountains that spilled into pools scattered with rose petals, the richly-colored Berber carpets and the detailed woodwork on the lobby columns. Then I headed to the bar and in a brazen act of cliché, ordered a coupe of the house champagne—maybe, it was even Pol Roger, the favorite of Winston Churchill, who, in 1947, decamped here, to this hotel, to write his memoirs.

We drove to the Atlas Mountains, to Meknès and the great Roman ruins of Volubilis. In the photographs, often there are others alongside me and my father, strangers who were in my life too briefly to remember their names: Moroccan physicians, their wives perhaps, the driver, who always joined us for lunch. But in almost every image in the album, I appear.

Here I stand behind my own bouquet of roses—hundreds of red, yellow, pink and white blooms bursting over a vase—on the terrace of my room. I am wrapped in a robe and my eyes are puffy. I had been crying and though we hadn't discussed it, my mother knew—how could she not? I had received a pleading telegram at the Mamounia from the man I had left, and my face bore the stain of anguish.

In another one, I am standing in front of a massive carved doorway, eyes puffy from sobbing, or sun, or my allergy to the microscopic particulate matter suspended in the air.

"Isn't it beautiful?" she asks as she shoots. She is impossibly slim, in tan trousers and a light blue blouse. She affixes the lens cap and stuffs the camera into her canvas tote. She hoists a bottle of water and takes a gulp.

"Are you thirsty, honey?" she asks. "Do you need sunscreen?"

Sometimes she photographed me doing business with the basket-makers in the souk, or buying a round of freshly-baked bread, or ordering a glass of tea jammed with mint leaves at the hotel restaurant. I am beside a donkey and my hand grazes the saddle. I seem intent while loading film into my own camera, or a tad awkward with a troupe of dancing girls in long brocaded caftans swaying behind me. Shoulders bared, I am in a sarong that is wrapped around me like a dress, seated on a mosaic fountain. In the pool behind me float thousands of roses cut from the stems. I look annoyed.

"Mom, please," I likely said to her. "All you do is take pictures."

"You look so pretty, honey," she would have said, and then sat beside me on the tiled ledge, listening to the splash of water into the basin.

There are many shots of my father and me at a restaurant, sitting around a table with her chair empty after she jumped up to chronicle the moment. As I look at the album now, I imagine her seated the second before the snapshot, opening our bottle of Sidi Ali water, mothering me to smithereens, asking if I like the stewed pumpkin or the lamb couscous I'd ordered for lunch. I am comforted with the assurance that when I smiled into the lens, I was really smiling at her. My mother.

She loved to take pictures when I wasn't looking, as I do now with my own children. She was fascinated by this entity she gave life to, and the sight of me seemed to never bore or tire her. In one shot, I lean over a pile of oranges. Looking at this photo, I experience a rush of the tart citrusy smell that traveled to my brain and remains there today. She snapped me with my eyes closed on a bench in the Majorelle Gardens. She captured me time after time with my face tilted up to catch the sun. I appear entranced, as if in meditation, but I was only grabbing a moment to turn myself a deeper shade of brown.

My mother was always there.

My mother is always there.

I returned to Morocco many times, several with my parents. I went to weddings and New Year's parties, but they were more rushed affairs, never with the desultory pace of my first trip with them. Occasionally I flew down from Paris, when I lived there. My parents returned countless times until King Hassan II died in Rabat in 1999. They had seen everything by then and still had never seen enough. My mother shot rolls and rolls of film on her travels there, but it was only during that first, perfect visit that she documented me with such persistence, as if she suspected I'd reach for these photos as an anchor thirty years later. Those photographs are aging more slowly than we are and in them, I feel not just the presence of the woman who loved me; more intensely, I sense a woman I knew, someone exactly my age now who was tackling her hard-earned freedom with wonder, openness, and a sense of abandon. She hurled herself upon the big, open landscape of Morocco and found her place in the world.

Twenty-five years had passed since she first landed in Casablanca, and she was well into her seventies, when she realized she wouldn't return. In truth, these cross-ocean voyages were trying, even in first class. Even so, she mourned the end of her travels there with enough grief and nostalgia to make it clear that the sense of loss was for something more than just Morocco and maybe a decent couscous (something that never quite made its way to Boston).

Then came her decline. It was slow, but inevitable. These days, my mother's sweet little room at her Alzheimer's home is decorated with a few things, now relics, from the souks she roamed so freely. Over the years, she amassed a lot of stuff, most of all carpets that seemed to be delivered with stunning frequency; she could not resist another tactile remembrance of the place she loved and belonged. There is a small woven basket, a little silver tea pitcher with a long spout. On the wall is a framed menu from one of the king's New Year's parties, engraved with gold and royal blue script, all in French. When I visit her there, I like to chat about her travels to Casablanca, Marrakech, or Fez, as if mentioning them might unstick a secret door to a clear, bright place.

"How many times did you go?" I ask. "A hundred?"

"That first trip with you and Dad was one of the best times of my life. Remember how happy you were to show me the Jemaa el Fna?" I ask.

"There must have been a million roses in those bouquets," I say.

"I hate the bones in pigeon pie," I say. "Don't you?"

Last time I went to see her, I brought a photograph. It's impossible to know what an Alzheimer's patient is seeing, and least of all remembering. "My favorite picture of me ever is from Morocco," I say. "You took it."

I open my purse and remove an envelope, which contains the shot of me on that great open terrace, under a brilliant slice of sky with the clay slopes behind me. Like all the others from that year, the picture is tinged a slight rusty brown. I was a young woman with a lustrous complexion and now, I am fifty-six with wrinkles and sunspots.

She looks at it. "Yes," she says.

"You can't see yourself, but you are there," I say.

She nods.

"You took this picture. You were wearing a gray flare skirt, a navy short-sleeved blouse and little blue flats that day."

She stares.

"In this picture, I am looking at you. You are younger and you are beautiful. You are my age, the age I am now. And you are looking at me," I say.

She stares.

"I am Marcia, your youngest daughter, and you showed me Morocco."

She tilts her head.

"Here," I say. "This is me, and I'm looking right at you."

She turns her face to me. Her hair is unruly, and though she is usually tidy, there are drops of soup on her sweater. She grasps my hand. Her skin is smooth and her touch is feathery, like the graze of a filmy scarf.

"Except I have no idea where this is. Near Marrakech? I just don't remember," I laugh.

She fixates on the photo again.

"Do you know where this is?" I ask. "You know Morocco better than anyone."

She turns her face up to me, suddenly alert, and a smile unfolds across her face. The gray creases brighten, her mouth unfreezes, her whole aspect alters in a millisecond from moribund to sunny. Her eyes a shattering blue.

"Yes!" she shouts, startling me. My mother takes the photograph from my hand, sets it on the table beside her, and closes her eyes. Her lips are still turned upward in a smile, but within seconds her face is glazed with tears. I reach over her and take the photograph, slip it back into the envelope.

She grasps my hand again and squeezes gently. Her fingers brush mine with a light sound, soft as the rustle of mimosa blossoms, yellow as the morning, on a warm night in Marrakech.

Chapter 31

Take Me With You

An hour from Marrakech, a car delivers my friend and me to Imlil for a day-hike in the High Atlas Mountains. Judging by the heavy-gauge North Face jacket and ice-climbing boots worn by our guide Abderrahim, it's clear I've miscalculated trekking in Morocco in February. I scan the snowy peaks and wonder how I will fare in my paltry jacket. And there he is. He sits patiently, about five feet from me, looking timid and cold. His head tilts downward, and although there is no eye contact, I sense he knows I'm there. I'm overtaken by a swell of tenderness. I say to my friend, "I think this guy just AirDropped me his heart."

I have fallen for a dog before, one whose face or spirit or gentle demeanor drew me in, but it was never like this. This time, it is instantaneous, maternal, and heavy with the twin yearnings of sympathy and empathy. Not to mention need. My grown children are away at school, and I am desperate for their company, even for a phone call asking for money or socks. My husband and I knock around our empty house, and I mother their rooms as I mothered them. I smooth out my daughter's duvet and dust my son's basketball trophies as if these barren gestures were direct expressions of love. And then there is my own mother, in her new dementia facility, issuing forth an incoherent streak of words with the same mouth she once coated with Revlon's Love that Pink, the same mouth she kissed my forehead with, the same with which she blew on a spoonful of spaghetti sauce before tasting it.

When I see this beautiful creature, I am not thinking of how supple a muscle is the human heart and how quickly it makes room for what it requires.

He is a handsome dog, medium-sized and in need of a brushing and a bath. When he approaches me, my arms ache with the urge to pat his black and white coat, so I reach for the dark matted fur behind his ears. He looks up, and I physically weaken over his expression of sadness and devotion.

"That's just how dogs look!" says my friend. "Look how his tail is wagging."

"Does he belong to anyone?" I ask Abderrahim.

"He's a village dog."

"Does he have enough to eat?" I ask.

"People feed him scraps."

"Does he have a name?" Abderrahim shakes his head. Now he does. I call him Gus, same as my dog at home, the sweet boy we found in an attempt to fill the void when the kids grew up.

He trots alongside as we set forth. Abderrahim hands us ski poles and, noting our pathetic outdoor gear, offers, "How about we cross the valley and have a meal at my house? It's still a decent hike."

The land spreads out before us. On the uneven trail, we cross the riverbed and I stumble on a wet stone. Gus stands by, concerned. Once, in the brightness of the ravine, the snowy path turns to packed desert sand. I drink in the spectacular scenery, the Atlas Mountains whose jagged folds gather up on all four sides. I throw a stick for him to fetch.

"You're such a good boy," I tell him. "Who's a good boy? Gus is a good boy."

We arrive at Abderrahim's terrace on the edge of another crowded village and are served almonds, bread, honey from his apiary. He places a plate of popcorn onto the large tray and tells us it's from corn he grows out back. A stream of mint tea is poured into glasses, and I cup mine with both hands. Above us, the graceful snow-covered cone of Mount Toubkal juts high into a deep blue sky. The air is almost warm.

We give Gus bread, and Abderrahim sets down a bowl of water. The dog curls into a pool of sunlight, plunks his head on my foot, and begins to snore. He is content. I am content. At this moment on earth, I need nothing more.

"Come on boy," I say. We begin our hike back through the valley, now a vessel filled with hard sunshine. He gets ahead of us and looks back frequently, checking on our progress. I dread the end of this day. There is no love as haunting as the one that is abandoned, and I know that he and I don't stand a chance. My steps are firmer on the way back, now that I have grown accustomed to the terrain.

Up the path is a group of schoolboys, and one of them throws a stone at Gus, and then another taunts him with a stick. The dog races back to my side. I am horrified at the adolescent cruelty and stricken with disgust. My hands inexplicably ball into fists, of helplessness and indignance. Abderrahim yells at the boys in Arabic.

"It's just stupid kids," he says.

"It's alright, Gus," I say. "Pay no mind."

Once, walking home from school, a boy pelted me with snowballs and one was filled with a rock. It hit my temple and my blue knit cap slipped off as I collapsed on the snow in front of my house. Once, a group of girls shut the door of their clubhouse on my daughter, after first calling her fat and dumb. On this day in the mountains of Morocco, I could not help this dog as my mother had soothed me, as I consoled my daughter. I could only whisper to him that he's better than all those boys.

Back in the village, our taxi idles. At my ankles, Gus looks worried and sits at the side of the road. His head is capsized again, gaze fixed on the ground. I scratch his ears, tell him what an excellent dog he is.

We edge into the car back to Marrakech. Out the back windshield, I see Gus begin to run after us. The driver accelerates on the sandy mountain road, and the dog accelerates too.

"I can't look," I say to my friend.

"He'll be okay," she says. "This is his home."

I look anyway, for two, maybe three minutes. He follows, follows, follows, a mad dash to keep up. My body is freighted with agony. He does not slow his pace even as the road smooths out and our car gains speed. Finally, he stops. He stands in a cloud of red dust frothed up from the car, and his beautiful head is raised high. We stare hard at each other as his face carves its way into my memory. In his eyes I see every regret, every loss, every desolate hour I've ever lived. But I hope that in mine, he can see sparks of pure, true, and urgent love. We had a sweet day, Gus and I.

"You sure live in a beautiful place," I say to the speck that is his face. The High Atlas peaks tumble across the horizon, and in the middle of them, Mount Toubkal rises like a giant.

Chapter 32

Signs of Life and Death in Africa

*I*t was the stillest of days, with no suggestion that bad news was barreling toward me in the ether. I had just settled back at our campsite with coffee and a handful of rusks, South African sweet biscuits. I was on safari, on assignment in Botswana, and after a morning hike, I paused to take stock of all I had seen. Bursts of yellow stockroses, baboons in lotus position, four-toed footprints on a hippo path, swooping bee-eaters with lime green jackets. It was a lot of beauty for one morning.

Two days prior, our guide Simon Byron had steered me here, with my photographer colleague Felix Odell, through swampy channels lined with papyrus reeds. We were deep in the labyrinth of the Okavango Delta's wetlands, sleeping in tents pitched on the banks of obsidian-black water.

This was my second leg of a three-part expedition. The first had been high luxury, dawn-to-dusk game drives and the singular thrill of wildlife sightings. It was the end of the rainy season, and animals were plentiful, contentedly feasting on spring grass. Elephant and giraffe calves wobbled next to their mothers, and tiny warthogs skittered behind their parents. The savanna pulsed with life, as if warm blood, rather than water, coursed through the floodplains. The only sighting that eluded me was a leopard, the stealthiest predator of all, but I had five more days in the delta.

This portion of the journey was about immersion in unspoiled wilderness, and I already felt my soul was recovering from something. Wild sage, jasmine and basil blew scent across the grasslands; I wondered whether they were some kind of sedative, so deep was my sense of calm. Simon reported the leopard call in early dawn, and though I longed to see the secretive beauty, today I was unrushed.

A message came over the satellite phone, our only means of communication. We were two airplanes and a boat away from the twenty-first century. "You need to call home," Simon told me softly. Another time, morbid fantasy would have clouded my vision, made me frantic that something happened to one of my children. But I instinctively knew why I would now measure time from the fractured peace of this morning.

Finally, a voice in the receiver pinged back to me from outer space. "She passed away peacefully," my husband said. "Her suffering is over." The call cut off sharply and I stared at the handset in my palm.

"My mother is dead," I thought. And I was clear across the world.

I had seen her in Boston barely a week earlier. New England was bracing for a late-winter nor'easter, and as I prepared the usual ritual of stocking up on coffee, wine and popcorn, my father called. In two days, I was due to leave Connecticut for Botswana. "Mom has declined," he said. "I wanted you to know."

"I'll be right up," I said and headed north to Massachusetts, straight into the storm.

My mother was approaching her fourth year at an Alzheimer's facility. For an illness marked by mercilessness, hers was unusually tragic. She had no intelligible language and seemed to be in a state of mortal terror. She lashed out at me and often at others. Did she know me? I certainly hoped not. There was nothing like recognition, even less of love. It was living death; I had lost her long ago.

It was warm in her little room. My father, one of my sisters and I played music she loved. I dipped a swab in lemonade and laughed when she bit down hard like a child with a lollipop. I narrated plotless stories about her grandchildren. Her beauty had returned in this liminal state. Her face was smooth, her color rosy. Meanwhile, Massachusetts had shut down. We were socked in for two nights and slept on a mattress near my mother, cocooned by 29-inches of snow outside. Even the Dunkin' Donuts across the street was closed.

My father, a physician, was not optimistic that she would wake, but it was Alzheimer's, an enigmatic disease rife with trickery, and there was no way to predict what even a day would bring. These dips had happened before, and I had said goodbye every time I left her for the past four years. My family urged me to go forth to Africa for the work I loved. My own justification was based on simple denial. I did not actually believe my mother would die.

"See you in two weeks, Mom," I whispered. "I'll find you a leopard. Promise."

She was a natural-born wayfinder who never needed a map. In another time, my mother could have led an expedition across the Congo, but she spent her decades as a stay-at-home wife and mother. Especially after her children left home, travel answered the call of her restless, curious mind. Her favorite journey was a safari in Kenya with my father, where she saw everything but a leopard—a "leppid" she called it in her Boston brogue. Those gorgeous cats fascinated her.

And now, it was unfinished business. I owed her at least that. I had been absent at her deathbed, and I wondered if the wound of my guilt could ever heal. But I was also in Botswana to work, and grief began to paint unexpected colors on my assignment.

Simon and Felix waited for me at the fire. I was numb. "My mother," I said.

"What would you like to do?" Simon's face was warm with compassion. We climbed into the boat and into the tangle of water and wilderness. My companions were gentle company. The universe has ways of offering comfort, and it was deploying them at every turn. Such signs are visible only to the willing, and in Botswana they were gracefully preparing me for loss. The delta was alive with lilies and flamboyant birds. As if my eyes were telescopes, I saw the cobalt feathers of a malachite kingfisher through a tuft of reeds. Under a charcoal cloud, strands of rain reached down to distant water. Simon opened a bottle of champagne and poured. "What was her name?" he asked.

"Ruth," I said.

We raised our glasses to life, to death, to light, to dark, to the earthly and the eternal. "To Ruth," we said.

That evening, I was seized by the reality of my complete displacement, and Simon lent me his satellite phone. I found service from a boat in our channel full of crocodiles. In the liquid darkness, I saw several pairs of yellow hippopotamus eyes across the bank. One of my sisters spoke firmly over the static. *"You are where Mom would have wanted you to be."* I retired to my tent and wept silent tears, listening for the sound that was described to me as a saw cutting through wood. The leopard's call.

When we moved on to the final stop of the safari, I was stirred by the pageant of death and renewal, so raw in the savanna, where the greens seemed brighter than when I arrived. A pack of wild dogs dragged an impala carcass to a clearing and feasted. A tiny Lechwe antelope leapt to meet his herd. My mother was everywhere, in the rays through the sea of mist as day broke, in the hint of breeze that grazed my cheek. Mostly, I saw her in all the protective female monkeys, zebras and elephants who kept their babies close and away from predators, as my mother did when I was small and she was my sole bulwark against the world.

The last full day was a wet and disappointing one. Our plane was leaving at 10:00 the next morning, and though there were storms in the forecast, I hoped for a final early pre-departure game drive. Nature gives no guarantees, but I went to bed hopeful.

I awoke at 4:30, drawn as if by hands to the waiting bush. I dressed, grabbed a thermos of coffee. Dave, our guide, said, "Let's go see what's out there."

Hours passed under a steely wall of sky and the drenched earth smelled fresh. The sun rose and clouds lifted to reveal pastel stripes on the horizon. Dave careened through mud and soaking gullies. There was urgency in his driving, and it made me nervous, because it reflected the percussive pounding of my own sinking heart. He shone a torch on cat tracks at the edge of the road. "Lion," he said. In an hour, I would be on my way home, to family and the empty space my mother's passing had left.

With a clatter of static on the walkie-talkie, Dave bolted in a direction only he knew.

I looked at Felix and we both raised our eyebrows.

"We must hurry," Dave said.

I clenched my eyes and fists. My lungs gripped a gust of air. When we stopped, I exhaled, looked up and saw the regal face of a leopard. She reclined on the twisted branch of a rain tree, her legs and tail draped languorously. "That's Marothodi," said Dave. "It means, 'raindrop.' Her mother is Pula. It means, 'rain.'" Every synapse in my body ignited in delight. I feared she would vanish if I blinked. She rearranged her limbs into a crook of the tree, looking relaxed and at ease. But I knew her power was greater than mine, than all of ours.

My body gave way to grateful, exhausted sobs and in an instant, I saw the pieces of the universe as if they were bathed in clarity. The relentless continuum, a New England snowstorm and African sunrise connected by the very same sky. Life's precariousness and impermanence but mostly, its astonishing generosity. I saw a leopard, who, for a moment, fixed her startling orange eyes on mine as if to tell me, *"You are where your mother would have wanted you to be."*

At last, she clambered down the trunk, into the tall grass and another brilliant day on Earth.

Chapter 33

He's Leaving Home

When I was a kid, the late-August appearance of yellow edges on the sugar maples brought on a sense of despair. It was a reminder that school was the price we paid for our sweet summer vacation, and that nature charges ahead even when the heart is reluctant. Since becoming a mother, this sensation grew only more profound. The end of summer is a crucible for those conflated feelings of joy and sorrow as my children come of age. The sense of loss tugged at me familiarly when I dropped my son off right before Labor Day.

When he was 13, he announced that he wanted to go away for high school. My husband and I were not prepared for him to leave home; I still regularly dusted off his dinosaur puppet, Reptar piggy bank, and the silver rattle given to him at birth—the various trinkets that composed a still life of babyhood on his bookshelves. I could not imagine the empty space his absence would create, in the house and in me. It was too soon.

But he was ready to bust out. Eight years ago, when we decamped from Manhattan, he was a second grader. On the route to school in Greenwich Village, we walked past delis, the fish market, and fetish boutiques. He had friends on every block near our apartment, and he loved to yell up from the sidewalk and wave to them behind the windows.

We moved here, two hours north, to our house surrounded by forest and patrolled by foxes and coyotes.

He adapted quickly to rural life, learned to drive his dad's pickup truck, grew a zucchini that won a prize at the local agriculture fair. He did his chores—shoveled the walk, weeded the vegetable garden—like a good country boy. He grew to 6'2" by eighth grade, spent endless hours out front with a basketball, and at thirteen, taught himself to dunk. The hoop in our driveway reminded me of the birch trees in Robert Frost's poem about the boy too far from town to play with other kids his age, who had to make do in his own yard. Even the much-desired snow days were lonely vigils—just he, his younger sister, and a couple of Flexible Flyers on the hill out back. We often logged two hours a day in a car, going to this practice or that, as he flipped between 95.7 and Hot 101.3 on the radio. His nearest friend was a fifteen-minute ride away in good weather, along dark twisty roads. Even when he grew quieter as he nudged toward adolescence, forced time with him and his sister gave us long stretches of concentrated intimacy.

A certain degree of cabin fever forged an iron bond between the four of us. Isolation gave him the space to think and work hard in school without the distraction of movie theaters within walking distance, Chinese take-out on the corner, sidewalks swarming with girls. But now that he was a teenager, he craved the round-the-clock parade of people he had known in his early childhood.

He got accepted to the school he loved with aid to make going there possible, and spent the summer energized, excited, and unafraid. Fourteen years old, braces, size thirteen feet: yes, he towered over me, and his room was carpeted with dirty gym shorts, size L, but I still woke up every night and tiptoed to his bedside, placed my hand under his nostrils to feel his breath, and did the same with his sister. Only then could I go back to sleep. Even though his smooth upper lip had turned to prickly fuzz, the ritual has not changed since he was a baby.

I tried to think of him as a man now, rather than my little boy. Alexander the Great had laid waste to Thrace by the time he turned sixteen. My own grandfather, like many immigrants, strapped on his boots in tiny Rosciolo dei Marsi, Italy when he was a teenager, got himself to the port of Cherbourg, France. There, he boarded a ship and said goodbye to his childhood, family, and country. He returned home once a few years later to collect the girl he loved and bring her back to America, where they would open their tailor shop. Neither of them ever saw their parents again. I often thought of his mother, Maria, and wondered whether she screamed a wild lament over the river beyond her house at the prospect of her son disappearing for what turned out to be forever.

Like the great-grandfather he never met, our son's readiness was not in his age, but in the certainty of his choices, and the confidence he had in knowing he could live day to day without his parents in the next room.

Some of our friends thought we were crazy. "How could you let him go away so young?" they asked.

Like every mother in history, I realized that now, it was time for me to bear up. I'm happy that our son felt self-reliant enough to go away, but nevertheless I feel duped by what this actually says about parenting. It's obvious, I suppose, what every parent of grown children knows: we can't hold on while we're helping them out the door. The moment our children are born, we gently plod them along, encourage them, await and applaud every milestone, not realizing that with every one, they need us less. This child, so wanted, so loved, had earned the assurance to break loose and go it alone. As parents, we had made ourselves almost obsolete.

Last September, my husband and I dropped him at school, forty-five minutes and a world away. I made his bed up as if it were in the Ritz Carlton, organized toiletries on his dresser. In the duffel bag, I discovered the dinosaur puppet and Reptar bank. I wondered what our son had been thinking as he placed them in his luggage. I dusted them off and put them on a bookshelf.

When we left him, he was already with a pack of boys, palming a basketball in the hallway. My husband and I held hands on the car ride home and barely spoke. We were both destroyed. I went right to his empty room. I remembered the generations of mothers before me who had to let their boys go when they said they were ready. Boys like my grandfather had been, who knew his best chance in life was to break loose and go it alone.

At least I would see my son again. At least I knew he was in safe hands, learning, thriving, holding books rather than a sewing needle as my grandfather did for the rest of his long life. But I was unable to bear the image of Maria, my great-grandmother, drifting through the house, thinking of her youngest son somewhere on the Atlantic. I wondered whether she had allowed her heart to break, or went mad with worry, or if she wanted to hold an item of his clothing against her face and inhale the scent of her baby boy now grown, whom she would never see again. I wondered whether she thought of him as any more of a man than I did my son.

I hoped she was able to give herself some credit. I hope she reasoned, one warm afternoon in the Apennine foothills outside Rome, that only if a parent does their job well is a child able to fly. If she could do it, then I could too. It was a family tradition, I told myself, a tradition of women throughout time. Strong mothers who raise strong adults, women who are stoic through the anguish of a child leaving home. But for the moment, I wanted to think of him as I had seen him the night before, my sleeping child breathing and breathing. I lay on his bed, but there was no pillow left to cry on. He'd taken it with him.

Chapter 34

Willa Cather's Lavandou

few years ago, while researching my book on France, I immersed myself in the country's rich travel writing canon, and retraced the itineraries (or parts of them) of many of my literary idols. With her 1908 road trip classic *A Motor Flight Through France* always stuffed into my bag, Edith Wharton was my frequent mentor and guide. In Nîmes, I imagined Colette dancing in the Jardins de la Fontaine; I conjured the ghost of a bored Henry James by the Rhône River in Arles, and in Chamonix, I pictured 16-year-old Mary Godwin unwittingly gathering inspiration for *Frankenstein* while hoofing it across the Alps with her future husband, Percy Bysshe Shelley. But no one lit my path as brightly as Willa Cather.

The collection of essays *Willa Cather in Europe: Her Own Story of the First Journey*, is a series of dispatches she filed for the *Nebraska State Journal* in Lincoln to help pay for her trip. It was 1902, and Cather, then 29 years old, voyaged overseas, accompanied by her friend Isabelle McClung. The book contains, to my mind, some of the most evocative travel writing in the English language. The stories bear all the elements—personal reflection, descriptive detail, observational insight, and cultural depth—we strive for when writing about place, and in perfect proportion.

At the time, Cather was teaching English and Latin at a Pittsburgh high school, while editing and writing for several local publications. She was also prodigiously trying her hand at everything: poetry, short stories, drama criticism, taking in every cultural input she could. "She was drinking from a firehose," says Cather scholar Robert Thacker of St. Lawrence University, due, not in small part, to her remarkable focus and drive.

She was not blue-blooded Edith Wharton, who had grown up in the first-class section of European trains with servants unpacking her trunks. Cather was of the American prairie, where her father ran a farm loan business, and she developed her love and scholarly knowledge of French literature not at Radcliffe, but at the University of Nebraska. When she finally went to France, she visited the graves of writers she long admired and the settings of great literary dramas, like the Chateau d'If—the island fortress near Marseille where the Count of Monte Cristo was held prisoner.

In 1902, she was on the cusp of her brilliant career. It is with this in mind—the writer on the verge of greatness, taking the journey of a lifetime that would also inspire much of her fiction— that I went to Le Lavandou, a village in the Var department of the south of France, where Cather penned the most beautiful dispatch of all, called simply *Le Lavandou*. That essay alone moved me to follow her tracks: to breathe the same piney air, look out at the same blue Mediterranean bay, and attempt to channel, or at least understand, the tranquility and bliss she described on that week in September.

There was something else in her communiqué back to Nebraska that caught me. It was these words: "Out of every wandering in which people and places come and go in long successions, there is always one place remembered above the rest because the external or internal conditions were such that they most nearly produced happiness," she writes. "I am sure that for me that one place will always be Lavandou."

Throughout the last years, I had made my living traveling in search of many objectives, most of them ill-defined or not defined at all. Over time, each journey's narrative would inevitably reveal itself, flicker and unspool in my mind. It could happen the morning I arrived in this or that place or it could happen after I got home, struggling to find meaning in the experience, just as I was ready to leave again. This time, however, the mission to pursue the memory of Cather came with an extra incentive: to sift Lavandou for the qualities that brought her close to achieving happiness and perhaps find myself in that exalted state, too.

Most of us were made to weave in and out of shadows. We wait for the pallid drone of life to be interrupted with episodes of transcendent joy. Perhaps this is happiness, rather than some permanent state, which I scarcely believe in, but which is a commodity valued above all else in our culture. My expectation was not transformation, like a pilgrim seeking a miracle. It was more to see if this quiet spot, singled out for its gifts by a writer I adored, might show itself to me in the same way. Mark and I had just left Ava in her freshman college dorm room and we felt the normal range of emotions: proud, excited, nervous, and even—for ourselves— free. But as I waited alone at a bus stop for my ride from Hyères to Lavandou, I felt bereaved. Unusually raw, I was also ready to receive the elusive grace Cather had found here.

She began in London, went through Paris and the papal city of Avignon, and found herself in this small fishing village about midway between Toulon to the west and Saint Tropez to the east. She arrived by the tiny train—the one whose arrival she would anticipate daily for its delivery of ice. (There is still a station there, where the bus from Hyères dropped me off, but the train is long gone.)

One day, Cather would see the landscapes of the southwestern United States through the prism of the south of France, and frequently merge the two cultures. Like Father Latour in *Death Comes for the Archbishop* and Thea Kronberg in *Song of the Lark*, all her senses were firing as she took in her revelatory new surroundings in a remote place that, though long inhabited, was barely on the map. She ate peaches, langoustes, and fish. The air was perfumed with lavender, which they spent hours gathering into bouquets; the landscape was of evergreens and sea "reaching like a wide blue road into the sky." Cather described a primitive place, a "principality of pines," where the soil was too sandy to grow anything but olives, grapes, and figs, and the people so poor she was uncertain how they survived.

Naturally, much has changed, as I saw when I arrived on a bright and sweltering September morning. There are few humble fishermen any longer, and the barefoot sailors are now stepping off their 65-foot catamarans into a massive and quite posh marina. The stores sell essentials for the yachting crowd, like rain slickers and rope. In Cather's time, there was one café; now there are dozens, all packed until late at night when the last revelers stumble out. The square remains lined with plane trees, above which a Ferris wheel spins dreamily. But the sky is still eternally blue, and the village sits in soft, shadowless sunshine.

The pair stayed at the bare-bones studio of a painter who was away in Paris. Some scholars believe it was Henri-Edmond Cross, who lived at St. Clair, just a mile up the shore from Lavandou. Many artists lived and worked in this remote idyll, most notably Théo van Rysselberghe. Both he and Cross famously painted the Bay of St. Clair. The town has created the Painter's Trail along the beach promenade, so the visitor can experience the vivid light and color that drew the neo-impressionists to this impoverished backwater. I paced the streets behind the shore for a while, trying to find any small hint of a hundred-year-old stucco house or what remained of it. But the home no longer exists, at least in any discernible way. Wherever she and McClung had stayed, it was difficult for me to place their location precisely, especially since the dusty, winding path that led to their humble lodging is long gone.

Cather and McClung spent hours on the porch of the shabby villa, which she writes was "good for one's soul," to "do nothing but stare at this great water that seems to trail its delft-blue mantle across the world." I imagined the writer so removed now from the high culture she had immersed herself in throughout Europe, where she connected closely with the great minds that helped form her. What a balm it must have been to turn down the pressure and lower expectations for a spell, to revel in an idleness she describes as "regal." Bathed in the breeze, with pine needles dropping on her reposing body, she writes of almost perfect peace, much as future opera superstar Thea Kronberg would do in *Song of the Lark* when she was sheltered by Panther Canyon in Arizona.

Cather describes a plateau on the flat top of a cliff extending out to the sea, on which stood a lone pine on the tip of a promontory. I walked the long, narrow path cut into the rocks from Lavandou to St. Clair, six times in all, hoping to see what mesmerized her for days. I never found the promontory, but when the light faded my first afternoon, I pretended I did. Sure, I thought, looking at the craggy formations that sliced into the bay. Waves slung over the outcrops and I watched them for hours without distraction, feeling an odd sensation as if I had forgotten something. This, I thought, is what it means to be unburdened.

She and McClung ate dinners at the Hotel de la Méditerranée, a grand old place that is no more, where a sad and solitary Parisian gentleman was the only guest. There is a new structure of the same name, a lovely modern hotel, where I might stay if I return one day. There are shiny villas, one-story apartment buildings, and buzzing cafés built into what was, in Cather's time, dense vegetation. But the pines—Aleppo and maritime—still grow mightily over this once-barren landscape, and fill the air with their heavy scent. The massive trees are bent from the constant wind, and the view skyward is not much different from any other shaded spot along the Côte d'Azur. But it is soothing to look up into the canopy and imagine that my eyes see what Willa Cather saw. These moments of reflection stir something deep in me, as I inhabit the very air that she breathed.

I had not managed exactly to retrace her steps, but the mission had put some pieces together for me, having read and admired Willa Cather for as long as I can remember. Words connect us all—the dead, the living, the great, the ungreat, but so can that which never changes: stillness under a stand of pines, the sound of waves meeting the shore.

"No books have ever been written about Lavandou, no music or pictures ever came from here, but I know well enough that I shall yearn for it long after I have forgotten London and Paris," she writes. "One cannot divine nor forecast the conditions that will make happiness; one only stumbles upon them by chance, in a lucky hour, at the world's end somewhere, and holds fast to the days, as if to fortune and fame."

In mankind's eternal, quixotic search for happiness, I was just another seeker those days in Lavandou. And indeed, I felt it and not just in the presence of sensate bliss, of the salty air that drifted with traces of lavender, of the sky spilling into a silver-blue sea, and of my ravenous hunger after hours exploring in the fresh air. No, I experienced happiness more as an absence of worry. In that and many other senses, Lavandou was lightness itself. But if this was happiness, it came entwined with the certainty of losing it. "One cannot really become acclimated to happiness," Cather wrote.

In Le Lavandou, she ate, walked, pondered and gathered. She drank brackish wine, fed on peaches and figs, chatted with passing fishermen, gathered blossoms. She observed. She rested before moving on for the "glare and blaze of Nice and Monte Carlo." She was firing sparks and making mental connections. She found a little place with much of what she valued, that gave her tranquility. She took a breath and leaned up against it, as if preparing for something. "She knew she was going to be Willa Cather, and the people around her knew it too," Robert Thacker told me. Her first book, *April Twilights*, a collection of poems, would be published the following year.

Chapter 35

Fear and Solace in the Big Bend

erhaps in my eagerness to grasp the essence of Big Bend National Park, I jumped in a little too quickly. Driving down from Marathon, Texas, 69 miles north, I aimed straight for the heart of the park: the Chisos Basin, a geological depression encircled by a mountain range of the same name. A friend had recommended the six-mile Window Trail hike; I reached the trailhead at high noon, disregarding the posted warnings not to hike after 10 A.M. because of the extreme heat. Blithely, I ventured into a dry canyon bed, past a surge of volcanic outcrops, and clusters of violet cenizos and bright desert asters.

Fifteen minutes in, the woman hiking a few yards in front of me turned and announced, calmly, that what seemed to be a remarkable painted stick bisecting my path was, in fact, a deadly Mojave rattlesnake. "Just step over it," she advised, as if there were any other choice. Thankfully, it ignored me, but the primordial threat and my acute, sudden fear forced my body into stress response. A gush of cortisol and epinephrine made my brain focus and heartbeat rocket, and the sensations refused to let up. By the time I reached the Window—a natural stone aperture at the lip of a 220-foot high cliff, through which I could see the Chihuahuan

Desert—it was 101 degrees. The woman I had been clinging to after the rattler sighting had veered off with her companion, leaving no one else in sight. My backup water bottle was emptying fast.

I proceeded cautiously on the way back, on the lookout for camouflaged reptiles and ducking for shade whenever I could on the uphill route. By the time I arrived at my air-conditioned car, dusty and dehydrated, I had learned my lesson. Big Bend was different from other national parks. One needed humility, stamina, a little courage, and probably *not* to hike alone, even if seclusion was precisely what I'd come there to seek.

"For the most part, people don't realize how hot it is, how isolated and vast," said Greg Henington, owner of the camp and tour operator that organized my visit. I was one of those people who hadn't realized it—but I was starting to. There's still something vaguely renegade about what has historically been one of the least visited national parks in the United States. It has no shuttle buses, and you won't encounter many easygoing rangers pointing directions or offering reassurance. It is also on the edge of nowhere: the nearest airport is an almost four-hour drive away.

The promise of adventure and remoteness is exactly why I went to Big Bend at the moment in history that I did. Because when the virus finally let up in the summer of 2020, I also desperately needed to get back to work. Carefully—tested, disinfected, tested again, and at a six-foot distance—I left Connecticut to seek refuge in the open vistas and astonishing stillness of far west Texas. The emptiest places on earth also appeared the safest, and in September of the first pandemic year, it seemed as if nowhere was quite as empty as this stretch of desolation along the Rio Grande.

Since I hit midlife, deserts, with their breathtaking quiet and pervasive sense of resilience, have been where I pursue solace. I am of solid New England stock, fully a child of the landscape that made me and where I choose to live now. The rocky coasts, moody mountains, and brittle winters have instilled in me a certain flintiness, too. But the influence of my father's boyhood with his Italian immigrant parents under Arizona's dome of stars also held sway, and has increased in recent years.

Every summer of my childhood, my family flew from Boston to Tucson, visited my grandparents (who still ran their tailor shop), rented a station wagon, and wove our way through the national parks and moonscapes of the southwest. My three older sisters and I crowded onto the sticky vinyl seats, playing word games and belting along to Tommy James & the Shondells out the open window. Even then, I was aware that the alien topographies and intense colors aroused in me a deep tenderness.

Now, late in life and full of wounds, I allow the intensity of these horizons to direct its mercy on me. It drowns my doubts and eases my sorrow, forgives all I regret, even when I cannot forgive myself. I ascribe these powers to the desert because of its relentlessness as well as its ferocity, qualities that are at once human and godlike. Light dominates all, inescapably, until the universe flips into the total void of black night. The simplicity of this pattern, the day in and day out of it, the sheer absurd dependability, is a template for endurance.

To be in the desert amidst its all-encompassing vastness is to encounter the sublime, a state that is dark, terrifying, exhilarating, and life-affirming. To experience sublimity requires subjugation to something infinitely greater than ourselves. It assumes a possible proximity to the divine, and "operates in a manner analogous to terror," and therefore produces "the strongest emotion which the mind is capable of feeling," posits the eighteenth-century Irish philosopher Edmund Burke in his essay, *A Philosophical Enquiry into the Origin of Our Ideas of the Sublime and the Beautiful.*

Burke differentiates between beauty, which induces delight and pleasure and inspires us to love, and the sublime, which provokes a tension between fear, wonder, and amazement and induces a response so powerful it is akin to pain. "The passion caused by the great and sublime in *nature*, when those causes operate most powerfully, is astonishment; and astonishment is that state of the soul in which all its motions are suspended, with some degree of horror," writes Burke. The sublime object exerts its power by filling our mind and subjugating our reasoning. To a lesser degree, he writes, the effects of the sublime are admiration, reverence, and respect.

What Burke deems the most sublime-inducing elements of the physical universe—vacuity, darkness, solitude, immensity, rugged terrain, the unknown, objects of great depth and height, infinity, light—were all present in Big Bend. Even snakes, with their enigmatic menace, bear mention in Burke's treatise as capable of "raising ideas of the sublime." There was nothing throwaway about my expectations: that through its grandeur, I might find comfort in my own smallness.

Disbelief, grief, terror, and maternal anguish. The gamut of fear and foreboding defined my emotional registry during the early months of the pandemic. Above it all were the atavistic instincts to stay alive, to protect my family, and to not be a danger to others. For me, there was no silver lining to having my fully grown children be forced to move back home, except being lucky enough for them to have a home at all. No, my heart broke all day, every day, as I grappled with a world now defined by sickness, death, and inequality. Within my own house, I knew what the pandemic was taking from my children and saw how preoccupied they were with the simple courtesy of not getting their parents sick. Their equanimity about it all stunned me, and how they maintained their humor I will never know, because I was in paroxysms of sadness.

I was also pushed back into their childhood and adolescence, the turbo-charged years of non-stop caregiving. Ray was now 25 and Ava, 22, and both had been living on their own. So, in a sense, had my husband and I. My pain for them was visceral, and I spoiled them, cooking their favorite dishes, baking the molasses cookies they loved, and changing their beds.

"Can I get you anything, honey?" I asked each of them now, as I had each morning when they were in elementary school. "I made some fresh granola and there are lots of eggs."

The familiar schism began to emerge, of selfless giving on one side and of selfish maternal fatigue (and guilt about it) on the other. Nothing was natural about this configuration enforced by the lockdown, but I was also jolted back into a time when all I desired was a long, solitary break. To eat minibar peanuts for dinner in some okay hotel and, without scraping a single dish, call it a day.

So when I was able to get on an airplane again, bestowed with health and good fortune, I did so, and vigorously returned to work. I emerged from the darkness of solitude and isolation imposed by the virus into even greater solitude and isolation in western Texas.

The day before my ill-advised solo hike on the Window Trail, I awoke to the nostalgic sound of railroad cars trundling east past my hotel room. I was staying at the Gage, on the main street of Marathon, the northern gateway to Big Bend. I brewed a cup of coffee, then ambled the town's small grid in predawn darkness, propelled by an elated sense of freedom. Though the temperature would soon soar into the nineties, I still needed to wrap myself in a woolly shawl against the cool desert air.

With one of the lowest light pollution levels on earth, the Big Bend region has the rarest of dark night skies—which is to say not dark at all, but shining white with bright planets and umpteen constellations. From the middle of the street, I watched the eastern horizon turn from starry black to flaming orange to powder blue.

I grabbed a breakfast of eggs and soft tortillas, and took my plate to an outside table. To the west was the contoured strip of the Del Norte Mountains, with Mount Ord pushing into the brightening sky. Back in the hotel, I took one last look around the artifacts and antiques the owner had amassed and displayed here in his lovingly restored corner of the Old West. In one of the common rooms, I found a mastodon femur uncovered at his nearby ranch. I brushed my fingers along it, the surface smooth as marble.

With adventure on the brain, I shot down U.S. Route 385 into Big Bend. So powerful and unexpected was the view that I had to stop several times to absorb it. The land before me contained nothing and everything, an all-encompassing vastness of mountain, desert, and, most dazzling of all, sky. Parts of Route 385 follow the course of the old Comanche Trail, named for the fierce nomadic horsemen who took this route from the central plains to conduct raids in the territories surrounding the Rio Grande, including what is now Mexico. Archaeological findings in the area record the presence of indigenous people dating back at least 13,000 years. By the 1880s, disease and the U.S. cavalry had suppressed, killed, or forced onto reservations the Mescalero Apache and the Comanche, who had established themselves in the southern part of what had become the state of Texas.

Later, the white population expanded with ranchers and mining operations that extracted mercury from cinnabar, until support swelled in Texas to acquire and deed this massive spread of land—dubbed by the Spanish conquistadors El Despoblado, or "the uninhabited place"—to the National Park Service. In 1944, Big Bend was designated the country's 27th national park, and today it covers more than 800,000 acres.

I was overwhelmed by Big Bend's scale, the geologic diversity, and the seemingly endless varieties of wilderness. It's the only national park with an entire mountain range, the Chisos, within its borders. There are canyons of limestone and smooth volcanic ash, craggy trails, abandoned ranches, and hot springs—all located within the Chihuahuan Desert. Anchoring it all is the Rio Grande.

The following day, I set off from the town of Terlingua, just to the west of the park, for my first encounter with the Rio Grande—the river that has, thanks in part to John Ford and Howard Hawks movies, informed our idea of the American Southwest. Big Bend's rainy season had been relatively dry that year, and the water level was unusually low; river trips were launching from the 311,000-acre Big Bend Ranch State Park, next door to the national park, where it was still possible to kayak. I traveled west on Highway 170. To my left, the river gurgled as it flowed east toward Santa Elena Canyon. Mesas loomed, as did whitish hoodoos, looking like they had been honed with giant sheets of sandpaper.

I did not grow up in an outdoorsy family. Visiting national parks, my parents relished the act of observation, the sanctuary in the landscape. At some point in midlife, I accepted the dares proffered by nature—for work, for my reluctantly aging self, just because. Less than a year prior, I had shot the Ganges River in Northern India on a narrow raft affixed with oars, so I was at ease now in the kayak as I maneuvered it into the water and sidled in. I almost instantly got a soaking, though not quite a dunking, on the first of several sets of rapids my small group encountered on our six-mile trip along the natural border between the U.S. and Mexico.

We floated between the opposing cliff faces through what the American side calls Colorado Canyon and the Mexican side calls Penasco. Looking south, to our right, we passed grazing herds of jet-black cattle. Dense walls of river cane flanked both banks, but I had other walls on my mind as I paddled through these fabled borderlands, absorbing the region's palpable mystique.

Most locals I spoke with derided then-president Trump's hypothetical barrier if it were even possible to engineer such a structure in this fluid landscape—for reasons humanitarian and otherwise. The wall would have interrupted the movements of animals such as Mexican black bears, cutting them off from their water source and migration patterns. Because the terrain is hostile on both sides, and often delineated by imposing cliffs, fewer asylum seekers tend to pass through here than elsewhere along the Rio Grande. Nevertheless, migrants attempting to cross into the United States are regularly discovered by border patrol agents, and tragedy too often befalls those who attempt to navigate this unforgiving desert.

Big Bend's location on the U.S.–Mexico border is a major thread in its complex history. Another is Terlingua: a town with its own mythical story, which became my base. In 1903, the economy there was thriving thanks to the lucrative cinnabar mining industry, but after several decades, with demand for mercury sagging, it stalled and then halted altogether. The industry left in its wake an abandoned town that, in the ensuing century, has attracted drifters, dreamers, and visionaries.

I sat with one of those visionaries, Lauren Werner, at the hotel she owns just off Terlingua's main thoroughfare. We chatted outdoors at a massive concrete table, looking east across a sea of ocotillo toward the warm glow of the Chisos ridgeline. We watched her rust-colored Irish setter mix, Waters, dart for a ball among the shrubs, while the sun continued its dance across the desert. "If someone asked me to describe freedom, it would be how I feel here," she told me. After just a single day at Big Bend, I already understood what she meant.

My casita at Willow House was a boxlike concrete structure, warm and earthy and velvety gray, blending into the landscape. From the patio, I saw an ever-transforming view of the mountains, which was overshadowed by even more domineering sky: its reds, purples, oranges, its wash of stars like a spilled tube of silver glitter. I reached in my bag for Burke's treatise and read: "Infinity has a tendency to fill the mind with that sort of delightful horror, which is the most genuine effect, and the truest sense of the sublime." The delight was obvious: beauty pervaded all while the sensation of reverence and awe penetrated my consciousness. But horror? Indeed, the vision also opened a channel of something close to dread. This example of nature's stoicism amplified my own sense of powerlessness. All a human being can be is a collection of the emotions our surroundings produce in us. Confronted with this degree of beauty, I felt simultaneously validated and vanquished.

For the next three days, I would set off from my casita at dawn to explore, which necessitated a guide, Randy De La Fuente. His function was multifold: he administered folklore and botany lessons, Texas-flavored bon mots, and the occasional gentle admonishment, mostly about hydration. Never again would I set off on a hike without enough water to fill a punch bowl.

"I do believe there is a bead of sweat above my eye," he deadpanned from the Lost Mine Trail near the Chisos Basin, a 45-minute drive from Terlingua. The five-mile hike is known for its panoramas, which shift bafflingly at every switchback. As we ascended, landmarks came abruptly into view. "There's my sweetheart," he exclaimed, gesturing toward Casa Grande, a statuesque volcanic ridge. He pointed out a lechuguilla, a spiny desert succulent with sap that is a natural probiotic, and showed me the scaly bark of the alligator junipers. Around us mingled the aromas of creosote bush, ponderosa pine, and Douglas fir. We turned another bend and there was Juniper Canyon and a lone, megalithic rock formation that reminded me of a ruined Scottish castle.

Later, as I drank an icy Pacifico on the porch of my casita, and the dry air blew over me like a soothing balm, there was almost a tactile sense of knots unraveling in my brain. Sizing up a kind of silence and darkness I'd never experienced before, I felt as if a spark had reignited something that had been extinguished during those first dark months of the pandemic. I had been wound so tight for so long, chained to the headlines and bleach wipes, worried about bills, the future of this tragic planet and my kids' place upon it. Mornings, I cried in the shower and at night, I wept in bed. It was as though the desert itself had expanded me into something more rational and whole. Trail by strenuous trail, vista by staggering vista—even in brutally harsh heat—Big Bend had transported me to the edge of tranquility.

The next morning, I hopped in the open back of a Jeep, and De La Fuente drove into the park from Terlingua as day broke. Surrounded by the ridgeline, which was still in shadow against the heavens, I got the feeling of being inside a gigantic black bowl. I had yet to see a cloud in Big Bend, but with its ever-changing palette, the sky commanded the land below it.

We turned on a dirt road to hike Grapevine Hills, a desert wash studded with boulders that sparkled with quartz. I stopped to admire tiny ripe persimmons and the dried stalks of the sotol plant, a relative of agave.

Motoring south on Ross Maxwell Scenic Drive, the 30-mile paved road that cuts through the western side of the park, we passed a series of mighty geological formations—Mule Ears, Burro Mesa—as we headed toward Santa Elena Canyon, Big Bend's marquee attraction, made famous by the Ansel Adams photograph that shows the imposing symmetry of the limestone gorge. From a distance, its walls blazed fiery red in the afternoon sun. I asked to pull off to the overlook, to absorb a view of this fearsome cleft in the earth. Sublimity, after all, is best encountered from a great distance. As the sky pierced flaming daggers into the cliff sides, I experienced a sort of fatigue, almost a swoon, from this viscerally human attempt to grasp the unfathomable.

"A hundred million years ago," explained De La Fuente as we began the hike alongside the canyon, "this was all under the sea." I lost my footing several times on the loose trail that skirted the water, winding past walls chock-full of fossilized marine mollusks. After our hike, bone weary, we made lunch in the Jeep.

Until recently, my beat was the great cities of the world. But as I crunched a peanut butter and Fritos sandwich, I was aware that I would scarcely be more content if I were eating *magret de canard* at Septime in Paris.

Shellacked with fine dust when De La Fuente dropped me off at Willow House, I showered it off there, though careful not to squander water, the hotel's—and the whole area's—most elusive resource. Feeling restored, I drove myself into Terlingua and turned into the former mining neighborhood still known, somewhat nostalgically, as Terlingua Ghost Town. I wandered the weathered cemetery and the cluster of original structures; at the Terlingua Trading Co., I perused the terrific book section as Willie Nelson's "Crazy" played on the sound system. I peeked into St. Agnes Church, which was bare-bones, but it moved me nonetheless, as these mysterious reliquaries of faith always do.

The next morning, I waited in the quiet, enjoying the last of the night's crisp, cool air. The prior evening, my last night, I had interviewed Bill Ivey, who owns the ghost town in its entirety—two hotels, the store, and the restaurant where we had dinner. Over chicken-fried antelope steak, margaritas, and vanilla ice cream, he relayed stories of his life growing up here in far-flung Brewster County, Texas. "Every day," he said, "I look at the mountains and say, 'I really am blessed to be here.'"

I stopped to consider us, this pair of strangers, having dinner together: a man raised in the desert, a woman raised in the forested northeast, and pondered how the land we identify as home shapes us all. How my father's boyhood in the southwest made him forever long for bubblegum-hued sunsets and the lonesome sound of a hot wind. And how enthusiastically he packed up his wife and four daughters every summer so he could transfer just a little of that equanimity to us. And how in the midst of a global pandemic, one of many that have stricken the people on earth throughout time, it was the desert I reached for to console me.

I had asked Ivey for his advice on the best spot to see the sunrise, as only he would know. He suggested following a dirt road to Indian Head, abutting the national park, just on the edge of Terlingua, leading to a path with millennia-old petroglyphs carved into volcanic boulders along the way. Though excavations continue in the region, only an estimated ten percent of the park has been surveyed for archaeological sites. At Indian Head, the pictographs of animal, human, and nature symbols are a reminder of the hands that created them, the ancient people who looked east and saw precisely the landscape I looked upon that morning.

Above me were the fleck of a waning moon, Mars, Saturn, the Milky Way, the heavens and all they hold. The earth, the sky, and the horizon wore their immortality with dignity, not mocking my own laughable brevity. It was all there—my terror of the infinite, and the vastness that telegraphed its tender, reassuring messages. Alone on this patch of Texas sand, I felt so small, but so—deliciously—alive. The night was swept away in a swift flash, lighting a pool of evanescent fire over the Chisos Mountains, giving way, as it always does and ever will, to the gentle curves of the Chihuahuan Desert. And with that—miles from anyone and a long way from anything—my arms shot up in a gesture of unadulterated praise.

Chapter 36

Brass City

*I*n the winter of 2021, after the pandemic had taken two million lives and stripped humanity of just about everything, I found myself commuting to a vaccination clinic in Waterbury, Connecticut. Almost immediately after I left my driveway, I steered past apple, peach, and blueberry orchards. Trees sloped gently over the hillside, resembling a perfectly uniform army advancing under the first light of day. Past this, if I timed it right, I would see a volcanic pool of fire in the distance, the reflection of sunrise in the local reservoir. Within twenty-five minutes, I would turn onto an unspectacular stretch of highway that took me to the hospital, where I would lace my ID around my neck and begin to check in patients.

If I were to be honest, it was not for the benefit of others that I signed up to volunteer. It was a personal rescue gambit, to save myself from months of all snow and no people, from the pounding inside my head, and from spiritual despair brought on by a world reeling with death, illness, and oppression. A decaying former manufacturing town on the banks of the Naugatuck River was an unusual place to find deliverance from the crush of loneliness and anguish. But deliver me it did, and not for the first time.

I first visited Waterbury in 1988, accompanied by a camera crew. Jane Fonda was filming *Stanley & Iris* there with Robert DeNiro, and the actress's presence in town sparked the embers of an old grudge. Some citizens of Waterbury—mostly veterans and their families—did not want "Hanoi Jane" in their city until she apologized for her actions during the Vietnam War, including being photographed, smiling, on a North Vietnamese anti-aircraft battery. For years, they had considered the actress and fitness mogul a traitor to America and the soldiers who fought and died for it. And so she apologized, in a high-profile interview with Barbara Walters on the ABC news magazine *20/20*, for which I was then a producer. After the interview, conducted at her home in Santa Monica, California, I was dispatched to Waterbury—about two hours north of New York City—to shoot B-roll and interview the mayor (not the one who, in 2003, was sentenced to 37 years in prison for soliciting sex with children). I still remember the line of script Walters read over shots of empty mills and vine-clad, abandoned factories on the banks of the Naugatuck River: "Waterbury, where the industrial revolution flourished and faltered...."

I could not have imagined that, fourteen years later, when I moved from Manhattan to a house on the edge of a forest, this husk of a city would, one day, become *my* city: the place I would go when I could no longer bear the woodpecker that, after a while, seemed to be drilling a hole in my brain rather than in an ash tree somewhere out back. After New York City and Paris, Waterbury at first seemed a sorry consolation prize of an urban respite. That is because at first, the adjustment from city to country had been drastic, the hurdles unscalable.

I missed friends, I missed strangers, I missed bad smells and brittle tempers. In my recent, former life, from the moment I awoke, I was conveyed through life by some unseen force that lifted me with a sense of power—mine and Manhattan's. The city's incessant, invigorating drumbeat was most noticeable after I left, when it cut off abruptly into silence. Suddenly, after the move, the loudest sounds were the wind ripping down my chimney, or the squawks of crows posted menacingly on upper branches. Until then, I had spent my adult years interwoven like some itinerant glass bead into the great cities of the world—living in some, exploring others. Now I was ensconced in the utter oblivion of arcadian New England.

One day, desperate for some semblance of people and even a quasi-urban buzz, I sought out Waterbury, resolved to give it the fascination treatment—a little wide-eyed wonder. I was surprised to experience the same sense of mission I had known as a traveler, of being displaced in the pursuit of discovery. Even more profound was the extent of my tenderness for the place. It was when I crossed the Green in the center of town that I remembered with a start that I had been here before, in my prior, younger life.

There are two world-class hospitals, but little else, on first inspection, to give Waterbury urban bona fides. No shopping area that hums with boutiques and espresso bars, no grand hotel to meet a friend for a cocktail, no great boulevard or plaza. Boarded-up shops and vacant lots line the sidewalks, along with a sparse sprinkling of tattoo parlors, delis, and mobile phone stores. Even the mall close to the center of town seems a strange behemoth with too much empty space, a monument to failed retail and the spurned optimism of the past.

There is even more neglect on the human level. Nearly half of the city's children live below the poverty level, and the city is chronically short of resources to take care of them. In a state with some of the wealthiest zip codes in the nation, Waterbury embodies the struggle of the forgotten, the disenfranchised, the unlucky. As such, it is the third most dangerous city in Connecticut, with a high rate of murder, assault, and other violent crimes. The DEA has Waterbury in its sights as a center of narcotics distribution for New England. There are myriad tragedies of the urban poor. But there is sweet life, too, on the streets. There are grand-mothers pushing strollers, couples arm-in-arm, bands of kids mak-ing mischief.

When I visited back in 1988, I discerned shreds of its for-mer grandeur; indeed, our cameraman panned up and down the Civil War memorial. Crowned by a bronze statue of a towering female Victory, the monument is complete with olive branch, lau-rel wreath, and cornucopia. Below her are four figures, including a teacher reading to two children, with a broken shackle at her feet, signifying emancipation. It dates from 1884, and this allegory of war and its human cost, even for the victors, would be very much at home in Washington, D. C., or Madrid. Or France. The artist, George Edwin Bissell, cast the monument's figures at the Parisian foundries where Auguste Rodin cast many of his works.

Now I see Waterbury's past in starker outline, perhaps because I have wandered the streets and seen up close what glimmers amongst its many scars. That is also what keeps me devoted to it. And like any city that struggles to redefine itself, the place beats with disparate kinds of energy. Waterbury is an acquired taste, but it is strangely my kind of escape. I gravitate to crumbling forgot-ten backwaters or mysterious port towns when I travel overseas, places where time has trampled memory and beauty, leaving the poignance of ruination. Plush hotels make me nervous; unless I'm on assignment, I like a two or three-star option in a dodgy neigh-borhood where the food is cheap and delicious, and a Coke at the lobby bar doesn't run me ten dollars.

Like a gorgeous woman despoiled by time and gin, Waterbury's bones are still staggeringly lovely. The back-road approach from Watertown leads you through tidy neighborhoods and lots of ram-bling, still-beautiful Victorians built by the city's founding indus-trialists. Until the 1940s, the thriving middle class—immigrants from Italy, Ireland, and Eastern Europe—turned out almost half of the brass manufactured in the United States (and many other things, including buttons, mattresses, machines, and the parts to run them) in the fortresses that lined the city's riverbanks. When World War II came, those same factories were repurposed to generate, among other things, most of the artillery and ammunition we used to defeat Hitler. The vision of so many handsome brick mills and their statuesque, dormant smokestacks makes me hunger for a simpler time, when these buildings were filled with people rather than ghosts.

Waterbury is a history lesson and a cautionary tale of industrial death, the human cost of white flight, of racist inequality—and the absolute necessity of perseverance. The centerpiece of its skyline is a 245-foot campanile built in 1909, a replica of Siena's Torre del Mangia. It looms over a McKim, Mead & White-designed brick building. Once the main train station, it now is the office of the Waterbury Republican-American, the town's terrific daily newspaper, which I will sometimes read over coffee and a slice of pumpkin bread in the diner near my house. There are too many stories about drug busts, but it is balanced by news of Jahana Hayes, the first Black congressional representative from Connecticut, who had been a history teacher in the Waterbury school system. My son had his photo in the paper once, sitting on Santa's lap. I bought six copies.

There are 27 green parks and a great museum, the Mattatuck (home of a cool button exhibit), which shows works by artists from the nineteenth century through today. But Timexpo: The Timex Museum, a cultural outpost that exhibited the history of Timex and the Waterbury Clock Company, that occupied the only remaining structure of Scovill Manufacturing, closed its doors. It absolutely broke my heart. I should have visited more than the one time I chaperoned a class field trip with my son. If I could, if I had all kinds of discretionary money, this is what I would support, if only to prop up a struggling city's dignity and to preserve the inventiveness in its DNA.

The grand buildings on Bank, Leavenworth, and Center Streets are living talismans of better days, a one-stop compendium of American architectural ingenuity. I stopped to photograph the majestic Citizens & Manufacturers Bank building, the creation of Henry Bacon, architect of the Lincoln Memorial. It is a magnificent, triumphant structure, and its formal iron work and lion heads spaced along the cornice are intact. The facade is plastered with "For Lease" signs, and this proliferation of bright pink and blue rouses in me a wave of compassion.

Around the block on Grand Street are the city's municipal offices, housed in Cass Gilbert's Georgian Revival masterpiece, constructed before he designed the United States Supreme Court Building. Greatness is everywhere. On the broad front staircase, I look for a shadow of the twenty-seven-year-old me, carrying a bag of tapes, rushing to the next location after interviewing the mayor.

As I followed unpeopled sidewalks and sought out these landmarks, I considered how reverently I wander through unfamiliar places—Barcelona, Saint Petersburg, Cuzco—but almost never spare a grain of awe for places close to home, rarely New York and certainly not in a place like Waterbury.

Before he left home, my son loved to zoom into Waterbury from our forested idyll, park along West Main Street, and play pick-up basketball in the YMCA that overlooks the Green. It beat shooting hoops on the driveway, and the lonely echo of a ball bouncing on tar.

To its right, at the corner of Prospect and West Main, is the magnificent copper-flashed Elton Hotel building. It was built in 1904 and is a temple of Beaux Arts symmetry and elegance. It is now a residential home for seniors. I stood on the Green, under a pair of honey locust trees, and took in the long view. So magnetic is its stature that were it in Brussels, it would be the very first thing I would seek out on my first morning in Belgium. John F. Kennedy gave one of his last campaign speeches from a second-floor balcony of the Elton two days before he was elected president. It was 3 A.M. and an estimated 50,000 people cheered him from below in the driving rain. In James Thurber's 1939 story *The Secret Life of Walter Mitty*, set in Waterbury, the main character waits for his wife in a hotel said to have been modeled after the Elton. After shopping for puppy biscuits and rain shoes, Mitty sinks into a leather chair in the lobby. When his wife taps him on the shoulder, he says, "I was thinking. Does it ever occur to you that I am sometimes thinking?" This, before he faces the firing squad in his reverie.

There are more bold-faced names, ones I once knew, or at least learned. To me, they scream: "This town still matters."

I have visited the Palace Theater many times, with its baroque, frescoed birthday cake of an interior, built in 1921 to the over-the-top specifications of the early Jazz Age and the dawn of cinema. Guys used to take their dates here to see Frank Sinatra and Bing Crosby, or so it is said. Decades later, in January 1976, Queen first performed Bohemian Rhapsody for an American audience live on the Palace's gilded stage. I cannot imagine the simultaneous gooseflesh that must have erupted in the theater from Freddie Mercury's penetrating voice.

My daughter once had a holiday concert there. Her choirmaster insisted the girls wear long black skirts and white blouses. We were so excited for her—it was a big deal to sing on stage at the Palace, Waterbury's Carnegie Hall. As she sang the first faux-cheerful line of *It's the Most Wonderful Time of the Year*, though, her face collapsed, her lower lip started trembling, and she wiped shining lumps of tears from her cheeks. We whisked her away mid-performance, and though I was worried about her fever that spiked later in the day, I was somewhat relieved that the onslaught of melancholy did not have a vague and mysterious provenance. As if my own sadness had already passed down to her during what was never, for me, the most wonderful time of the year at all.

Years ago, I attended the opening of Ken Burns' fifteen-hour documentary, *The War*, at the Palace. Waterbury was one of the four American cities featured in the film. It was bittersweet, at first, to leave the theater that night with images of vitality from the city's past still looping in my head and to walk in the winter cold past row upon row of desolation. Not a single bar or restaurant was open, there was no tinkling laughter of a passing promenade. The city seemed to be an empty shell.

But the current city, the one with busted-up storefronts below still-majestic Greek Revival and Romanesque facades, is the only Waterbury we know today. It is the one that welcomed me all those years later, when the pandemic was ravaging my sanity and my adopted state. The one that opened a large vaccination clinic in a performing arts high school, where I, along with multitudes of the virus-weary, found relief verging on salvation.

After spring finally arrived, I would occasionally spend my lunch hour venturing out to some unknown places within walking distance of the clinic. One day, I found Dylan McDermott Boulevard nearby, named in honor of the actor who grew up in the city and whose mother was murdered, just a few blocks away, when he was six years old. On the street sits the most extraordinary Second-Empire building, with a slate roof and belfry adorned with a cross. It does not appear to be a church, but it did appear to be empty and my instincts told me it is populated with ghosts.

But it is the living who make up a metropolis, and in Waterbury, they step with pride and sometimes, irritability. The sidewalks and intersections throb with music, courtesy of the newest residents: Ecuadorian, Cape Verdean, Brazilian, and the sounds are a joyous mix of merengue and hip hop, reggaeton, Lebanese pop and colazouk. These days, at the clinic, I check in many New Americans just moments before their vaccination. Often, they allow me to share the emotions of their personal pandemic turning point. They weep, they tremble, they make jokes. Sometimes a son or a granddaughter translates our conversation. "My grandma is very relieved today," a teenager of Vietnamese origin tells me.

The restaurants are similarly vibrant, and aromas—onion, chiles, roasting pork, and pungent café con leche—float like ribbons in the air. My son's favorite was Mikey's Jamaican, for tender meat pies, jerk chicken, and callaloo. But I still love the wood panels and tile floor at La Cazuela, 3 blocks west of the Y, and its Dominican pollo a la brasa and mofongo.

Best of all is La Tavola, a place outside the center of town in one of Waterbury's quiet residential neighborhoods. The maître d' is a standard-bearer of old-world courtesy, and the darkened booths and rows of red wine lining the walls call to mind the urban life I once led on the edge of Little Italy. Mark and I used to take the kids to La Tavola when they were still living at home, and feast on an absurdly tasty ricotta gnocchi with lamb, and my favorite, a succulent brick chicken.

Years later, during the pandemic, I would pick up paper bags full of take-out on the way home from the clinic, and sometimes bought an extra order of polenta fries to eat for lunch the next day. On the way home, at the end of a long and satisfying shift, I drove past a sign for Interstate 84 West toward New York City—the highway I took in a rental car thirty-three years ago when I was a young news producer who came to Waterbury to shoot a story. I steered my car in darkness along the back roads instead, toward the dairy farms, meadows, and gurgling creeks. Toward home.

Chapter 37

The Voyage

At 7:30 A.M., I found my way to downtown Bismarck from a hotel in the industrial fringe surrounding the city. Weightless snow spun in white concentric circles against the darkness. It had only been a few weeks since I returned from my last voyage, but I was itching again, called to a place, anyplace, where I could hide in my own company.

I had lived for almost six decades, but only recently had I rehearsed almost to the point of rote the global choreography I undertook at the age of fifty. It was close to the pattern I had lived in my twenties, back when my whole life was before me, and every week meant another story in some other place that was not home. Back then, standing still meant only standing still.

Now, the repetitive loop was made possible by desire: leave, return, stay, repeat. It was access to the spinning world I was after, because when I moved across and around it, I did not have to consider what to do with the hours that remained. Parts of me I never thought about had begun to go on the fritz: skin, hips, eyes, ears, teeth, the soft tissues of the organs in my abdomen. I did not want the next part of my life to be about disease, loss, and decay. There was one choice, and that was to stay only long enough to gin up the reason or the means to let go again. It was what a traveler did. Leave for the sake of leaving.

When I arrived home, the house stood dark and quiet. Autumn had sidled in while I was away, and dried oak leaves splotched the front walk. As I rolled my suitcase toward the door, desiccated pieces of what was once foliage, swaying green all summer, curled and gummed in the wheels. My assignment—sailing along the Atlantic coast of Europe and veering east to the Mediterranean—had come to an end that morning, fifteen hours ago, in Barcelona.

Port cities along the way had beckoned me straight into their pulsing veins, and poured purpose and delight back into mine. I eyed a medieval fortress off St. Malo, and crossed over to it against a rising current clutching a warm buckwheat crepe in my right hand. The relentless waters of the English Channel filled the tidepools with swirls and eddies and soaked my ankles as I hastened back to safety on the sludgy gray sand. In Bordeaux, the ship docked at daybreak, and I shot straight to the Pey-Berland tower. Up the twisted medieval stairwell I climbed, toward that which I was hoping to discover and that which I did not understand. Before me lay the red clay roofs of a city, the flying buttresses of an adjacent cathedral, a continent, the waves, a world.

In Bilbao, I bicycled to Done Jakue Square, breakfasted on sparkling wine and salty ham, and ducked into the Santiago Cathedral. Morning pierced the stained-glass windows and threw a multicolor mosaic against a massive limestone column. The light flashed purple, cobalt, fuchsia on the whitish stone, and as it did, I prayed for my mother, recently gone, and wept for knowing how much she might have loved to travel unencumbered and by herself, and drink Basque Txacoli wine for breakfast in Spain.

All I could offer was my openness, and I gave it freely. Everywhere I went, I swerved to meet my target, whatever it was going to be, the thing that slowed my footsteps and pried loose the ventricles of my heart. Andalusian domes in Cadiz, where I walked in wide circles, past the sea and stands of palms. I coiled up the spiral of the Tavira Tower, one of hundreds of watchtowers in the White City, where sentries once monitored maritime traffic after the conquest of the Americas. Flayed by wind for miles along a beach promenade in A Coruña, my feet pulled me to a hillside to corkscrew up another lighthouse, Torre de Hércules, to look over the sea and sky with the sting of sun on my face.

After days on the water, I had become nearly possessed by the color blue and the emotions it registered: smallness and tranquility, hope and apprehension. "So we love to contemplate blue—not because it advances to us, but because it draws us after it," Goethe wrote in *Theory of Colours,* and in the boat, chased by water and clarified by sky, there was no bleakness in the universe. Airborne, from that tower in A Coruña, I could see my vessel. Why, sometimes, do we prefer the beauty we are going toward to the one we are leaving behind? I longed again to stand on my balcony under the wide clear vault of sky as the hull violently cleaved the water, which frothed at the gunwales. How, I wondered, could such force induce such calm? Perhaps, I reasoned, it was because the barrier between safety and the abyss was just a humble railing and in my most deranged imaginings, I would never cross it.

In the presence of sublimity, I felt a swelling of tenderness and love and most definitely of terror. There is no escaping the prospect of death; it casts a shadow on beauty. The fearsome scale of the heavens and the power of an onrushing ocean pointed not to my strength but my vulnerability, and the vulnerability of everyone I love. This is what a traveler rushes toward, and this is what she retreats from, if only to shore up defenses to the simple act of living.

At home, there was quiet and work, and the space for me to fill the rooms and appreciate both. There was my husband of twenty-seven years, and the ease of the day-to-day, the love that coasts and doesn't have to toil for a living. But there were no children; they were long gone into their adulthood. Their absence fashioned a different kind of presence: a dull, aching void. Imposed solitude, rather than the chosen kind I regularly seek. Houses do not hold memories sweetly, they brandish them to taunt our abandonment and our advance toward old age and oblivion. It is the passage of time that hurts the most, and the house forces us to look backwards and to reckon with who my husband and I were, now that our children are grown. We were in this life together, but we were also two separate people, each of us alone. Outside, maple, ash, and oak leaves flitted and swirled, touching down and taking flight again.

"*Si tu peux rester, reste;*
Pars, s'il le faut," wrote Beaudelaire.
Stay if you can; leave if you must.

North Dakota! The election was two weeks away, and there was a candidate I hoped would win, who was in a fight to retain her Senate seat. I gave a small amount to the effort, and checked the box that asked, "Would you like to help?"

All I could offer was my openness.

To my surprise, ten minutes later, someone from the campaign wrote back. "Would you be willing to come to Bismarck?"

I could write a story. I could slide into the wrinkles of the universe. I could pitch in. I could seek the unknown and would surely find it, in time to return home, to my own bed and my husband's patient fold.

All Saint's Day, and it was snowing in Bismarck. At the coffee shop, I was served water in a tin tumbler. I ordered granola, an apple spice scone and a cookie made with lavender. Hot coffee in a paper cup, which I carried out into the flurries. The darkness refused to budge, and I navigated around one block and another and another. My yearning and my restlessness had brought me here and moved my feet forward. What I felt, what I knew I could feel, was a veer toward equipoise, a quest for unity. Joy and fore-boding, foreboding and joy, it happened at home and it happened everywhere, but they needed to be in balance.

I reported to work and was designated to a neighborhood of Bismarck deemed especially antagonistic to the candidate's plat-form. Talk, listen, persuade. Disappear, blend in, stand out—they all meant the same thing when I levitated to the sky and gyred back down. Time unfolded in circles when I traveled, and was not laid out in a straight, continuous line.

With a list of registered voters in one hand, I and my part-ner for the day, an electrician in a Carhartt peacoat, knocked on doors, gave a pitch if they were receptive, and retreated to the street and the wet cold. Though freezing, I kept moving, around corners and down cul-de-sacs. Bunches of snowflakes curled in great whirlpools like little earthbound Milky Ways. My toes, my fingers, my legs, my lips were chilled to numbness, and my jacket was draped with a million icy-lacy stars. On my feet were shoes I bought at the airport in Johannesburg six months earlier, and which I had lashed on to tear through port cities of Europe a few weeks ago. Such unifying elegance in sameness, as if it were my sneakers that validated my existence and made me whole.

I was busy, this was work, and the people from the campaign had welcomed me, no questions asked. At headquarters, we ate cold turkey sandwiches and sipped lime seltzer and pulled cam-paign hoodies over our heads. The next day, I worked the phones, calling voters in Fort Yates and Fargo, Devils Lake and Grand Forks, not letting on that I was there less to help than to trample the mud in movement and brighten the ennui of living.

I was a volunteer from the northeast alighting in this—to me—unfamiliar city, and when my workday was done, I tried to home in on my moment of contact. On breaks, and after hours, I drew myself to Bismarck's streets, searching for a scene that would spark remembrances, for a story in the limestone edifices, for a tower with worn stone steps that curved up its core, something to cut deeply within my psyche and hold it. Even here, I dreamed of unnamed raptures, and was conveyed through the city by curiosity. But here, I warned myself, it might be elusive. Boredom happens far from home, too. I carried the burden of my desire, making space in my consciousness for that which could unfold.

The candidate was speaking at a winery in Dickinson, and this was the chance I lived for taking. An evening round trip. Up close with the United States Senator, sure. I had a notebook and was, after all, more than an observer. I was a journalist. A trip across the North Dakotan landscape, definitely. I climbed in my compact Dodge rental and headed one hundred miles due west, across the state and into another time zone.

Even with the extra hour gained from the time change, I had to hurry. The event began at 6:00 and with no distractions, I needed two hours to get there. Along the way, I was tempted by detours and the mysteries they promised, signs that veered off to the Enchanted Highway, whatever that was, and the Old Red Old Ten Scenic Byway. To my right, an enormous steel form shaped like an eye with birds on it on it, black against the sky.

All I could do was glance right, peek left along the straight line of road. I guessed there were grain silos off the highway, abandoned Norwegian churches, a general store that sold ice cream in the summer, the country's biggest something-or-other. The humble past of the northern Great Plains. Flatness and horizons and the whoosh of a pickup truck blazing past me, its driver more accustomed than I was to high speeds on I-94, the freeway that cuts a 1,585-mile ribbon from Port Huron, Michigan to Billings, Montana.

In Dickinson, I snaked up a hill, found the place, and strolled behind the building to the actual vineyard. Rows and rows of vertical twigs that in the spring burst forth with greenery and fruit stood slack against the trellises. Looking east was a vast mantle of winter sky, a spectrum of clouds and grays. A sheer drape of snow was strewn across the dead ground from the earlier dusting.

Only a month ago, in Bordeaux, I left the boat one evening to drink red wine overlooking acres of vines, which glowed with autumn.

I drew into my jacket and went inside, to the warmth of camaraderie. The room smelled pleasantly of hot hors d'oeuvres, pigs in blankets, and cheese croquettes. I refused a glass of house white wine, and bought a bottle of Wind Chill Red, made out back with Marquette and King of the North cold climate grapes, to take home. I took out my pen, and interviewed a state representative wearing an American flag tie. But he was the one with the questions: "Why are you working on a campaign in North Dakota?"

"They didn't need me back east," I responded.

Stay if you can. Leave if you must.

When she addressed the gathering, the candidate spoke cheerfully, pumping her fist in the air. "We have to fight!" she said. "Our children are watching, and they wonder, 'Who are you?'"

A wall of darkness descended over the vineyards in the back, and before returning to Bismarck, I sidled over the candidate, hoping to get a word.

"I wanted to introduce myself," I said. "I'm a volunteer from Connecticut, and also wanted to wish you luck on Tuesday."

"Wow, I appreciate that," she answered, shoving red bangs to the side of her forehead. She was smiling, but the campaign had painted dark shadows on her face. Her opponent had been unusually cruel, and the fight she referred to earlier was relentless.

"I hope you get some rest," I said.

"Ha!" said the candidate. An aide whispered to her, and she fled to her waiting bus.

I exited to blackness, illuminated only by new and unexpected swirls of snow. My compact car would need to become a full-on workhorse, and the prospect of the drive gave me pause. It was practically a straight line across the state back to my hotel, so I could chug back to safety in just a few hours. My birthday was the next day, and I would be going home.

As the car warmed up in the parking lot, I looked up the colossal metal birds I had seen on the highway: "Geese in Flight." The 110-foot-tall sculpture marks the beginning of the Enchanted Highway, that I had seen signs for along the way. It begins at Exit 72 in Gladstone and leads south to the artist's hometown of Regent. He conceived it, and populated it with other of his monumental scrap-metal sculptures to draw people to this otherwise forgotten stretch of the world.

I weaved down the hill toward the highway and as I did, snow erupted into blurry trails, like a cascade of meteor showers beyond the windshield. As I drove, I clung to the far-right lane, wipers straining to keep up with the buildup. One tractor trailer after another blasted my woeful little sedan with a fusillade of frozen slush. Ten miles and an hour away, at Exit 72, I pulled far over onto the shoulder to rest my hands and mind, and look for "Geese in Flight."

At that moment, I experienced the crackling, the immensity of my curiosity, my bulwark against boredom and time, the lust and hunger for an awakening anywhere on earth.

If I drove past it, I could not bear the missed opportunity. Was this sculpture a wheel or an eye? Whatever it was, it was obscured by night. But as the squall quickened, wind gusts parted the airborne spheres of snow, dispersing them into shreds. And then, just across the highway, on the hillside, it flickered in and out of view. An edge here, a steel goose there, I felt a looming flash of strangeness. The sight of this giant had unanticipated power and judging from the dread and awe that pooled in my chest, something more lasting.

Carefully, I pulled back onto the highway, now almost abandoned, and proceeded back to my hotel on the outskirts of

Bismarck. The conditions were what they called in New England a whiteout.

In time, the unthinkable happened. A slick of weightlessness, an almost graceful relinquishment, and a force that pulled my tires to a blind and blinding spiral. My car and I, spinning, spinning, spinning through the celestial white. Spinning like the world I needed to move across. A counterclockwise loop, a succession of 360-degree orbits, a revolution a second, a coil of chaos. My hands attempted to steer in the direction of the skid, as I had learned in driving school.

A month ago, I stood on a ship as it passed through the Strait of Gibraltar, and from my balcony, watched the lights of Morocco twinkle to the south.

Six months ago, I ran through Johannesburg Airport and stopped to buy shoes. Three days later, my mother died.

A year ago, my children and husband sat at a beach café on the Adriatic coast, their bare feet tickling the sand. They smiled when they saw me and my daughter cried, "What did you find, Mom?"

I wound up the innards of lighthouses.

My memories were in frames.

I was saddened to think that my most meaningful acts were those I carried out alone.

In *Theory of Colours*, Goethe wrote that white represents light, and excites us. But as I burst through the flimsy veil of snow, and the tires carved circles onto the coated asphalt, I felt sharp mental clarity and a wave of tranquility. White, I thought, lays its hand on you. The sentry on the border of safety and the abyss.

"Tell us, what did you see?" Baudelaire asked du Camp.

When the car stopped, it was facing in the wrong direction. Such quiet I had rarely known, even on the open sea. I looked around for the eighteen wheelers and the pickups, but at this moment, they had left me to my pirouettes as if I were a dancer whirling alone on stage.

Through the scrim of gentle white flakes, I saw an exit to Bismarck, turned to face east again, and drove on.

Once, on the eve of her fifty-eighth birthday, a traveler set off in snow and darkness across North Dakota. What she saw there, in infinite silence and solitude, was so beautiful and terrifying it almost burned her heart.

Acknowledgments

I am beyond grateful to the team at Travelers' Tales/Solas House, who agreed to turn a selection of my essays into this book. James O'Reilly and Larry Habegger have been my literary north stars since they published my first travel essay in 2011. Without these extraordinary gentlemen, I would not be a travel writer. I thank them for all the opportunities and for being the most amazing, kind, smart and fun collaborators I could imagine.

I was incredibly fortunate to have Sumanth Prabhaker accompany me from the beginning, and help me make sense of ten years of essays. For his brilliant editorial guidance, I owe him all my gratitude.

I am indebted to Kevin Ford for his invaluable work on this manuscript.

In this book and in all my endeavors, I rely on Lavinia Spalding: her wise counsel, masterful editing, and patient listening. To her, I am grateful beyond measure. I offer heaps of thanks to Ann Hertberg for her important contributions to this book; to Erin Byrne for her writerly advice and friendship; to Don George for championing my work and editing it so smartly; and to Colleen Kinder, for how keenly and kindly she delves into the heart of a story.

To Lauren Cerand, I am grateful for so much. Above all, for believing in me and my work. Conversations with her embolden me, and every one of her ideas energizes me.

Many thanks to Kaye McKinzie, whose positivity and constant supply of wisdom and ideas never fail to buoy me. Kimberly Nelson designed the cover of my dreams, and for her work and vision, I am thankful.

At several turning points, Kerri Arsenault offered some key ideas, and I thank her. Dani Shapiro's generous spirit astounds me, and I am grateful to her. Christy Prunier has always given me such loving encouragement; Abby Pogrebin has been unwaveringly supportive of all of my writing endeavors from the beginning. I thank them, as well Susanna Salk, for her enthusiasm and countless solutions to my problems, Beth Kseniak, for helping me in so many ways, and Sarah Albee, for conversations that lead to clarity.

Thank you to the following people for the walks, the phone conversations, the tough questions, and the friendship: Chrissy Armstrong, Lisa Brown, Jasmin Darznik, Jean Davis, Blair Fitzsimons, Barbie Griffin, Lisa Huber, Jackie Levin, Wiz Lippincott, Kathy Mahoney, Martha McCully, Ellie Pitts, Kirsten Poitras, Elena Seibert, Harmony Tanguay, Wendy Walker, Lauren Werner. Thank you to the house on W San Antonio Highway in Marfa, Texas, where, for the first time, I envisioned what this book would be.

As this collection contains many previously published pieces, there is an exhaustive list of editors that have given me assignments, encouraged me, pushed me to write better, and published me. They may not realize that an email from them put wind in my sails, or that their edits and ideas contributed to my growth as a writer. But they did and here are some of the people to whom I basically owe my career: Ashley Baker, Jess Bergman, Ellie Cobb, Mo Duffy Cobb, Riza Cruz, Jay Fielden, Sara Finnerty, John Glassie, Anne Horowitz, Emma Komlos-Hrobsky, C. Max Magee, Lauren Mechling, Cara Parks, Jamie Rosen, Ben Ryder-Howe, Sally Singer, Eliot Stein, Flora Stubbs, Tom Tegart, and Hannah Walhout. I owe particular thanks to Doug Clement, who, as editor of *The Litchfield County Times*, let me write a column—and my heart out.

Very special thanks to my father, Roman, and my sisters, Ellen, Lydia and Andrea DeSanctis. They are the most selfless people, and they give me every imaginable kind of support—moral, financial, and intellectual. My thanks are not enough.

Finally, to my husband Mark Mennin and children Ray and Ava Mennin. I love these three magnificent people with all of my being. They have filled my life with joy, my heart with love, and my house with light. They have also pushed me to write honestly, even when it is not always easy for them to read. They keep me sane, safe, and always laughing. I am so lucky for them.

"Masha" is adapted from a piece originally published in *The Coachella Review* in 2010.

"To the Man in the Urinal in Prague" was originally published in *Off Assignment* in January, 2021. Reprinted with permission from *Off Assignment.*

"*Un Matin de Septembre*" was originally published as "A Mother's Snapshot from that Morning" in *The Litchfield County Times* in September, 2011.

"The Substitute" was originally published in *What I Didn't Know: True Stories of Becoming a Teacher* (In Fact Books, 2016).

"Love's Labour's Won" was originally published in *Vogue* in February, 2010.

"The Language of Sculpture, and of Words" was originally published as "The Slow Language of Sculpture, the Fast Language of Words," in *The Millions* in 2013.

"Waiting for the Sun" first appeared as "Waiting for the Sun in Vieques" online at *Gadling* in 2013.

"Strangers on a Train" originally appeared in *The New York Times Magazine* in 2010.

"Green Pastures" originally appeared as "Green Pastures and the Ghosts of Rwanda" in *Overnight Buses* in 2012.

"Twenty Years and Counting" first appeared as "A Grand Return" in *Town & Country* Fall/Winter 2011.

"Traveling Solo in the World's Most Romantic Country" was originally published on BBC Travel in 2015 and is reprinted with permission of BBC Travel.

A version of "Milk, Bread, Butter, Chocolate" was originally published in *Roads & Kingdoms* in 2016.

"Headlights" was originally published in *Entropy* Magazine as "On Weather: Tempest" in 2017.

"Falling" was originally published in *Cargo Literary* in 2017.

"Petra or Bust" is adapted from a piece originally published in Air Mail in 2019.

"Into the Cold" was originally published in *Overnight Buses* in 2013.

"Winter (With Apologies to Colette)" was originally published in *The Litchfield County Times* in 2011.

"Take me With You" was originally published in *The Common*, 2018.

"Signs of Life and Death in Africa" was originally published on BBC Travel in 2019 and is reprinted with permission from BBC Travel.

"He's Leaving Home" was first published in *The Litchfield County Times* in 2010.

"Willa Cather's Lavandou" is adapted from "Retracing Willa Cather's Steps in the South of France," that was originally published in *Lit Hub* in 2017.

"Fear and Solace in the Big Bend" is adapted from "Just Around the River Bend" that appeared in *Travel + Leisure* in 2021.

About the Author

Marcia DeSanctis is the author of the international bestseller *100 Places in France Every Woman Should Go*. She spent two decades as a news producer for ABC, NBC and CBS News *60 Minutes*. She has written for *Travel + Leisure, Vogue, Town & Country, Air Mail, Departures, BBC Travel, Lit Hub, Marie Claire, Off Assignment, Departures, Tin House, O the Oprah Magazine, Roads & Kingdoms, The New York Times* and *The New York Times Magazine*, among many other publications. She has won five Lowell Thomas Awards for excellence in travel journalism, including one for Travel Journalist of the Year, as well as the Grand Prize Solas Award in 2021 for Travel Story of the Year. She holds a degree from Princeton University in Slavic Languages and Literature and a master's in Foreign Policy from the Fletcher School of Law and Diplomacy. She lived and worked for several years in Paris, and resides in northwest Connecticut.

9 781609 522063